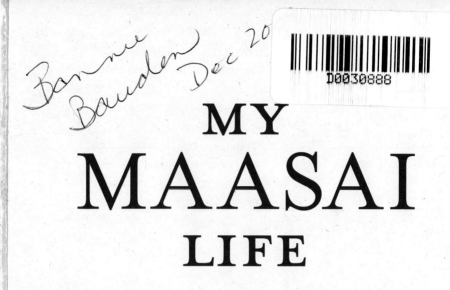

MY MAASAI LIFE

From Suburbia to Savannah

MY MAASAI LIFE

From Suburbia to Savannah

ROBIN WISZOWATY

me to we BOOKS

GREYSTONE BOOKS

D&M PUBLISHERS INC.
Vancouver/Toronto

ME TO WE BOOKS
Toronto

Copyright © 2009 Me to We Books

Greystone Books
A division of D&M Publishers Inc.
2323 Quebec Street, Suite 201
Vancouver, BC, V5T 4S7
Canada
www.greystonebooks.com

Me to We Books
233 Carlton Street
Toronto, ON, M5A 2L2
Canada
www.metowe.com/books

Library and Archives Canada Cataloguing in Publication
Wiszowaty, Robin, 1981-
My Maasai life : from suburbia to savannah / Robin Wiszowaty.
ISBN 978-1-55365-509-1

1. Wiszowaty, Robin, 1981-. 2. Maasai (African people). 3. Acculturation.
4. Americans--Kenya--Biography. 5. Kenya--Description and travel. I. Title.

HV40.32.W58A3 2009
305.896'5
C2009-902192-7

Have patience with everything unresolved in your heart and try to love the questions themselves as if they were locked rooms or books written in a very foreign language. Don't search for the answers, which could not be given to you now, because you would not be able to live them. And the point is, to live everything. Live the questions now. Perhaps then, someday far in the future, you will gradually, without even noticing it, live your way into the answer.

—Ranier Maria Rilke, *Letters to a Young Poet*, July 16, 1903

I feel tied to this life. Bound by decisions I never made, decided by people I have never met. Greeted with an outcome, beginning with an end, I am struggling to free myself of an upbringing I did not choose. Instead of looking at the world through the privileged eyes of an American, I want to broaden my vision and see life through a non-Western perspective. I want to discover for myself and break free from a worldview that I don't believe. I want to be cut down, sliced up, bashed and thrown this way and that . . . then rebuild myself into a shape that I dictate on my own terms, incorporating new meanings into my world. Until then, I am living someone else's decisions, thoughts and beliefs. I am ready to start living on my own.

—Journal entry, November 2001

Contents

Foreword

Dear Friends,

Today's world faces many challenges and divides. Economic catastrophe, the threat of terrorism and longstanding military struggles—with an increasingly sensational media bringing it to us twenty-four hours a day in real-time—have made us fearful of an imagined "other." While the information age has in many respects brought us closer together, it has in many ways cast us apart, forging cultural divisions rather than building communities.

We have globalized our technology and our economy. But we have yet to globalize our compassion.

That's why Robin Wiszowaty is our hero. Her journey has allowed her to become a true bridge between worlds. By embarking on her overseas journey from suburban America to rural Kenya, reaching out into the unknown, she made an incredible leap of courage, one few of us would even consider.

Everyone knows that old adage, "You'll never understand a man until you walk a mile in his shoes." Robin's own quest found her walking for miles barefoot alongside Maasai children as they headed off for school for the first time. She spent hours lugging water and firewood, brewing tea and gathering around a fire with families in their mud-hut homes, absorbing their customs and mastering their language.

In our frequent travels to rural Kenya, we've seen tourists and backpackers delight in the enthralling sights and sounds of this incredible land. But while they only briefly observe these scenes from afar, Robin wholly immersed herself in the true experience of life in Maasailand. And in return, the Maasai people accepted her as one of their own.

We've seen her sitting in hushed, intimate conversation with village elders, whose trust she earned through empathy and understanding. We've seen her astonish visiting students and volunteers with stories of her adventures. And we've seen her embraced by the teary-eyed mamas who are eternally grateful for her hard work in her role as Free The Children's Kenya Program Director.

In reaching out, Robin also discovered something within herself: the power to rise above limits, to break free of the status quo and to bridge worlds in a way that makes a true difference in people's lives.

Robin Wiszowaty is our hero. And by sharing her story, we know she'll become yours too.

Craig and Marc Kielburger
Free The Children / Me to We

Prologue

I am squeezed with dozens of other bodies into the back of a rusted, white Toyota pickup truck, bouncing along a dirt road toward the market town of Soko. A long hour's drive over the eastern slopes of lush and towering hills, it is a trek we make every Saturday to buy the week's groceries and supplies. On foot, the trip takes four hours along the dusty, arid spine of the hills' grasslands, then three more back down through the acacia-filled valley. But as one of the earliest passengers on the road this morning, I am lucky enough to stake out a seat on our community pickup truck. As usual, we squish as many people as possible into the truck's bed, pressed in until no standing room is left, even with many balanced on one foot.

I'm seated in the only available spot in the truck's bed, above the wheel well. Milk containers roped to an iron bar above thump against my skull with every bump in the road. An old man with long, stretched earlobes crams against me to my right, his wrinkled face and weathered feet telling of his many years of toil in the unyielding sun. To my left, a group of women laugh and talk animatedly in words I understand only occasionally.

The pickup jerks back and forth, bumping down the craggy road, kicking up a breeze of gritty dust. The combined reek of burning oil and close bodies, along with the ailing roar of the truck's engine, overwhelms me. With one hand I reach to steady a small boy as he takes a seat on my lap; with the other, I swat away a chicken pecking at my foot. As the boy burrows further into my arms, I squint into the sun and wind, watching the women's scarves blow freely in the breeze, waving in bursts of vivid ochre and blue.

I gaze out beyond this scene, at the valley stretching to a hazy horizon, and I ask myself: how did I, an ordinary American girl who grew up arguing with her parents, swimming for her high school team and playing kickball in suburban backyards, end up here?

My story began just a few years ago, but it seems a lifetime away.

1 My Ordinary Life

I grew up in the eighties in the safe and ordinary world of Schaumburg, Illinois, a large suburb forty kilometres northwest of Chicago. Schaumburg was proud of its reputation as the home of the sprawling Woodfield Mall—"America's Third Largest"—the state's number one tourist attraction and the anchor of the community's economy. Schaumburg's mainly white middle-class residents raised their families in quintessential American neighbourhoods, the kind where kids gathered on lawns for endless games of kickball and shooting hoops while parents watched from lawn chairs, or traded gossip over potluck dinners. In our neighbourhood, every summer the entire community would rally around a gigantic block party, with games, food and an annual talent show; when I was nine, I proudly shouldered the responsibility for finding raffle prize sponsorships and then wowed the crowd with a hula dance to the tune of the Beach Boys' "Kokomo."

I am the middle child in my suburban family. My older sister, Erin, and my younger brother, Adam, felt sometimes close, sometimes far away when we would battle through the shifting, always-complex power dynamic among us. As the eldest, Erin felt a responsibility to look out for Adam, even while I picked on him incessantly. His natural kindness made him vulnerable to my sneaky tactics, and I often managed to get him to take the fall for my own mischief. With Erin, I liked to maliciously flaunt my beloved Orange Tic Tacs and sour green apple Laffy Taffys and work up her jealousy—early on she had been diagnosed with juvenile onset diabetes and had to avoid sugar. Though our parents strove to treat each child equally, I felt I would never be as sociable and focused as Erin or as kind and creative as Adam. Despite our conflicts, in the end we bonded over our common appreciations: oldies radio, Pac-Man, lavishing endless affection on our dog Fluffy—the typical stuff of American teens.

At ten years old, my personal world-view was just starting to take shape.

Yet from an early age, I was unsatisfied with my ordinary life. I just knew there had to be *something* more exciting and significant than this transparent world. I could never find my niche or any comfortable sense of self. Looking around, all I saw were people doing only just enough to get through their lives. Household conversations focused on whether to buy Frosted Flakes or Cap'n Crunch, who won *Monday Night Football*, upcoming sales at clothing stores. My friends occupied their time either working toward promising futures—college, careers, marriage—or immersed in the escapism of fashion, rumours and Hollywood.

But wasn't there more to life than this? Why did this simple, day-to-day life seem to satisfy most people, but not me? I couldn't explain what I wanted instead or what kind of person I really wanted to become. I just knew it wasn't what I already had.

An inner anger that I could barely understand, let alone express, gradually began to build inside me. A fire of dissatisfaction burned within, a fire that lashed out in anger, against my parents, against my brother and sister. It was a fire that would only build and build, until I did something to quiet it. I could not be contained by high school's narrow hallways, my suburban streets, my ordinary life.

Was I the only one who felt this way? Questioning things aloud and refusing to conform within my social circle would only find me maligned as a "rebel," so I buried myself in constant activity, fighting to always push harder to wring experience from every moment. Starting in seventh grade, I became enamoured with singing in the choir and performing in musical theatre, and I joined every team or club I could. Tennis lessons. Drama class. Student congress. Swim team. Track and field. Softball. Model UN. A summer job lifeguarding at Schaumburg Park District. I filled every spare moment between practices or competitions by keeping a hectic social calendar with friends and my boyfriend—movies, restaurants, baking.

For most people, it seemed better to take the easy way every time.

And for the time being, so did I, grinning and bearing it, going with the flow, even as my anger simmered. But at the time I felt alone and I directed my dissatisfaction and anger at those most accessible: my family.

My father Tony comes from a Polish Catholic background. His grandparents, my great-grandparents, met onboard an ocean liner while crossing the Atlantic, arriving at New York's Ellis Island port in 1906 and marrying shortly thereafter. They spoke next to no English and had little money and, as the Great Depression loomed, they had to take any odd jobs they could find to support a burgeoning family of seven children. A middle child amid this brood, my grandfather eventually moved to the Midwest, founded a printing business that would support the family he raised there, but only with hard work, long hours and thrifty spending. My grandfather also believed passionately in the value of education and took pride in the fact that his daughters would be the first women in his family line to attend university.

But my dad, his only son, faced a number of challenges. At school a teacher told his parents that he was slow and that his parents should lower any expectations they had for his success. In fact, this teacher's prediction of failure did exactly the opposite, only motivating my father to work harder and dream bigger.

After a stint in the Marine Corps Reserve, Dad moved to a rough area of Chicago and into a tiny second-floor apartment facing a garbage-strewn back alley. The hallways stank of neighbours' cooking and the galley kitchen was so small he had to walk through sideways. The bathtub was a rusted wreck and, with no money, he was forced to pinch his cutlery one piece at a time from a nearby diner.

My dad worked an entry-level management at a bank while studying evenings to eventually earn a master's degree in education administration from Northwestern Illinois University, even serving as class president. Public speaking was his forte, and to this day he proudly recalls the best speech he ever delivered, addressing the student body on the occasion of Robert Kennedy's assassination. People in the audience wept openly as his words implored the power of unity, community and hope against all odds.

In the crowd for that speech was a young woman named Bonnie Rovin. She listened to his words and was profoundly inspired. I'm going to marry that man someday, she told herself.

My mother's upbringing couldn't have been more different from my father's. Coming from a wealthy Jewish family, she grew up on the richer side of Chicago. Hers was a life of country clubs, heated pools and fancy dresses. Hers was a life of comfort and ease until she was eighteen, when her father—the grandfather I would never meet—died suddenly of a heart attack. Distraught, she began to question her priorities, and she was actually in the process of dropping out of university when my father's speech that day stirred her interests. She immediately changed her class schedule in hopes of arranging a meeting with him and, she hoped, more.

Her attempts to win Tony over were successful and, despite their cultural and religious differences, they were married in 1971. Several years of financial struggles and hard work followed, both of them working low-paying administrative jobs at the university while fighting to make ends meet. Despite the odds, they managed to purchase a modest townhouse and, later, the house in Schaumburg where I grew up.

Erin was born in June 1979. Nineteen months later, on January 20, 1981—also Mom's thirty-first birthday—I was born. Almost three years later, Adam arrived. Other than early concerns with the discovery of Erin's diabetes, we were a normal, healthy family. Dad tried several careers, from working at universities to network marketing firms to real estate brokerages; Mom stayed at home with us kids. Dad made sure we kept a close relationship with our entire extended family of aunts, uncles and grandparents, with regular reunions bringing us all together.

Having clawed his way up to the comfort of a middle-class lifestyle, Dad was determined for his kids to grow up with the same dedicated work ethic. "We Wiszowatys," he insisted, "are leaders, not followers!" We were expected to always excel, particularly in academics. There were no Cs—I never received a grade below a B until eighth grade, when my distressed mother called my teacher demanding an explanation and afterward checked in weekly to track my achievements.

Dad was always fiercely determined to make his children feel powerful and confident. From an early age Adam, Erin and I fell asleep every night wearing headphones so we could listen to the motivational tapes he'd selected. These tapes played talks called "No More Excuses! Get It Done Today!" or "Get It Done and Still Have Fun!" We'd often return home from school to find self-help books on the kitchen table with a note: *Dear Erin, Robin and Adam, Read Chapter Three, we'll be discussing it at dinner tonight.*

Every morning before we headed off to school, we would recite my dad's scripted pep talks.

"Can you win?" he'd ask.

"I can win!" I'd say in return.

"Why?"

"Why?" I'd echo, following the script. "I'll tell you why! Because I have faith, courage and enthusiasm!"

We would recite these affirmations endlessly, repeating the lines ten times a day: "I am fearless! I am determined! I am powerful! I am *unstoppable!*"

As I got older, I began to object to performing these routines and told Dad I thought they were ridiculous. My mother seemed to take my objections in stride, always remaining mellow, even when my father was particularly motivated and pumped up. I could see his enthusiasm was only out of love, but I still ridiculed him and refused to be told what to do, and I reacted in outbursts that grew increasingly hostile.

One night when I was fourteen, our family had just returned from a dinner out, and the moment we got home my sister had taken over the family's only computer. I was irritated because I also wanted to use it, yet she refused. Suddenly, I was flaming with anger.

The next thing I remember is totally losing my train of thought. I heard myself screaming an incomprehensible spew of nonsense, something garbled like "hate everyone . . . computer . . . television . . ." Then, suddenly snapping out of it and realizing how crazy I sounded, I grabbed my jacket and stormed out into the winter night.

I headed along the wooded path where I usually walked Fluffy, trying to understand what had just occurred. *What's happening to me? Why did I do that?* I didn't even notice my dad behind me until he'd caught up and tugged gently at my arm.

As I fumed, he lectured me, saying he'd seen symptoms in me that he had himself experienced when younger: a feeling of helpless frustration, of not knowing how to control angry feelings.

"Sometimes you feel blank," he said. "You don't think straight, because you're in such a fury."

He was right. But I didn't want to admit it; I'd convinced myself I hated him and the rest of my family. He said he and Mom had discussed entering me in anger management counselling.

"No!" I refused. "I don't need that."

But as time went on, my anger persisted. I argued about anything and with anyone. I became unbearable to live with but no one in my family made any changes to quell my anger. Dad still treated me as an ignorant child who couldn't form her own opinions, and he forced his values of money and material success with disapproving looks and critical comments after every word I spoke. Eventually, rather than lashing out, I retreated further and further, building a wall of silence between us. Why keep setting myself up for the constant disapproval?

My mom hoped to be the family's peacemaker. Following one of the regular blowouts between Dad and me, I overheard her on the phone with my grandmother, confessing that one of her biggest disappointments in life was her inability to maintain a proper, loving relationship with me. Naturally, I felt terribly guilty, but in my stubborn pride I could never allow myself to bend to her wishes.

To make it worse, in comparison Erin and Adam glided by, untroubled by my father's expectations to excel, to be upbeat and outgoing, to "*Go get 'em!*" Erin and Adam had no problem doing that. But I seemed doomed to always be the black sheep.

My family also struggled to observe my mother's Jewish heritage. We were never particularly devout—unless counting our weekly Hebrew school visits, when, truthfully, we were more excited for the trip afterward to Burger King for Chicken Tenders (always the six-piece pack, until they expanded it to nine, which Mom found excessive).

I recall in my junior year we were celebrating Yom Kippur, the Jewish high holiday. Traditionally, Yom Kippur means an occasion of atoning and repenting for one's sins. In our family's version, we gathered at Schaumburg's Volkening Lake to sit around a picnic table, taking turns pledging our goals for the coming year. In my rebellious manner, I thought it was all tedious. I put on my typical sour attitude, thinking, *This is dumb. What a waste of time.* When Mom tearfully said her biggest goal for the year was to work on her relationship with me, I felt horrible. Of all the goals she could focus on in life, she focused on . . . *me?* When I barely gave her the time of day, a brief glance, let alone a smile or kind word? Yet in my defiance I could never allow myself to cry in front of her, or assure her doubts.

I hoped that going away to college would be my big breakthrough. I broke up with my boyfriend, looking to make all new friends and sever all ties. I refused to bring petty distractions from high school along with me to college. I'd be far enough away from my parents that I wouldn't have to do anything they said. I wouldn't have to answer to anybody.

Arriving at the Urbana-Champaign campus of the University of Illinois in fall 1999, the reality wasn't quite as I expected. Majoring in speech communications, I enjoyed my classes and quickly made friends. But the opportunities I'd imagined, the chances for freedom and to find an exciting new path didn't come as readily as I'd hoped. Student life was fairly mundane: classes, studying, eating pizza and watching movies with my dorm-mates, overeating at the residence's all-you-can-eat buffet to the point that I gained nearly thirty pounds. It was actually kind of a letdown.

One day I stopped to read one of the many flyers I'd seen around promoting something called Birthright Israel. The purpose of this international organization is to inspire young people to explore their Jewish heritage. They provide anyone born Jewish the experience of visiting their faith's spiritual home, all expenses paid, to help them to learn about their cultural history.

Birthright Israel seemed a blessing: an easy, low-risk way to break out with only English or French. Within English-speaking Africa, Kenya struck me as the most appealing. It was that simple.

Well, almost. In each of the programs I explored, participants would be surrounded by English students or placed in a cosmopolitan city—the very situations I hoped to avoid. I eventually discovered a program offered through the University of Minnesota that connected students with a contact in Kenya, who would then provide a link to a host community in a rural region. I'd be required to do a great deal of months-long groundwork at the University of Illinois, then develop a research topic and conduct field studies while in Kenya. I also had to convince the dean and college at my current university, the University of Illinois, that my Kenyan excursion would be worth an equivalent year's credit and allow me to complete my degree. Originally it seemed my professors would never agree to the idea, and I had to press hard for weeks to convince them. But to my relief, they eventually agreed.

The other issue was money. This trip was going to be expensive. Fortunately, I'd been working part-time jobs since I was fifteen: secretarial work, lifeguarding, camp counselling. All along I'd set aside eighty percent of every paycheque, always knowing that a time would come when I'd need funds for this eventual *something*. My friends threw away their allowances and earnings on movie tickets or dinner at McDonald's. Those things meant nothing to me. I had bigger things in mind.

So when this trip came up, I was able to cover my plane ticket, health insurance and most other costs. This was actually happening!

I knew nothing about Kenya. When I pictured Africa, all I imagined were the stereotypical *National Geographic* images of wild animals, rural huts, underfed children with flies crawling across their wan faces. I looked at photographs of the capital city of Nairobi, which was unlike anything I'd seen: crowded streets, drab buildings, certainly not a white face in sight. Those photographs only reinforced to me that I had no idea what to expect. I wouldn't know how to say "hello," "goodbye," "thank you," anything. But I didn't care. All I cared about was going far, far away. That was enough for me.

I might have asked myself once or twice, *What will it be like, to go*

of conventional expectations and get far away. Spots for their trips were very competitive, so I signed up without a second thought that I might actually be selected. Truthfully, I felt I barely qualified because of my family's relatively relaxed approach to our faith.

As it turns out, given recent events—I applied shortly after the attacks of September 11, 2001, and during a peak in the longstanding Israeli-Palestinian conflict—travelling internationally was widely seen as reckless, even dangerous, so very few people had signed up. To my surprise, I would be on my way to Israel that December.

I immediately called home. I hadn't spoken to my parents in a while, so I was eager to tell them about my plan. When my mom answered, I was prepared to gloat.

"Oh, Robin!"

I could picture her in her bedroom, idly watching television before nodding off to sleep. She called to my father. "Tony, Robin's on the phone!"

I heard him pick up the kitchen extension.

"Robin!"

I readied myself. "Guess what I'm doing over Christmas vacation?"

My mother sounded overjoyed. "You're coming home? Oh, Tony, she's coming home!"

"Ma, stop," I said, instantly annoyed. "I'm going to Israel."

I could almost hear their jaws dropping. They were of course thinking of terrorists and suicide bombers, the violence reported in the news every day. To them, this trip seemed insane.

They didn't really know what to say, and the conversation ended abruptly. I learned that in the following days they'd discussed my proposed trip with various family members. My aunts and uncles, all the family, all told them, "She is your *daughter*. She is your responsibility. If you need to tie her down to a chair, that's what you need to do. But you can not let her go."

But by then my parents were learning they couldn't tell me what to do. So they did the best thing they could. They both individually came to me on campus to privately discuss my plans. Why was I going so far away? Why couldn't I just come home? Why didn't we use this time to work on our family?

They asked with such sincerity, such intensity, I thought for the first time I could speak the truth and air all my feelings. But the truth was I didn't know why I wanted to go so badly. So I brushed off their concerns, still concerned with nothing other than my need to break free.

I promised my parents I would search my soul about exactly why I'd signed up for the Israel trip. So one gloomy evening, I showed up early to one of the nightly practices of the residence's Ultimate Frisbee team I had joined in my second year of university. With no one around, I sat under an awning against the cold stone of our dorm building, curled up with pen and paper in hand.

I had journalled since high school, but now something stirred inside me, yearning to be articulated. I felt on the verge of understanding what it was, but it was so big, just a jumbled mush, tied up inside me. Slowly I felt the knots loosening.

I started thinking, why? Why did I want to go? What would this trip mean within the larger picture of my life?

Just as I felt words approaching, my pen hovering above the page, the dorm hall's doors flung open and my Frisbee friends burst onto the field.

"Robin!" they called, "Let's go!"

One of them threw the disk long and the others chased it upfield. I instinctively moved to follow, then paused. Instead, I told them I'd catch up later.

As a soft rain began to fall, my pen raced across the page. I'd wanted to express these feelings for years, to scream them out, but never knew the words to use.

I feel tied to this life. Bound by decisions I never made, decided by people I have never met. Greeted with an outcome, beginning with an end, I am struggling to free myself of an upbringing I did not choose ...

I don't remember if I went back to practice that day, but I do remember filling most of that page, then returning to my room in Allen Hall to type it out into my laptop. By putting my feelings into words, I knew I was closer to some sort of conclusion. I needed to go as far as possible, to do as much as I could.

And, for better or for worse, the first step would be this trip to Israel.

Eventually, my parents gave me their blessings for the trip. Not that I was waiting for their approval, but I was glad to receive it nonetheless.

It was a fascinating two weeks. We visited the Western Wall on New Year's Eve at midnight and scaled Mount Masada at sunrise. We explored the old and new cities, repelled cliffs in the Negev Desert and swam in the Dead Sea. I was humbled by a visit to the Holocaust History Museum at Yad Vashem and later had the chance to meet both Israeli and Palestinian peers for long discussions of the region's longstanding cultural conflicts.

I was deeply moved by how attached these people felt to their spiritual lives. And while it didn't encourage me to pack up and move to Israel to become a devout Jew, it did remind me how fiercely I longed to break out of this Western mindset and find something else. But what that something was precisely, I still didn't know for sure.

When my parents picked me up at the airport upon my return, I could tell what they were thinking: *Phew! That's out of her system! Now we're done with that.*

Unfortunately for them, relief didn't last long. A few days later, I sat them at the kitchen table and told them exactly what they were most dreading: Israel was just Step One. I didn't want to just visit Israel, or any other western country, for only ten days. I needed to find a place far away and for an extended length of time. A space where I couldn't rely on technology or other people customs, norms, language—somewhere far from my current reality.

"If this first trip was a big deal for you," I told them, "then get ready because this is just a warm-up for what I'm *really* going to do with my life."

I initially considered three possible destinations: South America, Asia rural Africa. As a university student, I figured the best route would b study abroad for the upcoming semester, and I was pleased to find there programs available in each of these places. I quickly ruled out South Ame as all the programs I found required previous fluency in Spanish. I consi several possibilities in Asia, but they required the desire to learn an language. Then I found several programs in which one could study in

away, to not see any of my friends or family, for a whole year? But I never entertained such thoughts for long. When people asked how I would manage, I had my automatic answer: "It's going to be fun! It's going to be an adventure!" Adam and Erin seemed fed up with my incessant whining and complaining, so they clearly didn't take my ambitions very seriously. Friends told me I was foolish for even considering doing this. But I would just smile and nod while inside I was fuming, thinking, *As if you have any idea! You would never do what I'm about to do!*

The days leading up to my departure were full of excited preparation. Mom and I talked in heartfelt conversations, holding hands and discussing how it was going to be while I was away. Through tears she told me how much she was going to miss me and that she was scared to death that I'd get sick, even die. For his part Dad said he was worried I'd get caught up in political turmoil or even choose to never return home.

Yet when my parents asked me what my fears might be, I'd vehemently declare, "Nothing!" I denied myself the opportunity to think about what could go wrong. This, I was convinced, was everything to which my entire life was leading, my big, once-in-a-lifetime chance to show everybody I was more than just some angry, rebellious kid. This was my time to do something more daring than they ever would, and I would excel and thrive in it. In your *face!* I thought viciously. I had no idea what awaited me and I didn't care. I didn't even think twice about it.

But I did feel guilty, knowing how hard it would for everyone I was leaving behind. Thinking ahead, I collected birthday and holiday gifts for my entire family for the coming year, entrusting them to my grandma to deliver at the appropriate times. I hid small notes throughout the house so they'd be found at given times. For example, I knew Dad only read his Bible a couple of times a year, so I slipped a special note in there for him to discover later. I hid Christmas cards for everyone with the stash of decorations kept upstairs. I purchased cards from a florist and gave them to one of my mother's co-workers, arranging for them to be delivered with fresh flowers to Mom's office at the end of every month.

I had my friends go through my clothes and pick out what they wanted, then donated the rest to Goodwill. I squished everything I'd need into one backpack, figuring I'd buy clothes when I got there. I gave away my computer and my printer and whittled down my contact list to only those addresses I really wanted to keep. The plan was to rid myself of all superfluous things and people. I had only a few bare essentials—and my mission. That was enough.

I tried to set up these systems so that those I left behind would be okay, but also for selfish reasons—with these small reassurances, I could totally break all ties and wouldn't have to worry about anyone or anything while I was off on my adventure. In my mind, I was done with this place.

Before I knew it, it was time to leave for Kenya.

My flight was in the afternoon, so the last morning I slept in, unconcerned and in no rush for anything. A knock came at my bedroom door, and my father entered. He joined me on the bed, which he never had done before.

"Robin," he said, "if for whatever reason, you don't come back, if you're in some tribal conflict, or you catch some horrible disease . . . just know we love you, we've always loved you and we always will."

He was choked up, and his fears were genuine, but I was only embarrassed. I had seen my father cry only once before, at my grandfather's funeral. I wanted to properly honour what he was doing, reaching out this way, but I just couldn't. It was too much. I couldn't be seen as weak now, just when I was leaving. I needed to feel strong.

"Okay, Dad," I said. "Thanks." I didn't want to make a big deal of my departure, but at the same time travelling overseas was the hugest, most dramatic thing that had ever happened to me. At the airport, my dad hugged me and cried again. Then it was my mom's turn. She hugged me and also cried, just as I knew she would. Through her tears, she whispered in my ear.

"I want to leave you with some words of wisdom, but I don't have anything to tell you that you don't already know," she said. "You're ready for this. Go do it. Just call us when you get there."

Saying my last goodbyes, I picked up my bag and headed for the security gate. But before I'd made it through, I froze. I turned and ran back. For the first time in years, I shed tears in front of my parents. At that moment I felt such a sudden, powerful outburst of emotion. Yet despite my tears, I did my best to reassure them I was okay. They said they understood, and we held each other, sobbing together.

Then I headed off, this time for real. But as I was leaving, I realized I wasn't sure if I had my passport. *Do I need that?* I wondered. *You need a passport to go to another country, don't you?* I honestly couldn't remember if I'd checked it with my baggage or still had it on me. There, in the middle of O'Hare airport and in sight of my puzzled parents, I dropped to my knees and tore through my overstuffed carry-on bag.

Luckily, my passport was there. I waved it to my parents on the other side of the gate and called out to them: "It's okay, 'bye!"

Then I stuffed the passport in my pocket and hurried to catch my flight.

2 Culture Shock in Nairobi

Everyone is staring at me. A crowd of bodies surrounds at all angles, a collision of voices whisper and laugh at what I assume must be me. Wildly self-conscious, I shove my hands deep into my pockets, feeling my face grow hot, wishing I knew how to sink into the crowd, invisible.

It's like the first day of school all over again, only this September it's my first time taking Nairobi's public transit on my own. Up till now my host family has accompanied me, but from here forward I refuse to have my hand held as I find my way around the city—even though I'm not entirely sure which bus to take. I chalk up my uneasiness to an overactive imagination and compel myself to stand taller, trying to look as if I know what I'm doing.

Every morning at seven o'clock I embark on a two-hour commute across Nairobi, hopping a Nissan minibus—called a *matatu*—through town to the Nazarene Church on Ngong Road. There I meet with other University of Minnesota students for Swahili lessons, classes on Kenyan culture and sessions where we share ideas for our individual research projects. From my host family's home in a suburb on the west side, it takes about fifteen minutes by foot to reach the first matatu stop, called a "stage." There I join the crowd at the curbside and find shade from the sun—already blinding despite the early hour—beneath a signboard advertising a cellular phone company.

Calls and shouts from the matatus ring on all sides. Everyone is a potential passenger, the prey of aggressive matatu operators.

"Beba beba beba beba!" Be carried here!

The matatus don't depart until the operators had maximized their profit by squeezing in as many passengers and as much cargo as they can, so along with a driver each has a type of scout, working to get bodies in seats as quickly as possible. With pleading shouts the scouts yank urgently at the elbows of potential passengers, coaxing them inside. Once the cars are full, they surge along the four-lane Uhuru highway to their destination at the city centre, then refill all over again. The more trips the matatu operators make, the more money they earn. Each fare is ten shillings, about twelve American cents.

As I wait for the matatu for route 115 to arrive, I hear calls from vendors nearby.

"Kumi kumi kumi!" Come, come, come!

A small kiosk is set up next to the matatu stage, where a clever business woman sells cut-up papaya, pineapple, mango and passion fruit to those waiting. "Thirty shillings, fruit salad!" she calls. "Thirty shillings only!" Even though I've been told we're on the brink of the area's rainy season, the heat is still exhausting, and at the equivalent of about forty cents this fresh fruit is a welcome treat.

"Beba beba beba!" Carry, carry, carry!

With its engine revving and honks blasting like bullhorns, the route 115 minibus pulls up, trailing dirty exhaust. Men and women in business suits shove past me, cutting in line to board. I'm pretty sure this is my route, but amid the chaos I can't know for sure.

"Moja mwengine! Moja mwengine!" One more!

The noise is overpowering. Several more matatus pull up, each fighting to cut off the other, blasting music to attract potential passengers. Neon lights and graffiti drawings of American rappers colour the matatus, along with slogans ranging from *Jesus Saves All* to *Baby Got Back*. Lost in this disorienting scene, I allow myself to be hauled by the bicep into a matatu emblazoned with the slogan *We Be Jammin*. My feet are barely inside before the matatu pulls away.

The bus is jammed beyond capacity—as with all matatus, what would be typically a nine-seat vehicle has been refitted with benches for eighteen, though often more bodies spill from open doors and windows. I hold my breath against the thick scent of body odour as I climb toward the back, toppling into people as the matatu jerks, switching gears and hurtling off. My apologies go unacknowledged, and people simply give way the best they can. The experience is a far cry from Chicago's Pace suburban bus service or the shuttle buses at college, where every other seat would be free.

I squeeze into the back row, squished among three adults and two children. A stranger hands a bag to hold on my lap, though I can't tell to whom it belongs.

Conversations fly in all directions as we barrel down Uhuru Highway, voices raised over the blaring music. I have no idea what anyone around me is saying, so all I can do is concentrate on breathing through my mouth to avoid swallowing the clouds of black exhaust seeping from passing cars. Despite my best attempts to brace myself, hunched among these bodies and bags, my head slams over and over against the unpadded roof as we weave in and out of lanes. Holding my breath, I work up the courage to inhale, yet find it nearly impossible in the stagnant, pungent air. To my amazement, no one seems the least bit inclined to open a window.

Even with bodies pressing against me on all sides, I feel alone. Everyone is a stranger. These streets are unfamiliar. I am far from my friends, my bed, the familiar neighbourhood I could navigate with my eyes closed, everything I'd ever known. And yet, with total chaos surrounding me, pounding music playing so loud the entire matatu vibrates with pumping bass, a small girl absentmindedly clutching my leg for balance—here I am truly alive. *This is what I wanted! This is what I came for!*

The matatu hits a pothole and all of us are bounced from our seats, once again smacking our heads against the roof. The girl clutching my leg and I exchange smiles and she takes my hand. I inhale deeply, breathing in the smell of burning garbage, diesel fumes . . . and freedom.

Nairobi: the sprawling metropolis often called "The Green City in the Sun." (Photograph courtesy Lynda Kurylowicz)

The University of Minnesota had placed me for two months with a temporary host family in Westlands, a relatively affluent suburb outside of Nairobi. The family fed and housed me, but our relationship was generally icy. When I tried to make conversation or share stories, they were uninterested. I came to see that they were hosting a Western student for the money not to embrace a visitor from another culture.

Truthfully, that was fine with me, since my priorities lay elsewhere. Soon I would be matched with a new family in a rural area, where I would be immersed in the local culture and observe the conditions there first-hand. I didn't really know what to expect, but I knew for sure, once I got there, my real education would begin.

Before that, however, I had to go through eight weeks of classes and meetings across town with other American students like me, studying in a range of different fields and disciplines. My class was led by Professor

Mohamud Jama, associate professor at the Institute for Development Studies, University of Nairobi, and adjunct professor at the University of Minnesota. His encouragement had me excited about the months to come.

There was only a slight catch: unlike most of my classmates, I had no formal training in the field of international development and, to complete the course and receive full credit, I was expected to write extensively about the topic and eventually produce an eighty-page paper. The idea was daunting, to say the least. I hoped my time in this rural community would help me learn more about successful international development practices.

One afternoon I was walking through downtown Nairobi when I encountered someone who stopped me in my tracks.

A tall, thin man was headed down the sidewalk toward me, his colourful appearance standing in stark contrast against the grey backdrop of surrounding glass skyscrapers. Two long cotton scarves were draped across his bare chest, cascading all the way to his knees, held together at his waist by a beaded belt. To my shock, he was laden with weapons: a long knife encased in a red-dyed cow hide and a wooden club hung from his belt, with a bow and quiver of arrows slung across his back. He held a thin staff in one hand and a metal spear in the other. His pierced and stretched earlobes dangled almost halfway to his shoulders.

As he looked right and left, shrinking to avoid oncoming traffic, I wondered who this spectacular man might be and what had brought him to Nairobi. *What does he think of the wide streets, the big crowds of people, the running water or tall sky-scrapers?*

As we passed, the push of the busy crowd propelled me forward, yet I could smell from him a strong odour like raw milk and a smoky scent, like a campfire. The man seemed entirely out of place—almost as much as me.

I knew that in Kenya I'd be experiencing a culture and way of life unlike anything I'd seen. Leading up to leaving North America I'd been so focused on orchestrating my escape I hadn't anticipated the cultural differences—or how deeply submerged in poverty Nairobi truly was. The kiosk workers with whom I spoke every day didn't work to buy designer clothes; they sold bananas in the morning to put food in their children's mouths at night. Often they even lived in their kiosks with their children. Many bathed in an above-ground sewer system—the same one into which I often saw people urinating. They washed their clothes by hand, lived amid litter in the streets and breathed air so polluted you had to remove black build-up from your nostrils after a day on the streets.

Everywhere people pleaded for me to purchase their wares. Children followed me constantly with hands outstretched, begging in broken English: "Sister, sister, please. My tummy is hungry. Five shillings, ten shillings. Please, sister." Chatting with the guy who worked at the matatu stage in the mornings, I was surprised to learn he lived in a poverty-ravaged slum, just minutes from the comfortable home where I was living.

Walking Nairobi's streets, I manoeuvred around people sprawled on the trash-smeared concrete, their leprosy-wracked and underfed bodies, some missing limbs, sleeping in the middle of crowded streets—mistreated, neglected bodies that held human souls capable of compassion and love. Yet people simply stepped right past them.

I often felt numb, as though observing myself in the same way I observed these surrounding scenes. Every day I saw something that shocked me. I didn't know how to take it all in, or how to articulate it when I wrote to my family. Instead, I read emails from my mother about the weekly sales at Kohl's, how disappointing a new TV series was, how my alma mater football team was faring that season. How could I share what was going on here in Nairobi when I couldn't even explain it to myself? I pictured my mom at her office, seeing my name in her email inbox and then excitedly opening my message. She would call over all her fellow workers to share the news: her daughter was still safe and doing well.

But what if I wrote to her about the man with elephantiasis of the leg I'd passed on the street the day before? A chill shot down my spine and my breath caught in my throat when I saw him, slumped on the sidewalk. My face contorted as I fought to hold back tears and nausea at the same time. I fought to look away, but couldn't help but gape at the swollen, deformed figure lying before me. His thighs looked like the base of a tree trunk and his darkening skin was bursting at the seams, like a balloon ready to pop. His foot was so swollen that the toes nearly disappeared inside the distended flesh. I wondered: *How can he even turn over? His foot must be impossible to even lift! Can he walk? How does he stand the pain?*

Then he caught me openly gawking and met my gaze with a toothless smile and a trembling palm held out in hope of a couple of shillings.

How could I possibly explain to Mom just how gutted I felt in that moment? There seemed no way to share the flood of questions racing through my mind: Where does he sleep at night? What can he afford with just a few shillings? Or how do I even explain the unexpected contradiction, that even in agony his eyes held a gentle mystique, seeming to assure me all would be okay? Or how do I explain the bitter irony, that his smile was providing comfort and reassurance while I—healthy, with money in my wallet—stood stunned, unable to help him? And what about all the other sick, wounded Kenyans I saw? Do Kenyans have public health care? And if they don't . . . what did they do?

How could I possibly even begin to share all the disheartening scenes I saw almost everywhere I went in this strange city?

I was a part of it now; there was no turning back. I couldn't avoid the brutal reality; in fact, I didn't want to avoid it. Although there were no easy answers, no understanding, no logic—only corruption, greed and ignorance— this was a world I wanted to learn more about. Right now I didn't know how to share with my loved ones back home. Instead, I was learning to keep a million secrets with myself. But maybe someday I'd know how to tell them.

The days in Nairobi began to run into one another. Yet some experiences stood out, like the first day I was moved to actual tears.

I'd come to Kenyatta Market with my classmate Brenda to buy a sweater from the second-hand clothing market. It was a maze of stalls, vendors selling all sorts of used clothes, everything from fine-tailored business attire to Nike running shoes and Gap sweatshirts.

During my stay in Nairobi, I brimmed with anticipation while preparing to head to Maasailand for a full year.

As we strolled through the busy market, two street boys approached, asking for five shillings. Brenda took a glance at them, then declined casually, just as we both often did.

"*Sina pesa,*" she said. I don't have any money.

Clearly, this was an outright lie. I'd been taught to say the same thing, because when there are two beggars there are ten and, when there are ten, there are still more ready to pounce. But even after saying it countless times, it still felt wrong. Compared to the people we passed on the street, we might as well have been driving BMW convertibles with the top down, flashing designer clothes and sparkling jewellery, tossing stacks of cash . . . then saying "*sina pesa*" while craning our heads for a better view of the dejected locals.

One street man nearby overheard us. Missing most of his teeth, his clothes hung as if they hadn't been washed for weeks, and his hair was so dirty it was knotting into dreadlocks. Glaring at us, he said in Swahili, "What are you doing in Kenya, if you can't help us?"

Despite my halting comprehension of the language, I understood his question. What *was* I doing here? Was I here to help Kenyans? I couldn't remember any sort of altruistic impulse as my reason for being me here. I only pictured myself three months earlier, curled up on my family room couch reading books on cultural sensitivity, or shopping in neighbourhood department stores for appropriate clothing, thinking this was a chance for me to enlarge my experience and pick up others' points of view. I'd been driven simply by a desire to escape not to improve the lives of these poor people.

I had no answer for this man. His piercing stare lingered, awaiting an explanation. It was all I could do to turn my head to avoid meeting his eyes. Brenda and I quickly rushed away, still wishing there was some sort of answer, any answer, to give.

By the time Brenda and I parted ways to return home from our shopping trip it was raining, with a chill in the autumn air. I hurried down a side street to catch a matatu back to the suburbs, my rain-soaked pants sticking to my legs and my hands jammed in my pockets.

Then I heard it: a sharp yelp from an intersection about ten metres up the street. Drawing closer, I could see two street boys hovering over a third boy lying on the ground. Keeping my distance, I continued on my way. It wasn't an uncommon scene: I'd seen many street boys harass one another, stealing one another's little food or the glue they sniffed. Yet the third boy's cries echoed through the empty street, his quick yelps turning to desperate, wordless pleas as the others beat him with sticks. The sound seized my heart as I drew nearer, both with fear for my own safety and in alarm at the scene unfolding before me.

Then I saw what the boys were after: the fallen boy's jeans. He struggled on the ground, outnumbered and overpowered as they stole the only protection he had against the night's cold. He fought in vain until his attackers successfully yanked off his jeans and ran away, the echoes of their feet smacking pavement ringing down the empty street. Their victim tried to chase after them in his bare feet, but to no avail. For him, it was a harsh lesson in survival of the fittest.

No one helped the boy. I certainly didn't. I'd only watched in astonishment, not knowing what to do. I was clearly larger than his attackers and could probably have fended them off. But then what? More street boys would likely come to their help, and then it wouldn't be me against two; it would be me against eight, maybe more. And if I did get the boy's pants back, nothing would stop him from being robbed again minutes later, after I'd returned to my home—a home with running water, a stocked refrigerator, warm blankets and a window I could shut to keep out the cold.

Empathy was overruled by desperation, and desperation created chaos. It wasn't just happening here, at the corner of Koinange and Muindi Mbingu streets. It was happening across town, across the hundred various slums within Nairobi, across the country, around the world. I didn't know where I stood in this equation. I'd never been so desperate that I might steal someone's only pair of pants yet neither had I ever to defend myself against such an attack. I had never had to defend else from physical attack. I didn't know what the outcome would be if I did.

I had so many questions. The voices inside my head wouldn't shut up as I continually asked myself questions I couldn't answer. Why were so many kids living on the streets? What was the government doing about it? Were international aid organizations assisting? Did the kids make enough money to live even at a subsistence level? Did they make any money at all? What happened to them at night? How did they get this way? And, most of all, what could *I* do?

I met many children throughout Nairobi, as street children were unafraid about approaching strangers, begging for handouts. There was a group of boys who lived along the route from my home to my matatu stage and, after running into the same recognizable faces, I began to often stop and talk with them. One afternoon I met Moses, a ten-year-old boy who lived on the streets. He was immediately endearing, brimming with charisma. We made plans to have a proper chat, both so I could potentially include his story in my research and, because I was simply fascinated by his life experience, so unfathomable to me.

The next day he and a few other boys sat with me on the curb by an open-air market close by my host family's house. Their English was about as limited as my Swahili, but we still managed to understand one another. Each of the boys sipped small packets filled with milk I'd bought for them—a small price to pay, I thought, for fascinating conversation.

Because we'd arranged to meet in this upscale neighbourhood, Moses wasn't huffing glue today. But normally, he said, he spent most of his time in the slums and any money he could find on what he called his "gum"; huffing it took away his incessant hunger, made his body feel good and helped him forget the cold. It was, he said, the most efficient use of his money. Even though he knew inhaling the toxic substance could cause serious, irreparable damage to his young body and brain, in his desperation he clung to the numbness provided by its high. His father had died of AIDS and his mother was now also sick, so she couldn't afford to provide food for Moses and his siblings. With no way of surviving at home, Moses had to leave his village for the big city. Here Moses found other children who lived on the streets, having also fled their homes.

Moses pointed various kids out to me, knowing each of their stories. "That guy's parents both died. This guy just ran away from home for fun. This other guy doesn't even know how he got here."

Depending on the day and season, street life presented a range of serious dangers, from violence between street kids to malnutrition and disease from the brutal conditions. Later that winter, in January 2003, the newly elected government representing the National Alliance of Rainbow Coalition, or NARC, would send large trucks into Nairobi's streets, rounding up street children and taking them to state-sponsored facilities. I found out then that Moses himself avoided the trucks but later spent several intermittent sentences in city jail; he told me this never changed his preference to live on the streets.

Now, though, in those early days in Nairobi, I thought about how homeless people were regarded in North America, recalling how saddened I'd been to learn in school that children make up about a third of the homeless in America. It never made sense to me, when the commonly held stereotype of the homeless had more to do with mental illness or addiction, not a desperate underfed child on the street clutching a teddy bear, like one homeless child I'd seen here. How was this allowed to happen? How could people so young even *survive*?

Brenda was working with a development organization in the slums just outside of Kibera, and she invited me to tour the slum and see the true picture, away from the disturbing images shown in television commercials: children's wracked bodies, their open sores and bloated bellies, their weak efforts at swatting circling flies as they lay limp against flaking mud walls, while a groomed celebrity spokesperson pleaded on their behalf. Yet in the pit of my stomach, I felt apprehensive. Would I be welcome? Could I handle seeing such poverty?

Walking with Brenda through Kibera's narrow streets, it was impossible to ignore the suspicious glares of the slum's dwellers. Garbage was strewn along rows of tiny houses and through corridors formed by sheets of grimy, rusted tin siding. The stench of sewage hung heavy as we stepped carefully through red-brown puddles of dirt and recent rain. Green plastic bags were caught on rocks every few steps, leftovers of last night's "flying toilets"—Kibera's solution to a lack of public sanitation. I'd heard of people relieving themselves into bags at night, then throwing them out of the window; the evidence was all around us as we continued forward, careful not to slip in the mud.

But heading farther through the streets, a different story emerged. Echoes of children's shrieked laughter rang everywhere. Mamas in vibrant headscarves popped their heads from doorways, calling their kids for dinner, while other women worked makeshift vendor stands, selling fresh fried dough for five shillings; the smell of the cooking oil wafted mouth-watering aromas. Entrepreneurial men worked shoeshine booths and cobblers clustered on street corners. More and more children chased one another through these elaborate corridors, dodging the litter as they splashed through the streaming gutters.

A group of boys, dodging one another, accidentally bumped me. "Sorry!" they called back breathlessly, dashing away.

With Brenda as my guide, we visited some families' residences. The small houses, really only shacks, were made of corrugated tin walls and roofs with floors made either of hardened red clay or, sometimes, concrete. Some houses had simple, peeling paint jobs; many did not.

An average home was roughly three metres by three metres, half the size of my bathroom at home, with a curtain typically hung across the centre to fashion a bedroom separate from the sitting room or kitchen. Despite the close quarters, every home felt welcoming, personalized with decorations, wall-hangings or newspaper clippings. Floral patterned- fabrics were laid over couches and tiny televisions, tuned to whatever stations their limited reception could get, ran off car batteries. These furnishings almost masked my view of their unstocked cupboards, their ragged clothes, their unspoken desperation.

I tried to put myself in their place. Could I ever feel comfortable living in such a place, sleeping on a tiny mattress, with sewage streaming at my doorstep? A neighbourhood perpetually covered in mud and garbage and flying toilets? No running water, let alone no operating flush toilets or garbage collection? Could I ever call a place like this my home? Each family kept a twenty litre jerry can, called a *mitungi*, to carry water. It cost five shillings to fill it up at the shared water tank—roughly the equivalent of more than twice what my family back in Chicago paid for clean water piped directly into our home.

I was stunned, paralyzed, comparing the lifestyle I'd led back home with the experiences of those I saw in Kibera: those sick, starving, struggling just to survive. At home we raided our kitchen cabinets, which spilled with cartons of groceries, only to moan, "There's nothing to eat!" But here families often *really* had nothing to eat. Portions were strictly regulated and budgeted. Back in Schaumberg, my sister Erin and I often complained about having "nothing to wear," while piles of disregarded clothes tumbled from our closets. Here children wore cast-off clothes, most donated by Americans and sold in bulk throughout the developing world. Many wore clothes handmade by their mothers.

Nonetheless, for all that was different, just as much was the same between our worlds, half a world away. Families worried about their children as they slept, played, cooked, hosted visitors, hoped for the future—just as people everywhere, getting on with their lives.

My two months in Nairobi passed in a whirlwind of emotion. Everything was new and strange. But most of my time was spent readying myself for my true destination, only a few quick matatu rides away. As the end of my orientation period approached, I picked up the basic essentials I would need: a year's worth of tampons, a few loose-fitting skirts from the second-hand clothes market, a Swahili dictionary, malaria pills and not much else. I emailed a quick goodbye to my parents, saying I didn't know when I would be able to contact them next but assuring them I would do my best to be safe. Then, with my immediate future again uncertain, I was on my way.

3 My New Family

Weighed down by my stuffed backpack, I stepped out of the neon-green matatu into the street of Soko, a market town to the southwest near the Great Rift Valley. Morning was just breaking when I had boarded in Nairobi two hours before, but the sun now shone hot and unforgiving. The town was quiet, with the streets mostly vacant except for a few stray dogs, and the merchant stalls were empty. It was Sunday morning, and most Kenyans in this region, being devout Christians, were in church.

I wiped dust from my eyes as I tripped along the uphill road, thankful the rain was still holding off. My feet felt clumsy on the unfamiliar terrain and my pack shifted awkwardly as I staggered under the year's worth of supplies. The stares of local townspeople made me stumble even more as I made my way from the matatu stage to the main intersection. There gaudy advertisements for Coca-Cola and cell phone company Safaricom splashed across roofs, alongside crates of produce and other wares.

Heading west as I'd been instructed, I found a waiting off-white Toyota pickup truck, its rust and dents speaking of decades of busy transport. A few passengers waited in the back of the pickup while others hovered around, and I felt anxiety begin to burn in my cheeks. This truck, I'd been told, would take me down the valley to Nkoyet-naiborr, the community I'd soon be calling home.

The driver, looking to be in his early forties and wearing a tattered checked sport coat, leaned against the truck's hood. With my best attempt at a friendly greeting in Swahili, I explained how I hoped to join them on their way into the valley. I described my destination, a church with a name I wasn't sure I pronounced correctly. The driver eyed me with obvious scepticism. Then, without a word, he took my bag and motioned for me to climb into the pickup's uncovered bed. I hopped in. Unsure of where to sit between the shaky-looking benches and tightly packed sacks of groceries, I wiped red dust from a side rail and took a seat there. The driver handed back my bag, gave a nod, then returned to his place at the hood.

As time passed without any sign of motion, I began to understand the truck would wait until every visitor to town was ready to go. I tried to make myself comfortable, knowing it could probably be some time before we moved.

Gradually, the truck began to fill with passengers. A pair of young women, each with shaved heads and a child cradled in their arms, joined me in the back. Layers of light fabrics spilled around their bodies, accented with elaborate beadwork in every primary colour adorning their necks, wrists and ankles. The way they spoke in their high-pitched voices seemed almost like a shared game: soft, tender coos between intimate shared giggles, then bursting into a crescendo of laughter and celebratory clasped hands. I couldn't tell whether their boisterous laughter was directed at me, the stranger almost painfully sticking out, or something else I wasn't getting.

I felt myself retreating into myself, not knowing how to fit in, what to say or do. But this was clearly a bad time to become shy, so I tried to join the conversation in simple English. I said hello and did my best to make light of my failure to understand, shrugging comically. It seemed to work, and soon we were laughing together.

I settled in and tried to enjoy the scenery while we waited for the truck to depart. Soko was a charming small town, nestled against the green slopes and blue ridges of the Ol Doinyo Hills. Storefronts, some tin, some wooden and some concrete, lined the sides of the paved road, each bearing hand-painted and stencilled signs in English: "Blue Hotel," "Friend's Pub," "Barbershop & Saloon."

A convenience store was marked with a sign reading "Supermarket." *Supermarket?* It looked about the size of my living room back at home, with wooden shelves creating three aisles inside. Definitely different from the aisles of our Dominic's grocery store back home. Another read "Bookstore." *Bookstore?* It was about the size of my first grade classroom, with drab grey concrete walls on the inside—a far cry from the scene on Saturday afternoons thumbing through books in the cozy chairs of Barnes & Noble.

Three older men bearing walking sticks crafted from tree branches came over to greet the truck. The men walked slowly and deliberately, each with bright-red blankets—like the ones I'd seen on the man in Nairobi and which I later learned in my cultural education classes were called shukas—tied loosely across their chests and under one arm. I'd seen these blankets for sale in Nairobi's markets, but on these aged men they made a much more regal impression. The women in the truck immediately stopped their conversations to stand and bow down to these men, who then lightly touched the tops of each of their heads. The children did the same.

I took my cue to follow suit. The men laughed at my gesture. They and the women began an animated discussion about, I guessed, who this stranger might be. I caught one word I had learned in Swahili class: *wetu.* "Ours."

Chuckling hoarsely, the men beckoned for me to lower my head again. One after another they gently touched the top of my head, each repeating the same greeting that I barely understood. I really had to drastically improve my Swahili!

I brought my head back up, unable to wipe the goofy smile from my face. Everyone burst out laughing, talking over one another. One woman gave my arm a friendly squeeze, and I quickly felt less self-conscious. The older men were each given a boost and they, along with a few others, joined us in the back of the pickup. No one seemed concerned at how crowded the bed of the pickup truck was becoming.

Again my mind flooded with questions. *Would the truck drag its belly on the road from the weight? Was it safe to load the truck so heavily?* I had to stop myself from saying anything and trust they were capable of managing their affairs. After all, I had no idea what I was doing. It was best to fall in with the crowd, release myself of any worries and just sit back and learn.

As the busy chatter continued, my eyes returned to the street. Nearby young boys in both traditional and Western clothes knelt on the ground, playing cards and scratching their stomachs and arms. More stray dogs wandered idly, sniffing at patches of brush. The pace here was much slower than Nairobi's bustle. People moved more deliberately. I could feel myself being absorbed by the town's tranquil pace, the gentle grace of the people. It was like exhaling after a long held breath: my pulse quieted, the inner chatter that constantly filled my head seeming to silence itself.

Someone tapped me on my shoulder. I turned around to find the driver holding out a bottle of Orange Fanta.

He spoke his first words to me, in English: "Take it."

I could barely respond to this generous offer.

"Take it," he said again, smiling quietly.

I accepted the bottle, unable to fully express my appreciation as the driver again disappeared. I took a long swig to show my gratitude, then offered the bottle to the child sitting next to me. The other kids in the truck squeezed in around me, and we all took turns sharing this treat.

Over half an hour passed with no movement. The sun stalled overhead, its equatorial heat beating down on us. With the back of my hand I wiped the beads of sweat from my forehead. Just when it looked like we were about to leave, someone would hop out, shout something I couldn't understand, then more women would flock to the truck, loading their weekly shopping: huge bundles of corn flour and plastic bags of beans, cabbages and tomatoes. Men and children took the packages from the women and tossed into the pickup, then carefully arranged each package to optimize space.

People came and went. An hour passed, then another. More and more people crammed in for the ride, some standing. Others perched on a wooden bench arranged over the tires for more seating space, others on empty milk canisters. Some clung to the truck's roof or balanced themselves on the back bumper. I did a head count: amazingly, we had crammed *thirty-four* people into this small Toyota truck!

The driver finally returned to his seat, jangling a set of keys. Yes! We were finally actually going! I didn't know how long the ride would be, but I did know that my bum was already numb from sitting over the rail for so long.

But when the driver went to start the ignition, the truck only made a wheezing sound, refusing to start. The driver tried again. Another unsuccessful wheeze and foul smoke burst forth as the chassis shuddered. Three more attempts, then the driver popped his head out the window and called out something I didn't understand. Several men piled out, and I moved to follow, but a mama stopped me with a gentle hand. I interpreted this as an instruction to sit back down and did so, grateful that someone was looking out for me.

The driver shifted into neutral as the men pushed the truck forward. We rolled forward, slowly but with mounting speed, until the driver was able to pop the clutch and turn the engine over. Elated shouts rang out as the engine caught. Diesel smoke clouded the air as those pushing jumped back in, resettling themselves as the truck struggled uphill and forward into the valley.

As the wind picked up, the women pulled out more shukas to cover their shaved heads. An old mama wearing intricately beaded earrings smiled at me, again telling me something I didn't understand. I laughed and told her in English that I didn't speak Swahili—but I would soon! Whether she understood or not, I didn't know. But she laughed and outstretched her shuka to cover my head along with hers.

We bounced along the craggy road down into a valley of thorny flat-topped trees, whose yellow bark carried more branches than leaves, and small ponds as red as the soil. Cattle grazed in small sections of grassland, attended by young men enwreathed in shukas. We passed traditional huts, which I knew from my orientation classes were called *manyattas*. They were made of cow dung, mud and sticks. Many were surrounded by protective fences made of thick, thorny branches of the same flat-topped trees found everywhere, planted in circles. Tin structures sat topped with crosses; I realized these were churches.

I did my best to take everything in slowly, aware that the others were closely gauging my reactions. A bump in the road tossed us into the air, and we clutched onto one another, coming down on the side of the truck with a hard thud. I clung to the mama next to me, and we laughed at the ridiculousness of the rough ride. The entire scene felt daunting and enchanting at the same time.

Suddenly something disrupted the lively conversation, and a boy near the cab of the truck called out, pointing. The woman beside me seized my arm to direct my attention to something in the distance. I looked to see large, lean shapes ambling past on the roadside: one, two, three . . . five . . . seven giraffes, chomping dangling tree leaves, less than fifteen metres away.

"Wow!" I exclaimed. "I've seen them on TV, and at the Brookfield Zoo, but . . . *wow!*"

The entire crowd laughed at my amazement, even the children. They obviously saw giraffes all the time, probably more often than my family at home saw deer or any other woodland animals. I tried to reel in my excitement, afraid they were mocking me. But it was clear they simply wanted to share this incredible sight with me, even though for them it was familiar. One girl pointed and gave me a long, animated explanation of . . . something. Once again, I was reminded how I truly needed to become fluent in Swahili, and quickly!

We continued down the rocky road for nearly another hour before the truck began making intermittent stops to offload riders and their bundles of shopping. Luckily, the truck didn't need to be pushed to start again; then just as the constant stopping and starting began to make me queasy, we reached a church, the location where I'd been told to be dropped off. As the driver braked, I pulled up my pack and hopped out.

"*Kwa heri!*" I called to my fellow passengers. At least I'd learned how to say goodbye.

The family I was joining were of the Maasai people, an indigenous tribe occupying the southern region of the Great Rift Valley throughout southern

Giraffes roam the savannah: beautiful, but dangerous if crossed.

Kenya and north central Tanzania. During my orientation in Nairobi, I had done some brief research into this unfamiliar culture.

Maasai live as traditional pastoralists, herding mostly cattle, but also sheep, donkeys and goats. They are semi-nomadic, meaning their livestock is moved on seasonal rotation and in response to environmental factors, particularly drought. Cattle play a cherished role in their society, both in their economic and personal health. Maasai drink cows' milk every day as a staple of their diets, and they value not only the meat but even its blood, which they believe holds unique health benefits. However, since a cow represents an enormous financial asset for a family, slaughtering one for meat or blood is typically reserved for ceremonies and special occasions.

Despite the increasing modernization of Africa in recent years, the Maasai have still clung to many of their traditions and beliefs. They speak their own regional dialect, called Maa, though many also speak Swahili and English. Estimates of their current population range wildly, anywhere from only about 150,000 to almost a million throughout sub-Saharan Africa. Yet they still remain mostly marginalized from mainstream Kenyan culture, both economically and politically.

Professor Jama, my advisor in Nairobi, knew of a Maasai community in the Rift Valley who would welcome a visitor—me. I'd been told that district elders, together with Professor Jama, had assembled to decide on the family with whom I should live. The father of the family I was joining had past experience with various development organizations working in Kenya, and collectively they had decided how to welcome their American visitor.

The Maasai I'd seen so far—like the man in Nairobi—dressed in distinctively colourful clothing with ornate necklaces and earrings of fine beadwork. Many of them displayed long, pierced and stretched earlobes—a common body modification considered beautiful in their society. I wasn't sure if this was what I was to expect from my adoptive family. All I knew was that they were eagerly expecting my arrival. I had to rise above my nervous jitters and prepare to throw myself into whatever came my way.

And yet I was hesitant: could I reach out and cross the inevitable cultural gap? Would this family and I be able to joke, or communicate at all? Would the differences simply be too vast? Had my desire to flee a frustrating, ordinary upbringing been too hasty or too extreme?

I started toward the church, where I was to meet my "mama," the mother of the family with whom I'd be staying for the next year. The father of the family—my "baba"—was a teacher and one of the community's more educated men. He travelled often and was presently away, doing work with one of the many charities frequenting the region.

Then a stunningly beautiful, tall woman who looked not much older than me came toward me down the roadside. She wore multicoloured shukas draped around her slender shoulders and a bright blue skirt. Her feet were bare, but her face beamed with a brilliant smile. I hoped my own smile was even half as wide.

"My daughter!" she cried in English.

I wasn't sure how to react. "Mama?" I tried, trying to feign confidence.

"Welcome!" She hugged my shoulders, first on the left, then again on the right: a traditional Maasai embrace. My body was stiff, yet her movements were smooth and easy. She moved deliberately, with purpose.

Against my protests, she hauled my backpack onto her shoulders, then immediately dropped it back on the ground, staggering under its weight. She wiped her brow with the back of her hand.

"I'm sorry," I cried, coming to her aid. "Let me take that!" *Have I brought too much?*

I rushed to help her, but Mama then rose and effortlessly tossed my bag over her shoulder and continued ahead, laughing at my stunned expression. Finally I got the joke and hurried to catch up with her. Lacking the right words, I could only laugh to show my appreciation, and soon we were laughing together. I followed her lead toward a narrow, worn footpath running uphill through the brush. With her long legs, she kept a brisk pace, and I pushed hard to keep up with her.

"Where are we going?" I asked.

She looked at me and smiled. "Home."

I followed Mama up the dirt path, keeping a cautious distance. The long savannah grass and twisted, thorny bushes soon gave way to a clearing heavy with the smell of barn animals. I saw several small huts, then a fenced enclosure. Huddled at a distance, a group of small children watched. I gave them a wave, but they only scurried away.

Before I knew what was happening, Mama began a quick tour. She showed me a small structure made of mud and sticks that had a dirt floor on which stood a pair of small beds with wooden frames and thin blankets: this was the main house where we would sleep. Another smaller hut served as a kitchen, centred around a small, smouldering firepit, with a few wooden shelves and a number of long planks of scrap lumber set as benches. This must be where the family sits at mealtime, I thought to myself. There was a pit toilet, similar to an outhouse, located just outside the fence of replanted branches, roughly assembled from tin sheets nailed together. Nearby was a metre-square concrete block structure with tin sheets for walls, no roof and a large bucket inside.

"*Bafu*," Mama explained: where we would bathe. This would definitely be interesting!

Continuing our tour, we crossed through another fenced enclosure. *Ngombe yetu wanalala hapa*, she said: our cattle sleep here. She pointed to an enclosed area for the goats and sheep, another for the cows, indicating they were currently away being herded in community fields. A number of clucking chickens pecked around the yard. Mud caked on the bottom of my battered running shoe with each step, but I fought to show Mama I wasn't fazed, concentrating on each step.

Squish-sh-sh-sh. Something warm melted over my foot—I looked down and found my shoe sinking into the slurping quicksand of a huge cow patty. *Oops!* I raised my knee to try and save my shoe, but the suction was too strong. I pulled harder, forcing it out, and my foot came free—sending a spray of manure flinging into the air with its release.

Mama, ahead at the compound's edge, turned back. I snapped to attention and smiled as best I could, trying to regain composure even with manure splattered on my legs. A burst of high-pitched giggles broke out nearby. But when I turned, my small crowd of shy observers again fled before I could greet them.

Everything was hitting me so fast, I could barely process it. The isolation. The fire. A new bed. A new family. The powerful stink. What exactly was I getting myself into here?

"*Tuende uoge,*" Mama said, directing me to take a shower. After the long journey, I was more than ready to clean up.

By the bafu Mama arranged a bucket of water and swung a thin, threadbare towel over the tin siding. A yellow brick of soap sat on a narrow, wooden shelf. I closed the swinging door behind me, fastening it by twisting a bent nail over the doorframe. Stripping naked, I stood exposed to the open sky above.

My heart pounded from the day's frenzy of activity. This village was far from Nairobi's neon lights, pumping music and constant advertising. But I still felt overwhelmed.

With a deep breath, I splashed myself with water from the bucket and lathered up with the soap. Getting clean after the afternoon's long, dusty ride felt good, and I shut my eyes to review the day in my head. The bright red and blue of the women's clothes. The high-pitched chatter of a dozen competing conversations. The diesel smoke contrasting with the fresh air all around. The scratch of thorns in the tall, dry savannah grass.

Then I knew I wasn't alone. Turning, I was startled to see a cow's head was poking at my feet—and it was now drinking from my bucket of bathwater! I almost swore out loud in surprise. How could I shoo the cow away without someone hearing my distress and then coming to my rescue, only to find me naked?

"Go away!" I hissed at the cow. I bopped it lightly on its head and, to my relief, it began to slowly back out, trailing saliva from its mouth to my bucket.

I stood there, hands on hips under the open sky, afraid to look down at my bucket, now mixed with globs of cow saliva. Should I remain soapy, or rinse with water goopy with cow saliva? I could only chuckle to myself. Here was a choice I would never imagined having to make.

After my bucket shower, Mama resumed her tour. Past the manure field, we came across a second hut made of cow dung, sticks and mud, no taller than one-and-a-half metres high and three metres square.

"*Kokoo!*" Mama called. "*Hodi!*" Hello!

"*Karibu!*" Welcome! A hoarse, older voice whispered from inside.

Mama lowered her head and went inside, motioning for me to follow. I felt my way into the darkness, unable to see more than a metre ahead. A small fire roared in the centre of the manyatta and the stifling heat was overpowering. Stumbling forward, I accidentally kicked over an empty canister.

"Oh!" I cried, cursing my clumsiness.

Laughing, Mama took my hand and guided me to a mattress made of tightly woven sticks beneath a cow hide. Blind in the dark, I could only follow Mama's voice.

"Your grandmother," she said. "We say *Kokoo*."

My eyes gradually adjusted to the darkened scene, the only ventilation a thirty-by-two-centimetre window along the mud wall. Behind the fire, a small woman sat on a wooden stool. Squinting through the smoke, I discerned her tiny figure, wrapped in a ragged shuka with frayed edges, her shaven head shining in the firelight.

Speaking to Mama in soft, almost whispered Maa over the fire's crackle, Kokoo expertly prepared tea for us. Her dishes—cups, plates, a Thermos and pots—were kept on top of a pile of firewood that doubled as a drying rack and storage cupboard. She removed a steaming pot from the fire and dug out a plastic container, pouring a sugar-like powder into the pot.

I was staring at Kokoo's dangling stretched earlobes when she broke into a chuckle, catching me off guard. This was the first time we'd looked one another in the eye, and even through the darkness I was stunned by the glassy bluish hue of her eyes.

"*Ngoo shai*," she said, reaching over the fire to pass a mug brimming with hot milky tea. I thanked her and accepted the mug. The three of us sipped from our cups, eyeing one another through the rising smoke. Mama and Kokoo continued speaking, clearly discussing something related to my arrival. Then they both turned to me with expectant smiles.

"You must be given a Maasai name," Mama decreed.

Mama turned to Kokoo, prompting her. Kokoo looked at me as if she were the proud grandmother and I the grandchild, taking her first steps.

"We have decided on yours," Mama said. "*Naserian*. It means 'peaceful person.'"

Naserian. I repeated the name in my mind.

Kokoo cocked her head and repeated the word to herself, as if getting used to connecting my face to that name.

"Thank you," I said. I didn't know what else to say.

"Naserian, TUENDE!" Mama said, gesturing for me to come with her. I bid Kokoo farewell and followed Mama back out into the blinding light of day.

As my eyes adjusted to the sun's glare, we were met by those children who had before skittered away but now were gathered round. As Mama introduced them one by one, I was surprised to discover all of them lived in the compound with us.

Three boys stood leaning on one another: Saigilu, twelve; Parsinte, ten; and Morio, only five. Mama introduced another older boy as Kipulel, fifteen; she explained in English that they'd taken him in a few years ago, after his own parents' death, but she didn't explain the circumstances.

A girl cowered behind them, squatting on the ground with her skirt tucked under her knees, averting her eyes. Each of her features were perfectly proportioned on her slim frame; she carried a certain wisdom in her deep-set brown eyes despite her apparent youth. This was Mama's youngest sister, Faith—though at only thirteen she was more like her daughter. She'd come to live here several years ago to assist Mama with the sprawling family.

Suddenly I had four new brothers and a sister. No—*two* sisters! A tiny head squealing with glee poked from behind Faith. The daughter of a far-away relative, Metengo was four years old and lived with Kokoo.

As then Mama turned to explain the situation to the boys in Maa, I tried to gauge their personalities. Saigilu stood tall and slender, slightly in front of his brothers, respectfully nodding as Mama spoke, resting his hand protectively on Morio's shoulder. Parsinte, clearly the most animated of the bunch, laughed loudly, fidgeting playfully with his walking stick. He was about thirty centimetres shorter than Saigilu yet obviously had half the attention span.

Swatting away a fly, Parsinte accidentally bumped into Kipulel, who was leaning against the kitchen with his arms crossed. Kipulel quickly spread his arms and jokingly threatened to push back. This sent Parsinte and Morio into another fit of giggles as Kipulel eased back into his cool pose, a teasing half-smile on his face.

Morio bounced eagerly up and down, his arms swinging loosely in time to a song playing only in his head. His smile was mischievous as he tried to stare me down. When I squinted back, Morio exploded into giggles and let loose his song, singing loudly through the spittle forming on the sides of his mouth. Saigilu reached out to cover Morio's mouth and Morio dutifully stepped back in line, trying to stifle the laughter. I would have walloped Erin if she'd ever tried to quiet me that way in front of a stranger. Yet Morio seemed to find the attention he was looking for in Saigilu's mild reprimand.

Under Mama's watchful attention, the children's wariness of me as a new stranger gradually evaporated. Saigilu was the first to approach me, extending a hand in greeting. Parsinte and Kipulel followed close behind. Faith was last in line. She timidly shielded her eyes with one hand while extending the other to shake.

Morio danced around me, babbling giddily in Maa as he clutched my hand, making a game of not letting go. I played along, overwhelmed at all these new names and faces.

Mama concluded by introducing me to them: "Naserian."

All of the children echoed it back in unison: "*Naserian!*"

They led me to a plot of shade under a thorny tree near the kitchen. Saigilu saw me eyeing the tree and slowly annunciated: *A-ca-cia*, pointing upward. When I repeated after him, he laughed out loud, unable to hide his amusement. The kids gathered around me, tugging playfully at my blonde hair, fascinated by this unfamiliar colour, baffled by this strange person who had come to live with them.

This was my new family.

4 Finding My Way

Suddenly everything had changed. For so long I'd yearned to break free, to let loose that inner fire and seek out a new life. I'd thrown myself headfirst into an entirely new world, not knowing what to expect. Fleeing Schaumburg meant seeking freedom, hoping for something more meaningful, more real. My Maasai life was unlike anything I could have imagined.

That first night I lay awake all night on the narrow bed Faith and I shared, struggling to get comfortable. I turned over and over, the wooden frame digging into my lower back and my skirt sticking to the thin, foam mattress. I felt in bondage by my clothes, by the night's silence, by the uncomfortable bed.

Then a bone-chilling, high-pitched howl rang outside.

"*Faith!*" I whispered.

"Naserian . . . ?"

"What is that sound?"

Faith rolled over, annoyed at being woken. "Hyenas."

Hyenas? Now sleep was even more impossible. I tried to block out those echoing wails, but my mind flooded with questions. Was I doing the right thing? Was I just substituting one set of frustrations for another? Had I made a terrible mistake?

I winced at the thought of my parents seeing me filled with doubt or letting anyone see my apprehension. *Dad, you want me to be fearless? Powerful? Determined? Unstoppable?* They wanted me to be strong. I'd show them how strong I could be.

The next day I woke at the crack of dawn to voices and clatter coming from the kitchen. Stepping out from the manyatta, I stretched my arms and breathed deeply in the fresh morning air. The clouds hovered just over the hills' grassy peaks under a wide overcast sky. I felt light years from the congested freeways and glittering shopping plazas at home. Despite restless sleep, I felt ready for the day to come.

I was jarred from my reverie by Mama's shrill calls.

"*Naserian! Tuende!*" Let's go!

Back home, our family set aside Tuesdays for housecleaning, and I would inevitably gripe about having to do the dusting and vacuuming. Or throughout the week, when my parents asked me to clean my bedroom or wash dishes after dinner, it felt like a punishment, a little thing that felt like a life sentence. I'd whine and delay, thinking I had better things to do than help maintain our household. In my journal, I'd written, *I will never settle for staying at home, cleaning up after my husband and children. Please let me never live that life, centred around daily chores, maintaining the status quo.*

But it was quickly becoming obvious that my days in Nkoyet-naiborr would be defined by the many chores needed to maintain the *boma*, or household. Many of these were the same chores done for the upkeep of a North American home . . . but in a very different way. We still washed dishes and clothes, cooked meals, shopped for necessary supplies. But here, these daily duties weren't just to keep the place spic and span. Here, they were necessary for our very survival.

The day's first task was collecting water. In recent years, Western missionaries visiting the area had introduced piping projects throughout many areas of rural

Kenya, allowing more families across the land to enjoy greater access to water. Our boma's water was piped in from a natural spring up in the Ol Doinyo Hills down to a large metal storage tank about a kilometre from our home, next to the red-brick community schoolhouse where my brothers and sisters attended classes. Mamas from all across the community trekked there several times daily to collect water for their household purposes, from laundry to bathing to cooking *ugali*—a starchy, inexpensive cornmeal staple food for much of Africa.

As Mama explained, recent weeks had been dry, and water was scarce. It was the parched "white grass" of the prairies that gave Nkoyet-naiborr its name. During spells of drought that lasted anywhere between a couple of months to a couple of years, the daily water levels in the metal storage tank would be so low, the water could only be tapped from the spring at night. With such scant supplies, everyone had to reduce their overall usage, even as low as only one *mitungi* a day. Generally people were diligent about their usage, but it required community-wide participation to ensure everyone received their fair share.

In these dry periods, tough choices arose: should you wash your hair or your clothes? Can you bathe using just a cup of water? Can you prepare enough ugali with such limited cooking water?

I could tell Mama was unsure whether I was up for the task. She looked at my well-fed body and my soft, unworked hands, clearly sceptical as to my ability to do hard work. But I insisted I could do it—I just needed to learn. With a shrug, she picked up two plastic mitungis made from recycled cooking oil containers and motioned for me to follow her to the water source.

I followed Mama to the end of our property, marked by the fence fashioned from the thorny branches of felled acacia trees. With the fence in place, she explained, our sparse grass could grow protected from the grazing of the neighbouring cows that occasionally wandered by. We crossed the main road of red pebbled dirt and headed down the curved, worn footpath, weaving through the growth of sage bushes.

Rounding a bend in the path, Mama paused to twist a branch off what she told me was an East African greenheart tree. She snapped it in two and handed half to me, then continued on. I followed her example, shaving the bark off the branches' edges and placing it in my mouth to soften the phylum. After a few minutes, she showed me, their bristles could be spread out and used as a type of toothbrush.

As we came down the hill's crest toward the water source, I heard the high-pitched chatter of women's voices. My face flushed and my palms began to sweat. Until now, Mama had been my guide and protector, leading me through this unfamiliar experience. I wasn't a child, and I didn't want to be shielded or supervised through new experiences, yet a lump formed in my throat. Would I be accepted, or would the women band against me? Would they not all wink at one another and sneer at me as an outsider?

The women in their colourful shukas circled the tank, waiting to fill their mitungis. I followed close behind Mama as she joined the line, greeting the other women. Everyone knew her, and the mamas greeted one another as if they hadn't seen each other in years, even though they each came here every day. Mama was probably the loudest of them all; she called each woman by name, asking about their families, their livestock, any news heard along the way. The water source was the community's mass communication system.

The attention quickly shifted to me. Mama took the stage and began rattling off Swahili to her gathered audience of mamas. I didn't understand these words of introduction but tried to smile politely. I took my cue to bow my head to those older than me, as I had done with the elders in the pickup truck the day before. As the women looked me up and down, I felt horribly self-conscious and awkward. *Everyone's laughing! Are they laughing at me? Am I ever going to fit in?*

I tried to play along, following the flow without fully understanding what was going on. Occasional words leapt out from the flurry of conversation: *Chicago. America.* The mamas nodded, impressed by whatever Mama was telling them. I could see my concerns were unfounded; Mama clearly just wanted me to get to know my neighbours, and she wanted them to meet me. They weren't mocking me but discussing how they could best welcome me into their community.

As I watched the women talk I began to understand a bit about gender dynamics in this society. From my time so far, I could see that as a woman—and particularly as a young, unmarried woman—I would be expected to assume a very specific role in the family and in the community as a whole. At home I was used to laughing freely when a friend made a witty observation, or when a silly situation arose, yet now I was witnessing a new way for women to behave.

Back at the boma I learned to follow Mama's and Faith's examples, as I had been told that acting publicly in a flippant, overly enthusiastic and open manner would be seen as the behaviour of a promiscuous, easy woman. I had to learn to tone down my actions—not to be submissive, necessarily, but always remain conscious of acting respectfully. Men were the centre of attention, while women were meant to keep conversation going while sitting in very careful poses. Women maintained a humble demeanour, always staying vigilant of the family's needs.

Yet at the water source, with no men around, the women were free to behave much more openly. Fetching water is a woman's task, and this place was the women's domain. Here mamas could gossip, joke and enjoy the camaraderie of fellow mamas. They sat however they wanted, their usual composed postures now relaxed as they sat on their mitungis and waited their turn. They laughed uproariously with one another, and I laughed too—though, of course, I understood none of it.

Soon it was my turn. Transporting water, I saw from the women, is an art unto itself. The mitungi must be carefully balanced on two rocks beneath the spout and then held in place while the trickling water slowly fills it all the way to the top. And with water always in scarce supply, we could never afford to waste or spill a drop.

When the cylindrical twenty litre container was full, it weighed more than twenty kilos. I stood stalled, uncertain of what to do next.

"I will show you," Mama said.

She attached a long, woven rope to the cylinder and wrapped the other end around it once, then twice, securing it in an intricate knot. She then placed the rope around her forehead and reached down to knot the other end to the cylinder, creating a type of sling. I watched with wonder as she hoisted this heavy load up onto her slender back, adjusting the rope at a precise spot just above her hairline, so as not to pull at the skin, and at an angle that avoided strain on her neck. With the water stable, she shifted her hips, stood and was ready to walk. Her effort was definitely impressive, and I was amazed to see that some mamas even looped a second can below the first so they could carry two heavy loads at a time.

Then it was my turn to give it a try. On my first attempt I tied the rope wrong and, misjudging the balance of the weight, I let the rope slip from my forehead. I sighed and dropped the cumbersome mitungi back on the ground. Mama watched patiently, offering to take over as I sweated and strained. But I was determined to do it on my own.

While in Nairobi, preparing for my year with the family, I'd learned how drought is a regular and troubling reality for Kenya. Since water is vital to all components of daily life—cooking, cleaning, bathing, keeping livestock and staying hydrated in this parched land—scarcity, common during the regular seasons, can utterly devastate the population. Even if a family is well-off enough to afford adequate supplies of ugali flour and other staples, without the water with which to cook, they can't eat. Hunger then runs rampant. As Mama told me, in drought seasons one saw the fattest cows reduced to skin and bones. People's faces grew sunken and their bodies became emaciated.

Maintaining water supplies remains a mama's greatest responsibility and the most important duty she must perform, often from an early age as with Metengo. If I was going to prove myself capable of rising to the challenge, I would have to master this task. And quickly.

I took a deep breath and tried again. This time I took more care in preparing the knot and made sure to secure the rope on my forehead before rising. With Mama nearby I finally managed to level the weight and slowly stood fully upright. With the other mamas watching, I took one step, then another, and soon we were headed back up the pebbled footpath to the boma, carrying enough water for our entire family.

Faith and I return home after doing laundry—one of many household tasks for which, as a woman, I would be responsible.

In the rush of those first days I was introduced to so many new people that it was nearly impossible to keep them straight. Their names were all strange to my foreign ear, and at first all the kids' faces looked the same to me. Yet my new family was eager to introduce me to their community and into their lives.

I found the social world in Nkoyet-naiborr was much more structured than average American life. There was an elaborate system of customs and rituals, maintaining a regimented social dynamic. Luckily, my adoptive family worked hard to help me understand.

Maasai conversations and greetings are conducted in a very specific manner, with certain codes of decorum and rhythms of speech. For example, as Faith taught me through broken English, Maasai greetings are always performed the same way.

First, one calls the name of the person being hailed: "Naserian!"
The response is then, "*Ao!*" Yes!
In return, the person greeting the other answers, "*Sopa!*" Hello!
And finally, the response: "*Ipa!*" Hello!

Conversation could then continue freely, but at a much slower, more methodical pace than I was used to. At home, it seemed people spoke rapidly, as if constantly afraid someone would cut them off; conversations often ran over one another, intersecting and colliding impulsively and quickly. Among the Maasai, individuals take turns speaking, while the listener encourages them along, expressing understanding with the repeated sound, "*ay*." Rather than interrupting or finishing one another's sentences, people strive to state facts and ideas plainly and thoroughly, taking turns.

This sense of decorum applied not only to adults, but also to the kids. As I'd already seen, people met their elders with the head lowered as a sign of respect. The elder then lightly touched the younger person on the forehead with a brush of fingers. Between Maasai men, a generous handshake was the custom.

As an outsider I wasn't sure how I fit into this system. I was not a Maasai, so even though I was older than the children, the rules were different. The kids loved shaking hands with me, rather than being greeted with the touch to the head. They greeted me over and over: *Naserian! Naserian!* And every time I had to respond, *Ao!* Even as I grew tired of this game, they seemed to draw greater and greater pleasure from greeting me.

I loved being in this learning mode, especially in improving my limited grasp of Swahili. I was swept up in the experience; trying to learn the customs and daily rituals, while around me everyone spoke in an unfamiliar tongue, seemed overwhelming. I tried to remain unafraid to make mistakes. Here I was the new daughter of a new culture, and I was ready and willing to do my best to adapt.

But because my Swahili was so limited, and members of the family were themselves still in various stages of learning English, everything they said came out as a command.

"Go!"

"Come!"

"Naserian, *bring!*"

I felt I was always being ordered, never asked politely as I was accustomed. Even Mama, whose English was relatively sophisticated, spoke mostly in these sharp directions. I'd be hard at work scrubbing dishes or performing some other task, then hear Mama calling out: *Naserian!* Naturally, I'd come hurrying in response, only to receive more commands.

"Give me that."

"Get me the knife."

Do this, do that: abrupt, functional exchanges always took the place of meaningful, relaxed conversation. The language barrier was just too vast. Yet this challenge only drove me to keep working at improving my Swahili and helping their English. I was sure that soon I would be able to join in on the laughter, the jokes, the sharing of intimate feelings.

After the sweaty slog back up to the boma, Mama and I dropped off our mitungis at the kitchen. Faith was already hard at work on preparing breakfast and, before I had a moment's rest, Mama directed me to go help. Maintaining the family kitchen, including preparing meals, brewing tea, washing dishes and general cleaning, were also among a woman's many duties.

I crouched and entered. Faith beckoned to me through the darkness and, as my eyes adjusted, I knelt next to where she was breaking up twigs, preparing them for kindling.

As Faith demonstrated, the basics of preparing the fire, used for cooking and boiling water. A metal pot, charred with years of use, was balanced on top of three rectangular stones, placed at square angles in a horseshoe shape. The space left open allowed firewood to be fed underneath to create a bed of blazing embers. We then broke up several handfuls of bark from a tall pile of dried branches and logs Faith and Mama had previously collected.

Faith arranged the kindling in a small tripod, placed larger branches on the outside and then took a can of paraffin wax from a shelf and coated the smallest kindling. Placing the paraffin back on the shelf, she reached for the box of wooden matches that sat next to it, and with a quick movement she struck one and touched its flame to the wax. Once the fire had caught long enough for the wood to smoke, she dropped to the ground and blew several times to fan the flame. The smoke grew thicker, and I turned my head to cough,

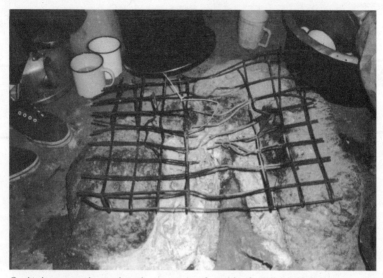

Our kitchen stove—three rocks with room to insert firewood and a grill to hold a pot.

squinting my smarting eyes.

When the fire was generating enough heat, Faith placed another pot, filled to a third with water, atop it—water to be used for washing dishes from last night's dinner. When the water began to steam, Faith removed it from the fire and placed it at her feet, dumping the dishes inside, along with the yellow bar of soap. A second pot was filled with a mixture of water and milk to boil for tea.

Maasai families typically only have chai tea with hot milk for breakfast, or occasionally fruit, if available, or on some occasions a small fried dough pastry called *mundazi*. Chai tea is a staple found in every Maasai pantry or kitchen, and brewing tea was considered another chore of great responsibility. It is considered essential to provide guests with tea, no matter the hour of day, and all Maasai—kids and adults alike—consider it an essential part of daily life.

Faith grabbed an unlabelled red container from the wooden shelf, unscrewed the yellow lid and poured loose tea leaves onto her hand to carefully assess the amount. Once the water and milk mixture had boiled she added the tea leaves and let the mixture boil some more. Faith then spooned in an equally diligently measured amount of sugar and sieved the completed tea into a plastic Thermos.

Just then the boys began to arrive for their breakfast tea.

"Naserian!" Saigilu, the eldest of the brothers, entered first, followed closely by Parsinte.

"*Ao!*"

"*Sopa!*"

"*Ipa!*"

With each family member's entrance, our voices rang with greetings, and a fresh cup of tea was poured. Next came Morio, who giggled shyly at me, followed by Kipulel, who beamed proudly at greeting me in Swahili and his rudimentary English.

Then their father, Baba, who had returned from his travels late the previous night, entered the kitchen. Morio's giggles came to a halt and everyone rose at once to greet him. He stood in the doorway, his head freshly shaven, wielding a long walking stick. He was clearly older than Mama, yet he had the slightly clumsy movements of a younger man. Though he was of average height and build, he possessed an aura of importance, and the children all met his greetings with hushed respect.

He and I hadn't yet met, and I wasn't sure what to expect or what he would think of me. I watched Faith to see how she responded. She bowed her head, as did my brothers, presenting the top of her head for him to touch.

Baba greeted me last.

"Naserian," he said in a deep, solemn voice.

"*Ao?*" I replied. He placed his fingertips gently on my head, then gestured for me to lift my chin. He leaned in, his dark, probing eyes close to mine. I looked over at Mama and Faith, but they were busy scrubbing dishes, soaping cutlery and plates in one pot, rinsing in another.

"*Sopa.*" His eyes crinkled in a wide grin.

"*Ipa . . . ?*"

My voice was so quiet I barely heard myself, and Baba have me a quizzical look. I cleared my throat and tried again.

"*Ipa!*" I shouted.

Baba laughed as my brothers scooted over, making room for him in the centre of the bench. Baba spoke loudly, his broad shoulders wrapped in two red shukas knotted around his shoulders, his chest dangling with beaded necklaces. The only non-traditional aspect of his appearance was the pair of jeans he wore under the shukas. The entire family was subdued and on their best behaviour in his presence. Mama poured a steaming cup of chai for him from the Thermos, reaching across the fire to hand it to him.

Mama was generally fairly protective about telling me about her past. She'd told me she had been born in Kuputei and came from a large family of farmers with three brothers and six sisters. She and Baba had been married for about nine years, and from the moment I met her I could see she was a dutiful, responsible mama and wife. I always tried to follow her lead when interacting with others in the community.

Seeing Mama and Faith's dutiful demeanour in Baba's presence, I felt myself also tighten up, even though he was eager to talk and ensure I was okay so far, and that I felt safe and secure in his home. Baba asked each of the children if they'd done all their schoolwork, then shared with us what had caused his late return last night: he'd visited neighbours whose cow had given birth, standing by in case his assistance was needed, and he'd helped another neighbour who was sick and needed to be escorted to a clinic in the market town. The entire family listened with admiration.

Soon Baba departed to check on the livestock, and the kitchen returned to its previous chatter. Faith snapped at Parsinte for almost knocking over her tea. Morio cried, complaining about not getting enough attention. Then Mama announced time was running out, so the kids hurried off to quickly wash up before their half-hour walk to school.

Kipulel lingered behind, and I asked if there was a problem. As if sharing a deep secret, he asked if there was enough tea left for a second cup. I laughed and poured him out the remainder of the Thermos. He chugged the hot liquid down in one gulp before running after the others.

As Faith and her brothers headed off for school, I settled in to finish the dishes, wishing them all goodbye in my best Swahili.

"*Kwa heri!*" Goodbye!

"*Haya!*" Let's go!

And off they went, excited for another day of school.

In the afternoon, Mama and I headed back out on foot. Though her days were typically occupied teaching at the elementary school, she'd freed time to show me around to all the community's important sites: the school, the dam where the cows drank, churches, the health dispensary recently implanted by the government, many nearby bomas, the spot on the highway where we could catch a bus to the market town on our weekly visits. She indicated useful shortcuts and introduced me to many of our neighbours, who greeted me with laughter and enthusiasm. We followed long, meandering paths—to me they all appeared identical, but Mama navigated them as adeptly as I could Schaumberg's winding crescents and avenues.

At each boma we were greeted with welcoming smiles and a fresh cup of tea. With hospitality and generosity toward guests at the cornerstone of Maasai culture, at each boma mamas and their families opened their homes to us, especially tickled at entertaining a guest from far away. No one thought twice about visitors dropping in for an impromptu visit, and they were always ready with a pot of tea, sometimes a plate of ugali at lunchtime.

News travelled fast in the close-knit community's chain of gossip and word spread that a girl from America had arrived in Nkoyet-naiborr. Wherever we went, people knew who I was before I knew them, and they met me enthusiastically.

"Naserian!"

But after the customary greetings, they'd break into exuberant conversation, sharing the details and dramas of their lives, even though I had next to no clue what they were saying. So one of the first things I learned to say in Maa was *mayiolo maa*: "I don't know Maa." They seemed to find this absolutely hilarious.

After a number of these visits, I was jittery with cups and cups of strong tea and my stomach was full to bursting. Yet I had to keep graciously sipping, nodding to show my appreciation even as the cup grew cold. Once again, I reminded myself to keep an open mind and, more importantly, to keep hope in my heart.

In the days to come, I met an endless procession of Maasai neighbours. Guests showed up regularly at our boma, with the expectation that I'd greet and serve them, just as they'd done for me. Usually, however, Faith was one step ahead of me and already brewing tea by the time it occurred to me to begin serving. Again, all I could do was just try and fulfill my role, perform my chores, then sit quietly and fit in as best I could.

I was expected to know and recognize all the people I'd met. But there were so many: stranger after stranger came by, each speaking in a foreign tongue. There were so many names to remember, so many faces. Yet my family was adamant: *How could you forget her name? You just met her yesterday! She's the sister of the neighbour's brother's market lady's* . . . I pretended to keep it all straight. But I really couldn't.

When guests left our boma, Mama and Baba would request that I walk them part-way back home. But I'd eventually get lost on the way back and usually ended up asking someone along the way for help. By accident, I learned my way around just by stumbling foolishly from one boma to another, helped along the way by friendly souls seeing this fish out of water scrambling to get home.

One time, after a late afternoon visit, I tried to lead a group of guests back to their home. After we'd said our goodbyes, I headed back in the direction I'd come, looking forward to relaxing after an exhausting day. Trudging home under the blazing sun, I was in somewhat of a daze and lost my way. Still getting used to meagre, basic meals and only tea for breakfast, along with a busy slate of daily tasks, I was left with little energy at the end of the day.

Then I stopped in my tracks. I was at the intersection of several footpaths, each stretching off into identical landscapes of rough brush and reddish dirt, well-worn by many feet. In my tired stupor I'd lost my bearings and had no idea which way to go. The sky was darkening, and dusk fell quickly here, and with dusk came hyenas. *If there were hyenas, were there other animals, too? Like . . . lions?*

I heard slow footsteps crunching in the dust behind me. I wheeled around to find a small Maasai man, draped in red, coming up behind me. Bracing himself with a walking stick, he muttered a few words I didn't understand, except for one: Naserian. Apparently my reputation had already preceded me.

Sensing my confusion, he gestured with his walking stick in several directions, speaking in a low, calm tone. I still didn't understand, but I caught the essence of what he was asking: *Where are you trying to go?*

I had no idea how to respond, except for a Swahili word I'd recently learned: *nyumbani.* Home.

He nodded, indicating understanding. My relief was inexpressible, and in my gratitude I momentarily forgot how tired I was. He led the way, down one of the several paths, and I followed closely behind. We continued at his slow pace as evening began to fall.

Night skies in Nkoyet-naiborr were a revelation of stars, a sweeping sky of twinkling constellations unlike those visible in the cities of America. While I gaped with amazement at the view overhead, my Maasai guide shuffled forward, leading me, and soon I recognized the trail that led to my boma. I thanked him profusely, but he simply continued on his way.

I knew Mama would be annoyed, and possibly concerned, at my late return. I was embarrassed that I'd gotten so lost so easily. But I was determined to feel my way forward on my own. After all, finding my own path was I'd come here to do. A little help along the way didn't hurt.

5 Samuel

After a couple of weeks, I mentioned to Mama my plans to begin running in the mornings. At first she resisted the idea and couldn't understand why I'd want to waste time running when there were so many responsibilities to manage. A leisurely jog wasn't exactly a typical Maasai way of greeting the morning. But at home I'd always been in the habit of playing sports and exercising to ease tension; running in the mornings could be a way of enjoying one of the comforts of home while still maintaining the duties of my new life.

With a bit of pressure, Mama gave her approval, though she didn't want me out in the wilds alone—you never know what, or who, you'll encounter, she said. She secretly contacted a friend of the family, Samuel, a young man about my age from a boma more than a kilometre away, and asked him to accompany me on my runs.

So one rainy Monday, Samuel arrived with my brothers on their return from school, then stayed for dinner. Afterward, as we all sat around the fire, we talked as best we could, despite our limits in each other's language. Samuel's home was near the water source, so we'd met before in passing, but had barely spoken. He was tall and muscular, with a quiet demeanour. Yet he was also quick to relax into laughter, and he listened intently to others when they spoke.

The next morning, after Mama, Faith and I had woken, fetched water and cooked tea, we sat together in the kitchen. Dressed in old basketball shorts, I began putting on my running shoes, when Samuel appeared wearing a red T-shirt and basketball shorts instead of the traditional shukas. He announced he was going to escort me on the run.

My eyebrows shot up. On one hand, I was glad to have him join me; running on my high school track team had shown me it was always more fun to run with someone else. But on the other hand, I didn't know why Samuel, a boy I barely knew, wanted to accompany me.

I looked to Mama, and she gave me a slight nod that told me he could be trusted.

"*Sawa sawa! Tuende!*" Okay, I said. Let's go!

Clouds overhead threatened rain as we headed down the footpath toward the dirt road beyond. As we ran, I periodically glanced back at Samuel, still unsure about his intentions. I hadn't been in Nkoyet-naiborr long enough to know what to make of Maasai boys.

Samuel seemed to sense my slight apprehension and gave me my space, running in silence behind me. Samuel wore the traditional Maasai shoe—with soles made of recycled tires and a crossover strap tacked on with rusty nails. Yet his breathing remained even and his pace steady, almost elegant compared to my clumsy steps and panting breath; I was still getting used to the thin oxygen of the region's more than 2,000 metre elevation.

We jogged together down the road more than a kilometre, then started back, arriving home as foreboding clouds gathered overhead. I showed Samuel how to stretch after a run: basic exercises like side bends and hamstring stretches that he clearly thought were peculiar.

While holding one bent leg, ankles behind our backs in a quad stretch, Samuel asked why I wanted to run all that way, just to turn around and come right back again. His eyes were curious, his smile almost mischievous.

"For exercise," I answered. "Don't you ever run for recreation?"

As soon as I said that, I almost slapped my forehead. *Of course he didn't!* Here there was no gym, no free weights; they carried huge buckets of water. Samuel didn't need to jog for aerobic exercise; he walked his cows several kilometres to the dam every single day. Maasai farmers didn't need to burn calories on a stationary bicycle in a gym—though they'd probably appreciate a mountain bike for their regular visits to neighbours kilometres away.

Suddenly, the sky opened in a heavy downpour. It was the first time I'd felt rain on the savannah. *Rain, finally!* As Samuel bolted into the kitchen for shelter, I remained outside. With a deep breath, I raised my face and outstretched my arms, letting the raindrops refresh my sweaty face. The bordering hilltops shone green through the driving rain, and the dusty, parched terrain became cool and quenched. I breathed heavily and again marvelled at this incredible place.

For the first time, I truly felt the blissful freedom of my new home.

Wringing out my T-shirt, I entered the kitchen only to find Mama had already cooked a steaming pot of tea. I plopped on the bench next to her, shaking my dripping hair while she handed Samuel and me brimming cups. She collected a machete and rope, preparing to leave to collect firewood.

"Do the dishes, then fetch more water so we can wash clothes this afternoon," she told me. "I'll be back to cook lunch."

Once we were alone, I asked Samuel if he would come to run again. He didn't quite understand my broken Swahili, and his attempts to understand English were even more futile. But eventually we managed enough communication to agree on keeping our running dates going.

Samuel downed the rest of his tea, then stood, saying he needed to head to school.

"School?" *Hadn't Mama said Samuel was twenty-two?*

"Class 5." He said it with pride, standing taller. I held back my surprise, and he promised he'd return after school to say hello.

Later that afternoon, while Mama and I washed clothes, I found a chance to ask her about Samuel's strange revelation.

"Mama," I said, bent over a water basin, "Isn't Samuel twenty-two, like me?"

"*Ay*," she said. Yes. Mama finished wringing out a blanket and plopped it into my basin.

"Well ... he said today that he was in Grade 5?" I unwound the blanket to scrub it between my hands, just as Faith had taught me. The detergent was so pungent my hands were beginning to feel as dry as a prune.

"*Ay*."

"So he didn't start school until he was *eighteen*?"

"*Ay*."

Plainly, Mama didn't see how I might find this strange. She stood, hands on her hips, stretching her back after bending for so long. She took a deep breath.

"Samuel is a good man," she said. "You'll see. Now, what are you doing with that blanket? Let me show you."

In the following weeks, Samuel accompanied me on visits to many sites throughout the community. We walked for hours in the nearby hills, where he explained the names of valleys and distant hilltops and how to identify different shrubs and trees and use them for their medicinal purposes, all the while sharing stories of times of awful drought. Samuel described one dry season when he'd had to migrate his cows to a distant hill—he pointed it out, so far away it appeared blue in the haze. Another year he'd had to lead the herd deep into the valley, nearly 150 kilometres away.

It was amazing that we could understand each other at all. Our friendship began at the most basic starting point: communication. My brothers and sisters were happy to help me learn Swahili, but my lessons with Samuel were much more successful. With his days busy at school and his many responsibilities to his own family, he usually could only come over to our boma in the evenings for dinner and conversation by the fire. Seeing how badly I sought to learn the language, Samuel obliged with patience and dedication, easing me through the basics and gradually increasing the level of sophistication, day by day, word by word. Soon we were able to understand one another much better as I became more and more fluent in the language.

Samuel told me that he felt these lessons, helping me to be safe and independent in Kenya, were the most valuable gift he could offer. And as I got to know Samuel better, we helped each other in similar ways, time and time again. He introduced me to other households and dozens of other Maasai, and before I knew it I'd gathered dozens of friends across Nkoyet-naiborr. Samuel shared his language, his culture, his family and his plate with me—everything he had.

I was used to having male friends and, while the gender roles within this community were clearly defined, it hadn't occurred to me to apply this thinking to Samuel—he was a family friend who spent time with *everyone* at my boma. Yet when I asked Mama for permission to leave behind household chores to make the day-long walk with Samuel to market, I saw in her a certain hesitancy, perhaps questioning my intentions. *Of course*, I thought. Young, unmarried men and women don't go around together on their own. If Mama was aware of this, others probably were, too. What about Samuel, what did he think about my constant enthusiasm for his company? Whenever he travelled from home I usually accompanied him. I enjoyed being introduced to everyone he knew and, on the times fellow research students Brenda and Eva had visited, I made sure he got to know them as well.

But I couldn't get Mama's assumption out of my mind; it followed me with every look she gave. *Have I done something wrong in the community's eyes?* I decided to ask Samuel to tell me the truth.

On our next Saturday trek to market, we were walking as always, Samuel a few metres ahead, whistling a Maasai tune with his walking stick in hand.

"Hey, Samuel," I called out.

"Yes?" He paused so I could catch up.

"I was wondering . . . do others think it's suspicious for you and me to spend so much time together alone?"

"Yes," he said quite casually. "Many people think we're going to get married."

I nearly choked. I was expecting he would say "they have their suspicions," or maybe "my brothers asked me if you were my girlfriend." But *married?*

"Don't worry," Samuel said. "I told them it's not like that. We are both still students, and students have to finish their education before thinking of marriage. Don't you agree?"

Samuel was so matter-of-fact about the whole thing.

"Well, yes," I said. "Absolutely. But . . . have we done anything wrong? Have I disrespected anyone?"

Samuel looked at me with his kind eyes. "Have we ever done anything you can't tell your mama about? No. We have not disrespected anyone."

With that, he turned and continued on. My concerns had been resolved, but from then on I knew I would have to watch what I said and did under the community's watchful eyes.

In weeks to come Samuel and I continued our hikes together over the hills, stopping at various households along the way.

One place we never missed a chance to visit was his grandmother's home, halfway up into the hills. Grandma Samuel's wrinkled face, hunchbacked posture and calloused feet told of a long, hard life, but by the old woman's feistiness and powerful voice, you would never have guessed she was more than a hundred years old. She'd been blind for several years from glaucoma, yet no one could pinpoint exactly how long—Maasai elders didn't keep track of years in the way we did. Even her age was only a guess; as they had only recently begun keeping track of their children's birthdays, most adults' ages were only estimates.

Grandma Samuel's wisdom and stories made her life a miracle in my eyes, and at any chance Samuel and I would stop in to say hello.

One afternoon, we dropped by at the same time one of her sons and his wife, Sara, were visiting. As was the custom, tea was to be served.

"I'm blind, I can't cook the tea!" Samuel's grandmother said.

"Not me, I'm eight months pregnant!" Sara said; she was due soon, expected to deliver twins.

"My leg is broken, I can't do it!" Sara's husband had suffered an accident a few days earlier, and his leg was swollen and wrapped in a shuka while he waited for a truck to deliver him to the clinic.

The absurd dialogue reminded me of a bedtime story: The Little Red Hen, maybe. The fact that Samuel and I weren't meant to cook the tea was understood, as we were visitors. Samuel in particular wasn't expected to, as preparing tea was a task mainly reserved for women and girls.

But as they continued their debate, I looked to Samuel.

"This is silly," I whispered to him. "Let me go start the fire!"

He nodded, and before they'd noticed I'd slipped into their kitchen and had a pot of tea almost ready.

"Where do you keep your cups, Grandma Samuel?"

She pointed to the top of the firewood pile. We all laughed at the ridiculous scene as she helped me serve the tea.

One afternoon, Samuel arrived at our boma saying he wanted to show me how to make charcoal. I wasn't sure why he wanted to do so, but I of course obliged his offer.

Charcoal was made by first hacking down branches with a machete, then breaking them into smaller pieces. The wood was allowed to dry out, then piled and covered loosely with soil so that small air holes remained, allowing a small fire to be lit inside. The fire burned for several days, gradually transforming the wood into charcoal. Once the process was finished, the pile was spread by a hoe to dry before it could be packed into large sacks.

As we watched the charcoal burn, Samuel gazed into the trickling smoke with a sombre expression. I asked him what was wrong, and he said the smell conjured up memories, reminding him of the sadness of his youth. Not knowing much about his early years, I asked him what he meant. In simple, slow Swahili so I could understand, he began to share his story.

Samuel was born in Nkoyet-naiborr and lived there all his life. Like most Maasai kids, he didn't know his exact birth date. He told me it was December 25, but I knew this was likely untrue since, as Grandma Samuel demonstrated, recording dates of birth was a custom the Maasai had only recently adopted.

The fifth of nine children, Samuel's was a life of deep poverty. As a child, he'd mostly worn cow hides, as his family was too poor to even buy shukas. If they were lucky enough to have maize flour, they had to struggle to make it last as long as possible; spread thinly, one kilogram could last their entire family for two days, one meagre daily serving each.

Despite owning one of the largest herds in the community—and therefore possessing the greatest potential for prosperity—Samuel's father also had a serious drinking problem. Moratina, a kind of honey beer, is the local Maasai brew, and Samuel's father spent most days passed out under an acacia tree with a bottle instead of herding his livestock or looking after his wives and children.

Maybe Samuel's father, like many Maasai men of his generation, drank because they bore the brunt of the social change the community had experienced during their lifetime. Modern developments, along with heightened periods of drought, have led to herds that are much smaller than in decades past. Men don't need to lead migrations to find water and grazing land for their cattle. Men are no longer needed to protect the community from cattle raids and other dangers that were so present in the past. Women increasingly bear greater responsibility for supporting families. As a result, men feel they have lost their purpose. But cultural change did not excuse the fact that Samuel's father was a man who had failed in his duties—he had chosen alcohol over his family.

To support his drinking, Baba Samuel began to sell off the herd. Over the years he had sold eighty-two cows and nearly 200 goats and sheep, leaving the family's stomachs empty of food, yet filling his own with all the alcohol he could find. He also preferred his first wife to Samuel's mother, and in his drunken rages often beat Mama Samuel. He also refused to treat both his wives fairly, selling only those cows belonging to Samuel's mama's home.

At only five years old, Samuel was already herding the family's remaining herd himself. *Go!* his father would order. *Herd the goats today!* Even if they hadn't eaten, he'd hear his baba's voice ordering him to go and threatening to beat him with a metre-long stick. Samuel often received brutal beatings at his father's hand.

Samuel came to hate his father, yet he felt guilty for feeling this way. While herding the cattle every day, he would continually ask himself, *What can I do to make my life, and my family's lives, better?* He feared betraying his father's wishes, though Baba Samuel didn't care to create any real future for their family. It would be years before Samuel could do anything about it.

Samuel grew up with a strong, unbending desire to attend school and gain an education, but his father strictly refused, believing Maasai were not meant to attend school but instead follow traditional ways. Out of Samuel's eight brothers and sisters, only Samuel's brother Joel, as the first-born son, had been permitted to receive any schooling, making it all the way to eighth grade. Samuel's three older sisters were all married off at young ages and his younger brothers had similarly been prohibited from school. The youngest of the family, his sister Sananga, was still under Mama Samuel's watchful guidance.

Joel whenever we were together, although only in his mid-twenties, seemed much older. Years ago, their father had forced Joel to leave his then-pregnant girlfriend, who he loved, and enter an arranged marriage with the daughter of one of his father's friends. Rather than be exiled from the family, Joel had sadly agreed. But Joel never saw their father as a bad man and, unfortunately, he followed the same path. Samuel told me how Joel had squandered many opportunities, engaging in reckless behaviour with drinking and women. Joel also began to shirk his responsibilities, drinking, beating his wife and failing to provide his children with clothes, shoes or food.

In time, not only Samuel's younger brothers and sisters but Joel's family as well came to depend on Samuel, the second-born son, for support. From an early age, Samuel saw that his family's future rested on his shoulders.

When he was fourteen years old, one man tried to reach out to Samuel: my adoptive father. Baba noticed Samuel's desire for an education, seeing that Samuel was a good person in a terrible situation. Baba—still yet to marry Mama and begin his own family—offered to arrange for Samuel to attend school and even pay for his uniform, shoes and books. But

Samuel's father intervened, steadfast in his refusal to allow him to receive an education. So Samuel remained forced to herd every day, forbidden from even learning the alphabet.

One day that same year, Samuel was working in the fields when he came across a cobra, coiled in the tall grass. Before he could react, the snake sprayed its poisonous venom. Samuel's hands and joints immediately swelled hugely, and he collapsed.

Hours later, concerned that her son hadn't returned at his usual time, Mama Samuel went out to the fields to find him. She found Samuel lying unconscious, nearly paralyzed. Without a moment to lose, she lifted him onto her back and, accustomed to carrying daily loads of water, carried him four hours over the hills to the closest clinic, in the market town. Only after much medication, painkillers and a week's rest did Samuel begin to recover.

But even as Samuel was healing, his father was making a deal with a man in a community more than 150 kilometres away. Samuel was to be sent there to work as a labourer, herding cattle for a thousand shillings—about fifteen dollars—a month.

"This money is not yours," Baba Samuel told him. "You will bring it all to me."

Samuel worked that job for eight months, never seeing one shilling for himself. His feet remained bare and he wore only a thin sheet wrapped around his scrawny body. The family for whom he worked often didn't feed him, and in his weakened condition he often became sick, especially when weather was foul. Baba Samuel made monthly visits to pick up the earnings; from the hills where he worked, Samuel would watch his father go into the employer's home, leaving an hour later, never once even saying hello to his son. The money would be drunk within a week. When Samuel described these long, lonely days to me, his eyes became misty and distant.

One day, Samuel decided he couldn't take it anymore. He walked all the way back home in his bare feet and told his father he refused to go back. In another drunken haze, his Baba handed him a herding staff and said, "If you will not herd over there, then you will herd over *here*." Once again Samuel's long days were filled with labour, herding the family's cattle on their land. By this time, he was fifteen.

Then Samuel had a brilliant idea. When heading off every day to herd the cattle, he began bringing a machete along for making charcoal. He still had to tend the cows and take them to water, but he found he could dedicate a small amount of spare time every day toward making charcoal for sale. In eight days of work, he could make nearly four large sacks of charcoal, each weighing about fifty-five kilos. Mama Samuel then came to haul the sacks to market, earning eight shillings—about twelve cents—per bag. If two bags sold, it earned enough to provide the family with a kilogram of maize, an article of clothing or another small essential household item.

However, making charcoal is hard, dirty work, and Samuel's respiratory system suffered from the smoke. His throat was ripped apart and he often coughed up blood. His physical condition, already weak, deteriorated even further.

Samuel's father resented seeing his family gradually becoming independent of his domineering presence, the children eating porridge regularly and dressing in untattered shukas. If he checked on Samuel and saw him making charcoal instead of focusing on the cows, he would lash out with his fists. All the time, Samuel remained dedicated to providing for his family.

But Samuel's father still had his own plans. He told Samuel it was time for him to become a moran, a Maasai warrior. Becoming a moran meant proving his strength by killing a lion, as well as stealing cattle from non-Maasai neighbours. Samuel had seen bitter conflicts rage over cows being stolen, then reclaimed, then stolen again. And many young men had been mangled, or worse, in their attempts to kill lions. To Samuel, becoming a moran meant sacrificing his morals—and possibly his life.

"These are pointless fights, left over from grandparents' grandparents," Samuel told me. "Death without purpose will not occur by my hand."

Seeing Samuel's defiance, his father made another demand: if he wouldn't become a moran, then he must marry and begin a family. But time had passed, and Baba Samuel had grown weaker with age. Samuel, now almost eighteen and no longer a timid boy, was able to stand up to him. He objected: if he got married, what could he possibly offer his wife? He would have to sell the remaining cows and end up poor, just like his father.

For the first time, he told his father, "No."

Samuel wanted to go to school, to learn Swahili and English, to learn of the world he knew existed beyond his difficult life.

"School?" his father scoffed. "Maasai don't need school."

"I want to go to school," Samuel insisted. "I want an education."

So, at eighteen years old, Samuel entered first grade. He attended school by day and made charcoal in the evening and at night, oftentimes not going to bed until long after midnight, then waking before dawn. Often so exhausted he couldn't concentrate, his grades suffered, and he barely passed his subjects. Sometimes his father would demand he herd cattle instead and, despite everything, he still had to respect his father. He would herd the cows one day now and then but always returned to school the next.

Yet he persevered and wasn't ashamed at being eighteen in a classroom of six-year-olds—in fact, many others in his community admired him for his dedication to his studies. Many younger boys saw him as an example of how, with hard work and dedication, even Maasai boys from the poorest families could pursue an education.

Though Samuel was realizing his dream of receiving an education, he still needed to feed his family. As a student in the early grades, he only attended classes in the mornings. But as he advanced to fourth grade, he no longer had afternoons and weekends free for making charcoal. To make ends meet, he began sweeping and compacting cow manure from around the property. By market day, the pile could be sold for fertilizer. This way, he was still able to provide some food for the family.

Around this time, Samuel began to suffer sharp pains in his ribs. He began to feel sick—seriously, persistently sick. But to afford a doctor visit, he had to work even longer hours, which only made him sicker. Even worse, the doctors with their limited resources at the community health care clinic were of no help. He didn't know what else to do, other than just keep working as hard as he could.

By the time we'd met, Samuel was twenty-two years old and proudly working his way through fifth grade. As he poked at the smoky charcoal with a stick, I could see the pride he took at his many accomplishments. Yet there was also weariness there; after all, huge responsibility had fallen on his shoulders at such a young age. I couldn't imagine what it was like.

"Thank you for telling me this," I said.

He nodded, stirring the coals. "*Ay.*"

As I came to be accepted by my new family, I was also accepted into Samuel's. We became known in the community for always being together. When I asked him why he was so open to a stranger from practically another world, he said he'd never been sceptical about my intentions in visiting his community, simply because from the start he could sense I'd be a genuine friend. Still, I couldn't help but occasionally wonder how these closely knit families saw me, an outsider and foreigner, trying to join their community. Did they think I was trying to steal Samuel away? Were they suspicious of me, imagining I was out to exploit him, or all of them, for my own gain?

I wasn't the first foreigner to visit Nkoyet-naiborr. In 1972 an American missionary had come to the community and stayed for twenty years. From when Samuel was a small child, he remembered this tall, strange man who hoped to learn about Maasai culture and who even learned the Maa language. In return, he taught local families how to plant tomatoes, cabbage and carrots and how to build a water collection dam, which allowed their livestock to have reliable sources of drinking water and spend less time migrating. He also taught them about Christianity, which many people embraced wholeheartedly. His motives didn't seem suspicious or underhanded. He simply came to help the community learn and prosper.

The next foreigner to arrive was also from America, a man who too came under auspices of learning about Maasai culture. But this man introduced negative influences to the community, disrupting households by influencing women to engage in what Samuel vaguely referred to as "bad manners." A group of elders were forced to confront this man and tell him he was no longer welcome and that he should go back to his country. He didn't leave Kenya, but he found himself shunned by most families and moved to another region of the country.

Others had come, then quickly departed. Years passed before any other outsiders joined the community. Now, here I was: the latest to try and assimilate into the culture. But one of the major tenets of the Maasai way of life is a belief that visitors are blessings, and outsiders should be received with hospitality and kindness. So with full, open hearts, they welcomed me into their community.

Since Samuel had shown me so much from his community and his culture, I felt I should share some of mine with him. Nairobi—bustling with traffic jams, skyscrapers, movie theatres and so much more—was the most Westernized place that was accessible. Few people from Samuel's community had been to the big city before. No one in Samuel's family and none of his neighbours had ever made the journey. One weekend, we decided on the spur of the moment to visit the city together. With no idea of what to expect, Samuel was enthusiastic but also anxious about what complicated, unfamiliar things he might experience there.

Samuel could only guess what Nairobi might be like from what he knew in the village. In Nkoyet-naiborr, the landscape was rarely busy. Cows wandering freely through the compound, grazing in pastures, but other than on special occasions, one rarely found more than a few people gathered at a time. One car passed in the morning, and then the same one passed again in the evening on its return. Samuel imagined, he told me, that when we went to Nairobi, he might see four cars, maybe even ten. He thought perhaps he'd see a house the size of an acacia tree. He was in for a shock, and I was nervous about how he would view this shock. I was also afraid that, if the city was too overwhelming, he would think less of me by association because I come from a land of similar excess. *Will he see me differently? Will his image of me as a respectable, modest girl be wiped away?*

Yet I was eager to share more of my world with him. I watched Samuel borrow a pair of Joel's jeans and a neighbour's white button-down shirt so he could fit in, wearing city clothes. The village boys were almost giddy in anticipation for Samuel to see the big city. And I admit—Samuel looked pretty good in stone-washed jeans.

After a four-hour walk and two matatu rides later, we pulled into Nairobi in the late morning. As we entered the city's downtown, Samuel's face froze with shock. The noise and stink of the crowded city was far beyond his wildest imagination, and the sensory overload immediately made his head hurt. He marvelled at the size of the city's skyscrapers and, when we saw one made almost entirely out of glass, he was convinced it would collapse at any moment. Samuel was particularly amazed by Nairobi's roads, where four cars could drive side by side in one direction—going both directions, eight cars might pass at once.

"There are so many people, Naserian!" he cried.

We walked up Kenyatta Avenue, pushing our way through the maze of oncoming crowds. If it wasn't for the awestruck look in Samuel's eyes, turning around every ten steps to take in the panorama of skyscrapers and hulking buildings, Samuel would have looked right at home in the city. But eventually, as is inevitable on any busy city sidewalk, someone bumped roughly Samuel's shoulder. Samuel turned to speak to him, but the man only kept on walking. Samuel turned to me, confused.

"Naserian, why didn't that man stop and apologize?" His eyes lit with curiosity. "Or why didn't he at least say hello?"

His voice rose, his tone almost becoming hurt and angry. "Why doesn't anyone say hello?" His chest heaved with agitation. He was simply unable to grasp why people could choose to treat one another this way.

I tried to comfort him. *How do I explain this?* "Well, this is a big city, Samuel. Things are different than at home. But I promise we can talk about it later."

We headed down Kenyatta Avenue toward the city's parliament clock tower when Samuel spotted a fellow Maasai man on the other side of the street. Shukas draped around his slender body, the old man walked with authority down the street, on his belt a *rungu*—a wooden club that many Maasai warriors carried. Samuel moved to cross the traffic-crowded street.

"Samuel, *wait!*" I called out.

I caught up to him and seized his shoulder. "You can't just run into the street!"

Samuel stared at me blankly.

"You have to cross at an intersection or wait until the cars brake for you. Go to a crosswalk if you want to get to the other side. Do you see those white lines painted on the pavement?"

"Oh! *That's* what they're for."

We smiled together, him out of newfound enlightenment and me in shared happiness for his enjoyment. The Maasai elder had already departed before we could cross the road. We continued our stroll until we came to Uhuru Highway, took a left and arrived at the Haile Selassie roundabout, a busy traffic intersection with a large public fountain at its centre.

Samuel watched with wonder as water cleaner than he'd ever seen spouted into the air; his mouth dropped open as he stood stunned, staring at the continuous water flow. Seeing no one hurrying to fetch the water, Samuel jerked his head to the right and left, searching for a mitungi. His first instinct was to bring the water back to Nkoyet-naiborr, where we were experiencing a drought.

I put a gentle hand on his shoulder. He turned to face me, breathless with anticipation. I had to explain it to him . . . *but with what words?*

"I know this water looks beautiful," I said. "It's clear, fresh and clean. Yet this water is different from the spring in Nkoyet-naiborr. It doesn't replenish itself from underground; it is only for decoration, for show. See those pipes underneath? They bring the same water back up."

Samuel still found this idea unfathomable. "But ... *why* can't we bring this water back for our mamas?" The crowd of passing pedestrians began to push up behind us and honking cars came from every direction, startling an already flustered Samuel. I again told him things were simply different here. "But I *promise*, we'll talk about this later." Samuel's trust in me allowed us to forget the fountain and continue on.

To show Samuel as much of city culture as possible, I suggested we catch a movie. I tried to explain the concept.

"We enter a large room with many seats, all facing a big screen. The lights go down, the sound comes on and a picture appears on the screen for our entertainment. It tells a story, through sound and images."

He seemed to understand the concept, though not why we had to pay so much for it: 200 shillings (about three dollars). But he was up for giving it a try.

The only film playing was a Hollywood action movie. We bought our tickets and entered the darkened theatre. For Samuel, it was a huge and strange place, and he paused at the top of the staircase facing us; he'd never walked down stairs before. He clutched my arm as we carefully crept forward and found a pair of seats. As we sat in silence, waiting for the lights to go down, I could sense his nervous anticipation.

The lights dimmed, and I could feel Samuel shifting uneasily next to me. Loud, overbearing trumpets enveloped the theatre; at this, Samuel grasped my arm so tightly I thought it would leave a bruise. The screen lit up with crashing cars and blazing gunfire, and Samuel clasped his other hand over his eyes, refusing to look. He contorted in his seat, almost curling into a ball; his senses were too stimulated, too overwhelmed. *Okay*, I thought. *Enough.* I had to get him out of there.

We snuck out of the theatre only minutes into the movie. Back in the light of day, Samuel gradually calmed down, and we wove our way back through the crowded streets as the sun began to set into evening.

We stayed the night at the home of my original host family, most of whom were away visiting relatives. I let Samuel get some much-needed sleep on a mattress in the living room, while I slept in my old bedroom. We left early the next morning, both of us eager to escape Nairobi's chaos and clamour.

By the time we'd arrived back at Soko, Samuel's headache had worsened to throbbing pain, his thoughts going a mile a minute. I tried to discuss what had happened with him, but he could barely speak. His mind was spinning. The cars, the skyscrapers, the roads, the noise and crowds—he'd seen things he hadn't imagined even existed. As soon as we got back to his manyatta he headed straight inside, and I left him alone to clear his mind.

A few days later, Samuel took me on a long walk up the nearby hills. We sat together on an outcrop of rocks looking over a vast expanse of brush-covered land.

"Naserian," he said, "this is the land I will one day inherit from my father. This is *my* land. But honestly, I don't understand *your* land."

Perched there, high up on the craggy rock, we went over our experiences in Nairobi. He filled me in on what had happened after his return. After he'd holed up in bed, Mama Samuel had brought him food, but he couldn't eat. At night he'd talk aloud in his sleep, waking his mother, who was convinced he was hallucinating because he had contracted malaria.

Everyone tried to talk to him, to hear about his adventures. *What did you see in Nairobi? What is it like there? Is it a happy place?* But to Samuel it was all a blur. He couldn't answer any of their questions; his mind was still spinning.

His entire family came to visit—all his brothers and sisters, half-siblings, nieces and nephews, neighbours—people flocked to him, all dying to hear about the big city. Yet Samuel still couldn't formulate the thoughts to describe what he'd seen. Nothing made sense. Everyone wanted to understand the city and assumed Samuel now knew all there was to know about Nairobi. They expected him to come back full of enthusiasm and joy. And inside, he was glad he'd made the trip, but he was too overwhelmed to tell the story. He'd slept until morning.

At school the following day, he'd been swarmed again. *How was Nairobi? What is it like?* Even the elders pulled him out of class to ask about it.

By then he was able to muster up a sentence or two. He explained Nairobi was a great place for big, important people. He told them about the roads, the cars, the clamour of activity. He told them he even almost saw Moi, then the current president. Everyone was amazed and impressed, even if Samuel was stretching the truth somewhat.

Seated there on that peak, looking down on the land that would one day be his own, Samuel said he was truly happy to have learned about Nairobi, mostly so he could now access the government hospital and help others make the trip when necessary. Even though it'd been overwhelming and frightening, we knew it wouldn't be his last journey to the city. And it was definitely not the last important experience Samuel and I would share.

Samuel, just before our first visit to Nairobi together.

6 Chop Wood, Carry Water

"Naserian! Amka!" Wake up!

I rolled over in bed in response to Mama's sharply whispered command, careful not to wake Morio or Faith, sound asleep next to me. Slowly shifting my weight off the bed, I placed my feet on the ground and felt around in the dark for Faith's plastic flip-flops. Finding only one, I fell to my hands and knees to feel under the bed for the second shoe.

"Naserian! Tuende! Saa ya kuenda maji!" Time to fetch water. I quickly stood, adjusting my skirt and grabbing a sweater before running out to join Mama.

"Entitai, sopa." Good morning, my daughter.

"Ipa." Acknowledging her salutation, I bowed my head in respect for Mama to touch—our daily greeting. She handed me my mitungi and rope and we headed off in the early morning's darkness to fetch water.

Away from the sleeping family, we began our usual morning conversation. Thanks to the help of Samuel and others, my grasp of Swahili had steadily improved, and conversing with me was refining Mama's rough English.

"Did you sleep well?"

"Like a rock. And you?"

"I slept well. Morio kept me up, though, with his wheezing."

I loved sleeping with my younger brother Morio but at the same time it was extremely difficult. He suffered from a lung infection, and his breath was slow and laboured. I'd lain awake most of the night, listening to him wheeze, constantly afraid his next breath would never come. Sometimes I spent the night counting the intervals between each of his inhalations, terrified they would slow even further, unable to think about what I'd do if they stopped.

"Should we take him to the dispensary again?" I asked Mama, hurrying down the footpath, trying to keep up with her long strides.

"We'll see."

The dispensary in Soko never seemed to have the right medication or be able to provide a reliable diagnosis. We'd been there four times in the last months, but none of the medications provided had eased Morio's constant flu-like symptoms. He'd been prescribed cold medications and painkillers when they said he had the flu. Next he was given antibiotics for pneumonia. Then, malaria medicine. Then they said they'd run out of medication and had nothing else to give us. What would they tell us the next time?

We wove with water jugs in hand through the sharp whistling-thorn acacia trees, careful not to snag our skirts or shins. The morning's clouds hung low next over the hills and a light mist clung to the ground.

At the waterpipe this morning, we find other mamas already hard at work. There were so many strong, beautiful mamas, and I am getting to know them all: Leah, Linda, and Lydia, who is an unmarried thirty-something woman considered to be a pillar of strength among the community's women; tall and robust, she keeps the nicest house. It was no surprise she was elected counsellor of the area council. Another young mama, Nalamite, stands out for her striking hair and beautiful clothes. Then there's Mama Toti, Mama Naomi, Nalotuesha, Nalamayi, Shosho, Mama Skola, Mama Sawoi—a close-knit community of women, supporting one another while making daily tasks a lot more fun.

"Naserian! *Sopa!*"

I caught sight of Mama Samuel, waving from the line, her smile showing the wide gap between her bottom teeth. I set down my can and headed over to greet her.

Seeing her every morning was one of my favourite parts of the day. She radiated a contagious energy, despite her petite five-foot figure. Her daily presence in my life, loving affection, and giving personality made her like a second mama to me. As neighbours, our two families enjoyed a close relationship. I called her "Mama Samuel," even though Samuel is her fourth child.

I lowered my head for her to touch. "*Ipa.*"

I brought Mama's mitungi along with mine and took my place in line while Mama continued her greetings. I wished I'd woken up earlier. The line would take another twenty minutes before our turn, and we still had yet to cook tea for my brothers and sisters, and ensure they bathed and dressed in their uniforms to make it off to school before seven o'clock.

When our turn arrived, we hurriedly filled our containers from the tap. With practice, I was gradually learning some of the many subtle intricacies of a successful water run.

First, the thin rope we used was made of very fine, coarse fibres. With the weight pulling on your back, the rope chafed and dug into your skin; I often saw old Maasai women with dents trenched into their foreheads from a lifetime of carrying water. Our family had another rope that was twice as wide and much more comfortable. When that rope was free to be used instead of the thinner one, the chore was much less painful.

The second technique I discovered came after I'd continually spilled water when mounting the filled mitungi on my back. I found it was important to ensure the cylinder was completely full in order to keep it from bouncing against my back, which is not only uncomfortable, but slowed me down on the walk home. I used a second, smaller container to pour in enough water so that the water reached a level that allowed it to seal.

The third thing I learned was that the top would never screw in perfectly on its own. To avoid any spillage—not only wasteful, but making for an unpleasant trip with water dripping down your back—I had to use a plastic sheet to tightly seal the opening, then close the lid around it. Then a rock or other object can be used to cram it even tighter, until it can't possibly come loose.

After a while I'd become less of a liability for Mama and more of a genuine help. In our sprawling home we needed six mitungis over an average day, unless we were washing clothes, when we'd need more. This meant twice a day we'd do two or more visits to the water pipe, just under a mile away.

I only felt I'd succeeded in learning this task when I could be sent on my own, with my own mitungi and can. When I could fill it by myself, tying my own rope and executing each task, step by step, on my own, I knew I'd proven myself capable. And when I first carried two mitungis on my own, I'd fully graduated.

With our ropes looped around our foreheads, balancing the water cans on our backs, we headed back up the footpath. We shouted our goodbyes to all the women, knowing we'd see them again later that day.

Fetching firewood and hauling water were tedious daily chores that I gradually learned to master.

Returning to the boma with our mitungis of water, I went to our kitchen to start a fire and boil tea using the milk Mama had already coaxed from the cows. Inside the house, Mama woke up my brothers and began tidying up as they prepared for school.

The family was supportive as I tried to master the techniques of proper chai brewing. Just as the milk began to boil, I used some paper wrapping from last night's ugali flour packet as an oven mitt and removed the pot from the fire. I set aside some for the afternoon tea, leaving just enough for this morning. I added water and measured out tea leaves. Again, waiting for it to boil.

Seeing the tea was ready, I removed the boiling pot from the fire, mixed in sugar and poured the liquid through a sieve into our large Thermos. I then put yet another pot of water on the fire; this would be for our brothers to bathe with before they left for school.

"Naserian!"

It was Faith, coming to assist in the kitchen. After our greetings, I sent her to fetch the soap.

"Where is it?" she asked.

"In the bafu."

"No, it's not," Mama called from her bedroom, where she was sweeping the floor. "It's in the basin behind the cow pen, where I did laundry yesterday."

We went through this routine often, as we shared a single block of yellow, coarse Ushinde soap for bathing, laundering our clothes and washing our dishes. Once we'd located the soap, I began scrubbing dishes while Faith swept the dirt floor in the kitchen with our only broom, a market item crafted from long, thick dried grass we'd bought for a few shillings. In minutes she'd masterfully transformed our kitchen's dirt floor, littered with last night's cabbage cuttings, chicken poop, scraps and ashes, into a clean, even surface.

Soon the family poured into the kitchen, ready for their morning tea. I handed out steaming cup of the tea I'd brewed, watching for the reactions to my concoction.

"Naserian," Saigilu said, "This tea . . ."

"Yes?"

". . . is very good."

"*Asante*," I said. Thank you.

I smiled with pride to myself as I grabbed another cup to pour some tea for Morio. Another small victory.

At about this time Mama got a new job as one of the school's community-sponsored teachers, and she would head off with Faith and the boys to school every morning. The government employed too few teachers to meet the needs of Kenya's rural schools. The school in Nkoyet-naiborr had 350 students but only six teachers; some schools had as many as 500 students with only eight teachers. Each community had to seek its own solutions.

In Nkoyet-naiborr the parents each contributed a small amount to a collective pot, used to employ educated community members to act as teachers for the early grade levels. Mama, had been in school as far as Form 2, or the equivalent of Grade 10, and she became the sponsored nursery teacher. She taught a half-day of school every morning, Monday through Friday. With her new responsibilities away from home, I had long given up my morning runs with Samuel; I didn't have the luxury of time for it anymore. I didn't really mind, since running for water and firewood was definitely keeping me fit enough!

This left my mornings alone with Morio. Barely six years old, he wouldn't begin nursery school until next year. He didn't speak Swahili, let alone English, and I still hadn't caught on to his mother tongue, Maa. Yet somehow, through his good nature and my best efforts, we enjoyed our mornings together.

He knew it was time for his bath, so we returned to the kitchen to restart the fire. I fed the fire just as before, bending to help the wood catch with my breath. When the flame caught, I turned to Morio with tears running down my face. He was shocked for a moment, then laughed, realizing it was only the smoke in my eyes that caused the tears. He began babbling fast, probably telling me he was too clever for my dumb jokes. Or so I guessed.

After Morio was washed, dried and clothed, we headed over to Kokoo's house for her to look after him while I went again to retrieve water.

Morio, ready for his bath.

Today was when I had to wash the family's clothes, which would require several trips to the spring.

"Kokoo!"

"*Ao!*"

"*Sopa!*"

"*Ipa!*"

She came to meet us, touching my bowed head. As was our habit, we pretended to converse briefly. She spoke to me in Maa, and I said "*ay*" at the appropriate times to show I was listening. Then I responded in Swahili, explaining that I needed to go to the river. Could she watch Morio? She responded with "*ay*" in acknowledgement.

I knew full well Kokoo didn't completely understand, but that she would catch the drift and care for Morio until I returned. Then I heard the sound of small feet from behind me, and little Metengo, who lived with Kokoo, came scurrying up to greet Morio and me.

I'd been told on my first day that Metengo was not Kokoo's daughter, but only later did I learn the true story. Here was a classic example of the complicated family arrangements that emerged in extended Maasai families. Metengo was the granddaughter of one of Kokoo's husband's several other wives, whose family lived far away in another region of Maasailand.

Metengo had come to live in Nkoyet-naiborr so she could help in the coming years as Kokoo grew older; in return Kokoo would teach Metengo everything there was to know about keeping a home, so she could eventually carry on these traditions. This was a common traditional Maasai practice and demonstrated how anyone of a certain age can be considered a parent to a younger child, or a sister to another woman, or any other kind of domestic arrangement.

Metengo was four, almost the same age as Morio, and the two were fast friends. Kokoo and I watched as they dashed off to play together.

After two trips to the spring and back, I had enough water to wash clothes for the entire household. Currently there were eight of us at home, though the number always fluctuated with Baba's frequent travels and visitors always arriving from far-off regions.

Following the commotion of the early morning, I enjoyed the momentary silence. Morio and Metengo played outside in the compound field, climbing trees and jumping down, over and over. *Perfect*, I thought; they'd occupy one another while I finished my chores. I had another hour before I needed to start preparing lunch—just enough time to do laundry. Gathering the familiar yellow soap, a faded orange bucket and two plastic basins, one of which we had to sew with thick thread to seal a tear, I headed to the area by the cow pen where we did our washing.

Settling in on this next task, I crouched to soak the clothes in the soapy basin, then stood to wring out the soapy water. Then back down to rinse the clothes in fresh water before standing to wring them once again. Wash, wring, rinse, repeat, over and over again. In high school, my flexibility had been so poor I could barely touch my toes, despite being on the track team and stretching diligently every day. Here, so many chores, like washing clothes, building fires, preparing meals or cleaning dishes, were done bent over or on my knees, that I spent half my days bent at the waist. By sheer necessity, my flexibility and strength were improving dramatically.

An hour later, just as I'd hung clothes to dry on the twigs of an intricate bush, the kids returned from playing. Metengo dashed off to return to Kokoo's as Morio and I began preparations for lunch. From the storage next to Mama's bed we gathered half a cabbage, a tomato, the other half of last night's onion, a spoonful of cooking fat and some salt and corn flour and brought it all into the kitchen to begin making cabbage and ugali. After I'd chopped and washed the vegetables, Morio assisted me in again restarting the fire. Embers still glowed inside, so all it took was for Morio to peel dry bark for fuel, and soon the fire was raging anew.

A pot quickly went on with the cooking fat, half an onion, tomato and salt. We added the shredded cabbage and after a few minutes I removed the pot from the flames with a makeshift oven mitt of paper wrapping. Another pot went on with some water and, once it was boiling, I poured the corn flour into the pot until my now-trained eye saw it was just enough to make the ugali.

In mere minutes we had transformed a pile of discarded wood into a

Mama demonstrates how to cook chapattis. Along with ugali, this thin, unleavened bread is a staple of many African diets.

blazing fire and lunch for an entire large family. Not exactly like making macaroni and cheese on an electric stove back home, but delicious nonetheless.

Just as the ugali was nearly ready, I heard the other children returning home for their quick lunch break, Mama close behind but stopping by to visit Kokoo before returning home. Almost immediately the kitchen was full of people, laughter and the clatter of plates. Baba was the family's biggest eater, but he wasn't there, since he was away again, this time visiting elders of a neighbouring region. As the ugali was divided into portions, it released steam into the air and solidified into slices. The first time I had tasted the cornmeal mixture I'd found the clumpy, mostly flavourless maize nearly inedible, but I was getting used to its filling appeal. Ugali was such an integral part of the Maasai diet, dinners were practically considered incomplete without it.

I added cabbage on each plate and served the boys first. We were lucky to have vegetables for lunch; many families, like Samuel's, could only afford tea for breakfast and plain ugali for both lunch and dinner. Some ate only once a day—one of the reasons for the high levels of malnutrition in the region.

Faith was next; then I prepared a plate and kept it aside for Mama. Metengo, even though she would eat later with Kokoo in their manyatta, sat gazing at the food, silently hoping for a bowl. I retrieved a bowl from the shelf and served her part of the remaining ugali, along with some cabbage.

Her eyes lit up. "Naserian!" she squealed, eagerly snatched the bowl and ran outside, Morio close at her heels, to eat seated in the dirt.

We all ate in joyful chatter. Parsinte sat with his bare right foot propped over his knee, working a long acacia thorn into his skin to remove a sliver that had poked his ankle on the way home from school. I asked the kids about their morning classes.

"Today, we learned about the science of the inner ear," Saigilu proudly told me. "Test me."

I tried in vain to think back to my own elementary school science classes. It had been a while since I'd given much thought to the ear's anatomy.

"Name the different parts of the ear and their purposes," I said.

Without hesitating, Saigilu rattled off terms I honestly had no idea were right or wrong. His confidence was enough assurance for me.

I turned to Kipulel, asking what he learned in school.

Kipulel, despite being three years older than Saigilu, was a few grades behind. Kipulel's story was a sad one. Orphaned at a young age, he'd fallen behind others of his age. Baba took him in and started him in school, but since Kipulel hadn't started until two years before, he was fifteen but only in third grade. Like Samuel and other poor Maasai children, Kipulel knew that education would create a better future than the cattle and goat herding that was traditionally expected of boys and the household chores that were expected of girls. Kipulel was enthusiastic about his studies and top student in his class.

"*Tulisoma fractions kwa maths.*" Learning fractions, he explained in Swahili.

Faith always ate the quickest, eager to get the cleaning done before she went back to school. She wasn't the top student, but her effort was unmatched.

"Faith, how about you?" I asked. "What did you learn in school today?"

Already working on the dishes, she shrank from the sudden attention, taking her time to answer.

"Today our teacher taught us the science of germs, and how they spread. We have germs on us all of the time. It is important for us to wash our hands after going to the bathroom and before we cook or eat. See?"

Faith displayed her hands, wet from cleaning, dripping with fresh suds.

I smiled to myself; she always made me proud of her.

"Faith, you know so much more than I did at thirteen years old."

"Really?" she asked, turning her wide eyes to share a look with Saigilu, who sat scarfing down his ugali beside her. "Thank you, Naserian."

The two of them giggled together as we continued our lunch. Then Mama's tall shadow appeared in the doorway. We all made way as she threw herself upon the wooden bench, letting out a deep breath and tossing up her arms for dramatic effect.

"Whew, I'm tired!"

"Take this, Mama," I said, handing the plate of food to her. "This will give you more energy."

While eating, Mama explained a new song she'd composed that morning to teach kids how to tell time. In a matter of minutes, all of us were singing along. We gave Morio a chance for a solo, and he took centre stage in front of the fire. Metengo, never one to be left out, hopped up and down next to him. As they took turns dancing to the catchy tune—Saigilu like a true Maasai dancer jumped high in the air, then paused slightly every time he hit the ground, and Parsinte performed his own interpretive dance, bouncing on one leg to carefully keep his wounded foot out of the way—Faith and I laughed as we gathered the remaining dishes into the washing pot. Kipulel chuckled as well, good-naturedly making fun of his siblings from the sidelines.

Soon the dishes were done, the children had rushed back to school, and Mama had left for the afternoon to herd the goats, sheep and cows. My brothers were lucky to have Mama; whenever necessary, she took on their chores of herding the cattle so they could attend their classes. She did everything she could—waking early and staying up late, rarely taking a break for herself, always working—so they could concentrate on their studies.

With Mama gone I was left to tend to the kitchen and the house. Faith and I had just stocked up on firewood the day before, so there was no immediate need to go again. Metengo and Morio were again playing outside. I watched their curious game with fascination: they pretended rocks were like the trucks they'd seen on the main road, steering them over clumps of grassy dirt. In many ways it was just like the way kids in North America played, emulating exciting things they'd seen in their days. Yet Metengo and Morio seemed completely happy playing in the rough, dusty clearing, with no video games or gymnasiums or shopping malls.

Cherishing this momentary break, I went inside the manyatta to read, one of my only solitary escapes. What I *really* felt like doing was enjoying a nap. But if anyone caught me snoozing when left in charge of the household, I would be seen as lazy; in a place where struggle and strife were a part of daily life, sitting around idle was a serious no-no. Reading was not considered lazy, yet it afforded me a chance to sit and rest. I took out a book—Jared Diamond's *Guns, Germs and Steel*, an interesting story of culture and history that had helped me on my research paper—and sat outside by the manyatta to let my mind wander while blankly gazing at the pages.

I loved this simple life. Yes, it had its struggles, but life at home also lacked in so many ways. Perhaps in our world of instant convenience and leisure, not much was missing financially, but I'd seen emptiness of another sort. I recalled a quotation attributed to Mother Teresa, who said she'd never seen such emotional poverty as she had in America. "The most terrible poverty," she'd written, "is loneliness, and the feeling of being unloved." The quotation had stuck with me, but it had never really made sense while I was surrounded with the wealth and comforts of suburban life. Now it was starting to make sense to me. Here in Nkoyet-naiborr, we had little in terms of material possessions but plenty of love for all.

Maybe I did miss some of the comforts of home. Did I miss my favourite vegetable, broccoli? No. Did I miss candy or junk food? Not really. Did I miss going to the movies or eating in restaurants. No. What I did miss, though, was privacy and independence, both of which were thrown out the window the first day I'd arrived.

I also missed conversation. For a long time I hadn't been able to talk to anyone in a way that allowed me to fully express myself. Few here spoke English fluently enough to discuss feelings, and after these past couple of months I still didn't know enough Swahili to express deep emotions. Samuel was of course my closest confidant, but our conversations, though emotional and honest, could never touch upon the philosophical or emotional cross-cultural issues that perplexed me every day.

Unable to voice anything of any true meaning, I could only stew thoughts over alone in my mind, trying to understand what I was seeing. All I could do was diligently record all my thoughts in my journal, so someday I could share this new reality with my family and friends back home. But not until the time was right.

Every afternoon the heat brought swarms of flies, attracted by my perpetual sweat. Even when I shooed them away, they returned seconds later, crawling all over me, on the back of my knees, buzzing by my ears. They barely gave me a moment to relax and think! I knew screaming wouldn't get rid of them, but I couldn't help but sigh with frustration as I stepped outside.

Momentarily blinded back out in the glaring afternoon sun, I scanned the yard for Morio and Metengo. Seeing them playing by the fence, I called them over, secured the home with a padlock just to be safe and together we headed past the cow pen toward Kokoo's house. We told her we were going for a walk. She seemed to understand.

Metengo and Morio followed me down the path behind the house toward the hills, then rushed ahead. I hoped to escape the flies by heading to a shady area down this way that might provide some relief.

Suddenly, the kids froze at the small clearing down at the path's bend. I too paused, then saw what they were gaping at: just ahead, three giraffes, towering over five metres, blocked our route.

The kids ran to hide behind me, cowering with fear. I stood paralyzed in awe of these wild animals. While they were beautiful, I knew they also could be dangerous. The giraffes stared at us, these three intruders: we'd surprised them just as much as they had surprised us. I recalled Mama's warnings of giraffes' violent tendencies when they felt attacked. A giraffe could even kick a lion's head off!

The first time I'd seen a giraffe, travelling for the first time through the valley between Soko and Nkoyet-naiborr, I'd watched with utter astonishment at their long necks, their graceful movements. I'd been so stunned in the moment I could only look on in disbelief. But this time I was facing them head-on and, instead of admiring their beauty, I had to take action to protect the children. Mama had left me to take care of the home—to not just sweep, cook and clean, but also to care for the children.

I took the kids' hands, leading them as the three of us slowly and methodically backed away. The giraffes gave us an annoyed look, flicking their tails. But they didn't seem to want to linger and we watched them gallop away into the bush.

Amazed that I had been able to stand my ground in the face of wild animals, I took a second to collect myself and then led the children down a different path. Morio and Metengo seemed to forget the moment of fear almost instantly, running ahead. As for me, it wasn't until I'd found the reprieve of some shade before my heart could stop pounding.

The children began playing around a large, gnarled tree. They seemed to understand my weariness and happily began climbing its branches while I relaxed in the shade. I forced myself to lie motionless, almost daring any fly to land on me. I waited five seconds, silent and still. Ten seconds, then I exhaled. Fifteen seconds, thirty seconds—no flies appeared. *Finally.*

Just as I was letting my mind wander, finding the first peace in what felt like forever, I heard a voice call out.

"Naserian!"

I winced and opened my eyes.

"*Ao!*"

"*Sopa!*"

"*Ipa!*"

It was Joel, Samuel's older brother, passing by. He took a seat next to me, clearly eager for conversation. Despite my disappointment in again losing an opportunity for privacy, I was glad to see him. Joel had been arrested about a week ago and thrown into a local jail. I'd heard he was released two days ago, but I hadn't yet had the chance to stop by and see how he was doing.

With the acacia tree sheltering us and a light breeze cooling my skin, I listened as Joel shared the events of the past week. He'd been taken to the town jail for reportedly tearing down a politician's posters. Despite his pleas of innocence, the police were unwilling to give him the benefit of a doubt, so Joel had spent two nights with his legs chained to the cell's cold concrete floor. He'd been beaten and the only food he'd been given was so dirty it was inedible. With no toilet and the chains allowing only a half-metre radius, he and several other detainees sharing the cell were forced to sleep in their own waste.

Two days previous, Samuel had finally shown up at the jail with money to bribe the police into releasing Joel. His plan worked, and Joel had spent the last couple of days recovering at home with his new wife. He was shaken and weak, but mostly unharmed. I had some suspicions as to his innocence, as Samuel had told me of Joel's reckless behaviour, but I kept my mouth shut.

Our conversation was cut short by Mama's voice, calling me back to the boma. I invited Joel to come for tea at our home later that week, and he accepted. I quickly called down Metengo and Morio, and we all rushed back together.

Hearing Joel's story left me in a distracted daze for the rest of the day, as I went through the motions of again starting the fire, preparing and serving tea, washing dishes and preparing and serving dinner—again, ugali and cabbage. I couldn't stop thinking of how safe we felt at home in Chicago in our calm suburban neighbourhood, assured that the police would protect us and defend us in times of crisis. I kept hearing stories of the corruption of Kenyan police and about how justice was too often meted out in bribes and violence. Happily, the vibrant bustle of my family gradually lifted me from my disturbed state.

With the day's work done, I could finally relax. The fire blazed, lighting the glowing faces of Mama, Faith, Kokoo and my brothers, all gathered in the kitchen as Mama shared stories and news she'd gathered that day. Samuel's smiling face appeared in the doorway, greeting everyone again. I offered him a small plate of ugali and he joined us at the fire.

"Tell us a story, Samuel!" Parsinte cried.

"Yes," Saigilu said. "Tell us about when you killed a lion."

Killed a lion? Samuel had never told me! I looked at him with astonishment. He only shrugged and stretched out his legs, resting back against the pile of firewood as he prepared to tell his story.

"One afternoon," he began, "I was herding our cattle at the base of the hills, bringing them to the water to drink. My friends Salash and Leshinga were with me. The five dogs we went with for protection encircled our herd, as always, helping to keep them in line. Then, in the tall grass, we spotted a lion on the hunt, eyeing our cattle.

"When the cattle saw the lion, they scattered across the fields in every direction, kicking dust into the air. The dogs' barks echoed off the hills as the lion sprang into an acacia tree, about ten metres away. Salash threw his spear. But the lion saw it coming and dodged out of the way. The lion's roar echoed across the savannah and the cattle bellowed in fright.

"Our loyal dogs are used to defending us against hyenas or leopards. But they knew they were no match for a lion. Seeing Salash's spear miss, Leshinga, who is known for his accuracy, threw his spear directly into the lion's ribs. Its tan fur immediately burst with blood. In surprise at the pain of the spear the lion almost fell from the tree, then saved itself by catching hold of a branch with one paw. Our dogs ran and hid in the tall grass when they caught the scent of the lion's blood. They knew that if the lion fell it would eat us."

Glancing around, I saw the kids on the edges of their seats, enthralled by Samuel's tale.

"I tightened the grip on my spear, brought it behind my back, took a few running steps and threw my spear with all my might at the lion's stomach. The spear pierced it straight through. The force of the spear caused the lion to fall backward but the spear caught in the thick branches, pinning the lion in place.

"Salash hurried to grab his spear from the ground, then handed it to Leshinga. Leshinga again heaved it and pierced the lion in its heart, just below the neck. The lion wrapped its legs around the tree and fought with its claws to keep from falling. Its blood poured onto its fur, all over the tree, dripping down below. But still it lived.

"Then Leshinga and I both threw our *rungus* at the lion. Leshinga's hit its head and mine hit the paw it was using to keep itself up. At this, the lion gave a great roar and fell to the ground. We rushed forward, and I used my machete to cut the lion's throat, ensuring it was dead. Then we cut its tail off."

Samuel turned to me and said: "*Hii inaonyesha sisi waMaasai tulishinda.*" This was the sign that the Maasai had won over the lion.

We were all stunned by this story. There was a brief silence, then we all cheered. When the din died down, Mama turned to me.

"Naserian," she said, "Now it is your turn to tell a story."

Me? Everyone looked to me, gathering in closely by the fire.

They knew I was making progress with my Swahili, and they were encouraging me to improve my grasp of Maa. Our fireside gatherings were my chance to put these new languages to use. But what story to tell? Even if I had an interesting story about life back in America, they would never really understand it. And what story from home could follow the drama of Samuel's lion kill? *My high school graduation? Winning the 100-metre swim race? Surviving my first week at university?*

Then I had an idea. I asked for a volunteer to help me tell the story; of course, Parsinte leapt to his feet. I whispered in his ear that, as I told the story, he was to act it out with whatever came to his mind. Saigilu and Kipulel looked on, ready to join in, while Mama cuddled Morio in her lap. Faith put down the final dishes so she too could listen. Samuel folded his arms and watched with amused curiosity to see what I'd come up with.

They were going to help me write the story, I explained. First they were to tell me what the least sturdy kind of house is around here (*grass!* they cried), a middle-ground home (*mud!*) and the sturdiest, most reliable of them all (*stone, like the school!*).

Line by line, Parsinte stood before the fire and acted out my words of the Three Little Pigs, recast for the kids as the Three Little Goats. Parsinte's silhouette danced on the firewood piled behind him as the neighbourhood lion threatened to "Huff and puff and *bloooooooow* their house down!" Everyone laughed loud and long as the evening came to a close.

Far in the distance a cow lowed. Settling into our beds, Morio appeared at my bedside and I held up the sheet to let him crawl in beside me.

I kissed his forehead, asking him to sleep well that night and to try and breathe deeply. He responded with words I once again couldn't interpret, and I could tell he didn't quite understand me either. Yet we both fell asleep with smiles on our faces.

7 Traditions in Change

Back in Schaumburg, leaves would be changing colour and the first hints of snow would be appearing on branches. While at home the Chanukah menorah and Christmas tree would be going up, here in Kenya our community was preparing to celebrate a much different time-honoured tradition.

December is traditionally the season in which young Maasai, boys and girls alike, are circumcised. The ritual typically occurs when community fathers decide a child is ready to be considered an adult—usually between twelve and eighteen years old. Though the details of these ceremonies vary from region to region, for all Maasai this initiation and the ceremony that follows represent the symbolic entry of a young person into maturity, and it is always a momentous occasion.

Kokoo and other women had invited me to join them at an upcoming circumcision ceremony. Those who attended would offer encouragement to the young girl through this difficult rite of passage. If I declined, I'd be seen as not extending my support. So I agreed to go and began to prepare myself emotionally, because I was definitely wary of what I might see.

Faith had regaled me with accounts of her own circumcision, which had taken place only a year before, when she was twelve. I cringed as she bragged of how she'd sat with legs spread, arms crossed in defiance to the coming pain, her neck cocked with attitude against the discomfort. She hadn't cried or even winced and after a couple of minutes it was over. Such composure was admired and widely seen as more than just putting on a brave face: her stoicism was considered an expression of honour for family and community. When she proudly described the scene to me, I wasn't sure how to react: approval, or pity?

I asked Samuel about his own circumcision ceremony, again a delicate subject I felt uncomfortable broaching. But, like Faith, he spoke of the day with pride, describing how he and his friends Salash and Leshinga had revelled on their day of initiation and basked in the feasting and excitement of the ceremony. The pain of the actual procedure was long in the past, but the respect he'd gained from his kinsmen would be everlasting. The whole process was something I found hard to understand, which only made it more important to me that I attend.

The circumcision would take place in Orpurlkel, Mama's home village, about a four-hour journey to the southwest. The rest of the family was too busy with school and other responsibilities to come, so Baba, Kokoo and I set off on Friday, arriving late in the afternoon after another lengthy, squeezed-in ride in the back of a pickup truck.

The boma held about fifteen manyattas, and 200 or so people had gathered across the compound. Steaming pots sat atop roaring fires in preparation for the coming feast of tea, cabbage, potatoes, beans, rice and chapatti. Cattle, goats and roosters wandered freely. Baba immediately joined a group of men socializing under the shade of trees, leaving me and Kokoo with the women. It was all in celebration of the initiation, which would take place tomorrow morning at the break of dawn.

I would have little to do with initiating the three boys. Instead, I was expected to join the women in supporting the twelve-year-old girl who was to be circumcised. She spent the entire day inside her manyatta. Her head was cleanly shaved, and the women of her family comforted her in preparation of this momentous occasion, advising her how to behave during the "operation," showing a brave face with no outward expression of her physical pain. A few months after her healing, she was to become the fourth wife of a sixty-four-year-old man, who I saw stumbling drunkenly across the compound throughout the afternoon.

Meanwhile the three boys—dressed in black from head to toe—prepared themselves by spending the morning together herding cattle. All morning they were in the fields, pumping one another up for the next morning's ceremony, encouraging one another to be strong men and not flinch, gasp or betray their fear when the pain inevitably came.

When they returned from herding in the mid-afternoon, the rest of the boma bustled with anticipation. The mamas were overcome with tears and cries of exultation. I was surprised to see these strong, hardworking women, the backbone of every household, suddenly trembling, huddling together as if warming themselves against an imaginary cold.

For their part, the boys worked themselves into hysteric ecstasy, screaming and yelling, flailing their arms above their heads, dramatically falling to the ground. Over and over, they helped one another to their feet, only to collapse again into a heap on the ground, shouting words I couldn't decipher. I had no understanding of what was happening, where this emotion came from or what it all meant. Baba was nowhere to be found and Kokoo had joined the older women in gushes of tears.

I later asked Mama why the boys were acting this way. This process, she explained, was called *mori* in Swahili, or *orkorio* in Maasai. It's a mental process that flows through their entire body and, in this elevated state, they're ready for anything. Their toes can be placed into a fire, or their fingernails burned, and they barely feel it. In this transcendent state, they can endure the fear and agony of the actual ritual. For boys, even twitching slightly in reaction to the pain is a sign of cowardice.

Just before being circumcised, young boys go through a trance-like process, emitting high-pitched staccato yelping of the syllable *iyie*, inducing hyperventilation that also serves to numb the pain. Then a bucket of cold water is splashed all over the body, and from that moment until the end of the operation they remain silent.

It is an emotional experience for the women to see their sons in *mori*, and they too enter an elevated state of controlled hysteria, hoping to help them to show their bravery and give emotional support to the boys. Their tears are not of pity, but of joy and expectation.

Regaining their poise, the boys strode through the crowd, the sea of women parting to let them pass. Each boy headed to his own designated manyatta. They ducked inside, only to emerge moments later having changed into elaborate outfits made from animal skins. Each stood on a black oxen hide lain on the ground as elders traced their feet, sizing the boys for special slippers to be crafted from the hide.

In the meantime, the boys' mothers had concocted a shaving cream from a mixture of milk and water. Holding the boys close, they dabbed this cream on their heads before shaving away all the hair, including their eyebrows. Additional shaving cream and a razor were then given to the boys as they headed into the bush to privately ensure all other hair on the body was completely removed. In many ways, it was like the mothers were giving their sons a new birth. The shaving process is symbolic of leaving behind everything youthful, shedding one's skin to be remade as a man. Sometimes other women close to the boy also helped to show their support in this powerful moment.

Then the celebration truly began. Moratina brew was served liberally and the gathering erupted in song and dance. Children's laughter echoed from every corner. Smoking fires indicated a feast was pending, and elders' drinks were filled over and over as they gathered under acacia trees. From early evening into late at night, no plate or cup went empty. More rice was served, more brew was poured, more cabbage was dished out and more chapatti triangles were offered. Men and women, young and old, feasted, drank, danced, sang and played into the wee hours of the morning. As the hours grew later, I found myself wishing Samuel was there. He would have patiently explained everything—the meaning of every piece of jewellery, the significance of every step of the ritual, every lyric to the songs being sung.

At around two o'clock, I noticed the knife to be used for the boys' circumcision had been left resting unattended in a corner next to the firewood, its blade rusted and dirty. I ducked into an empty manyatta, lit a quick fire and placed the knife in a small pot of boiling water. I replaced it again next to the firewood, but lying on a plate in a plastic tub, feeling a little better knowing tomorrow's procedure would be a bit safer.

As people gradually headed to bed, Kokoo and I crawled onto a hide with another mama and her eight-year-old daughter inside a dark manyatta. We huddled together under a wool blanket against the cold night's wind, readying ourselves for the big day ahead starting with the initial cuts at sunrise.

The sky was still dark when we awoke early the next morning. Kokoo brought me a cup of tea and I sat gazing at the stars, thinking how different my present reality was from that of those kids, in the last minutes before their initiation.

As I was identifying the Orion constellation—my sixth grade teacher, Mr. Cook, would have been proud—Kokoo came rushing over. She seized my arm and insistently dragged me across the compound. She directed me toward one of the manyattas and, when I didn't move fast enough, she pushed my head down and shoved roughly me inside.

Inside I encountered a scene I would never forget. The young girl was leaning back on the dirt floor facing me, her naked legs spread wide. Crouched before her was the circumciser, her knife at the ready. Positioned directly behind the circumciser, mere feet from the operation, I watched as the first cut was made into the young girl's flesh.

My mind was ablaze. *Oh, my God!* Almost fifty women were cramped into the manyatta, and the heat was intense. I could vaguely hear stifled chatter in the background, but my concentration was fixed on the girl in front of me. She was being supported from behind, with two women's arms linked under her shoulders. The circumciser braced the girl's left leg, while another mama leaned against the girl's right. Still another mama lay sideways across her body, comforting her with a soothing hand on her forehead.

I made a fist and bit my right index finger, not knowing how to react at what I was witnessing. It took roughly two minutes to complete the procedure that brought the girl into womanhood. But from this moment on, she would be forever revered by her family and neighbours as a brave woman, and everyone would speak of her with incredible esteem, knowing she was able to endure the most difficult struggle, and she could now be counted upon as a true woman of the community. She didn't utter a sound, only shed two single tears.

A hollowed-out gourd, called a *kibuyu*, containing milk was placed next to the girl on the mud floor. The circumciser splashed milk on the girl's fresh cuts in order to coagulate the blood and honey was applied with a finger. The women exploded into high-pitched cheers as the crowd poured out of the manyatta, arms raised in triumph.

I staggered away, afraid my knees would give out with each step. My mind was consumed by visions of raw flesh. I shook my head, trying to clear it of the dizzying images I'd seen, but I was unable to delete them from my mind's eye. A warm pressure built up in the bottom centre of my back, bringing waves of nausea.

Even as I headed away, stunned, joyful exclamations reverberated across the compound as word travelled of the girl's courage. Message of her success was quickly sent to the river, where the three boys had just undergone their own initiation, and a messenger returned with news of all three boys' bravery. Not one had flinched, cried or hesitated in their moment of honour. The parents cherished the display of courage from their children—who were, as of this day, adults.

Everything about the boys was now reborn: they were men. All the trappings of youth—their clothes, their walking sticks or weapons, even their shoes—would be left behind as they became this new person.

As the returning men returned to the boma, an arrow was taken to a young calf's neck, creating a stream of blood that was directed into a kibuyu. Each of the four initiates were given raw blood to drink; the belief was the blood would return proteins and nutrients to their body lost in the circumcision.

A massive bull was then prepared to be slaughtered. For many, this rare sacrifice would be the only time they would enjoy meat all year. All the elders and young males followed as a cow was herded from the homestead to be killed. Baba found me and summoned me to come. While I was still woozy from what I'd seen, I felt obliged to follow; this was typically an activity attended only by men, but as a special guest I was allowed to witness the ritual.

The cow's front legs were bound together, then its back legs, forcing the animal to lie on its side. Its eyes were wild as it grunted with panic and fear. After a quick slaughter, an incision was made from the base of its jaw along the neck, stopping just before the chest. The skin was then peeled back to create a bucket-like receptacle, used to collect the blood after the main artery was pierced. The men formed a line as one young man dipped a cup into the filling basin and handed it to each man in turn.

When all the men had filled their cups, the blood was not quite drained. A faded orange plastic pitcher, just like the one Mom used for iced tea during summer barbeques back home, was used to save the extra blood. I watched as one man cut a branch from a nearby bush, picked away the leaves and twigs, then used it to stir the pitcher. I first assumed he was doing this to prevent the blood from coagulating. But a moment later he withdrew the stick, and the blood had clotted onto the stick. To my horror, he proceeded to take a generous bite of the solidified blood, then passed the stick around for others to chew off bites of this bright-red treat.

At this point I began to feel sick to my stomach from all of the blood, both human and animal. My vision began to blur; all I could see was the first cut of the girl's skin played on repeat in my mind.

"Naserian!"

Hearing my name snapped me out of my trance. As my eyes focused, I found a hunk of goopy, clotted raw kidney being extended to me from one of the men.

Expectant eyes stared at me. I gulped and reached to accept this offering. It looked harmless enough, and I fought to remind myself that I'd come here to challenge myself, to try new things. The piece was small enough to pop in my mouth in one go. It was chewy and warm, and my stomach almost sent it coming back up—but I kept it down. *I did it!*

The festivities continued into the night. More meat was cooked, and

At the circumcision, two Maasai men enjoy coagulated cow's blood on a stick!

the singing, dancing and children's games continued as I joined the women in cooking. We peeled carrots, onions, tomatoes and potatoes as the succulent aroma of freshly roasted meat filled the air, summoning all to the feast. An assembly line was formed, serving roasted, fried and boiled meat, stews, rice, potatoes, cabbage, beans and chapatti. We all ate until full, then ate the same amount again. Cups were filled with Maasai brew and chai. The celebration continued long into the night.

By the time the roaring fires had faded to coals, the remaining meat was portioned out for guests to take home to their families. Pots were covered to be stored in manyattas. Drunken men were ushered to their beds and lanterns were extinguished, house by house, as the community went to sleep full, proud and hopeful of the new initiates who lay inside their own manyattas, healing.

Days before the circumcision, I had written an email home, sharing with family and friends news of this ceremony I would be witnessing. My university roommate Sara told me it was perfect timing, as she was writing a paper on "female genital mutilation"—a term I'd not heard used at all in Kenya. She asked me to assist her in gathering some primary research.

Over the following few weeks, I led a series of conversations in both formal and informal settings with a range of community members: educated and uneducated, men and women, young and old, circumcised and uncircumcised individuals. On the topic of circumcision, our discussions mostly surrounded the basic question of "Why?"

I learned that circumcision provoked many diverse opinions. Mama said she would never want to undergo something like that again. Another woman of the same age told me she couldn't relive the traumatic incident, even in words. From several women I spoke with, it seemed it was mainly the younger generation, many who had been exposed to Western ideals, who condemned the practice.

Talking to the people of an older generation, grandmothers and grandfathers, was a different story. Mama Samuel was excited to talk about her own circumcision day and requested we not limit the conversation to the two of us alone. So one morning, eight women elders and I gathered over tea. As the fire embers relaxed into smoking red coals inside the small manyatta, each woman took a turn recalling her own special day. When asked to describe the pain, each said the physical pain was long forgotten, but they still retained the pride of being accepted as an adult by the community and to be seen no longer a child. To be initiated from a girl into a true mama was the highest honour. Through circumcision, they'd passed the ultimate test: to know they could be a grown woman in the community. Once cared for, they could now care for others.

One had to wonder: would the tradition die out with this older generation? Or would it continue being practised for generations to come? Or would it evolve into an entirely different process of initiation? Samuel had a different opinion that his mama. Having attended school and learned of the health complications that might emerge later, specifically during childbirth, he'd begun to wonder if this was the best thing for his future daughters. But for his sons, it would go without question that he absolutely wanted them circumcised. To him, this was without question.

Around that time a Maasai development worker from the Transmara Region of southwest Kenya came to Nkoyet-naiborr to investigate what techniques the community was using to preserve its culture against potential threats of encroaching development. As a gesture of welcome, I volunteered to lead him on a hike up through the Ol Doinyo Hills to visit a tree nursery. This opened my way for an uninterrupted exploration into the worldview of a knowledgeable Maasai man, who had received an education abroad, then returned. He said he agreed with the view that circumcision was barbaric, and he said, if God should bless him with a daughter, he would never circumcise her.

We discussed how, since 2001, female circumcision was officially illegal in Kenya, which while an encouraging sign of progress, created many side effects. Families could now bring their boys to hospitals to be circumcised sanitarily, under anaesthetic. But with this legislation, girls didn't enjoy that more hygienic option. Their operations often occurred hurriedly in bushes at night, to avoid being caught. Discussing the issue with nurses, I'd learned that the skin healing from such an operation later tears more easily, rather than stretching, during the birthing process—a significant side effect in a culture where childbirth is already often a dangerous experience.

Up in the hills that afternoon, my guest from Transmara asked me a poignant I hadn't anticipated: if I ever chose to stay and fully become part of the Maasai community, keeping a home and raising a family here, would I circumcise *my* daughter? Mere months before, I would have been able to answer this question without a second's hesitation: of course not. Yet when he asked, I paused. How could I deny my daughter an enormous part of her cultural identity and heritage, for the rest of her life? But at the same time, how could I possibly wish my daughter's genitals unnecessarily cut?

How could I form an opinion on a rite of passage with a long history I couldn't fathom? Yet, when someone as intelligent as Mama spoke out openly against it, there must be another way.

One interesting development I'd heard about was a new idea being promoted by some rights agencies called "alternative initiation," or "circumcision through words." It was a process which offered girls the same honours, along with education about human rights, without actual surgery taking place. All sorts of varieties existed, some that took place over a couple of days, others for weeks, sometimes within in homes or schools, but the foundational concept was the same.

As in a traditional circumcision, female family members and neighbours came together to celebrate their introduction into womanhood through songs, dance, feasting and education. Yet the girls are given more of a chance to express their individuality in the initiation process. Maybe there were less damaging ways, such as this, to nurture girls as they grew into strong, capable women respected by their communities. Whether through a knife or shared empowerment, these girls still would maintain an irrefutable sisterhood for the rest of their lives.

I still didn't entirely know what I personally thought about the circumcision debate. Reading about these experiences was one thing; actually witnessing them up close was entirely different. Was I doing my fellow women a disservice by not raising objections—"sanitizing" the idea in my mind? Whose role was it to sanitize these wounds in society?

I had only spoken with a small sampling of one community, of one ethnic group, of one nation, one continent. I was in no position to universally judge those who continued this practice. But what I did know was that more and more I was taking these Maasai traditions, and their significance, to heart. Every day I spent with this family and this community brought us closer together.

8 Research

With all that I'd experienced and seen so far, worrying about fulfilling my university credits had been the furthest thing from my mind. But I'd been neglecting the field research that I was supposed to be conducting for school, and I had scarcely even begun thinking about the lengthy paper I was required to write.

From my months in Nkoyet-naiborr, I'd learned there were too many complexities surrounding local issues, such as female circumcision, for a development worker to barge into a community, crying, "It's barbaric and shouldn't be done!" That aggressive approach wouldn't prevent women from circumcising their daughters, and it wouldn't create healthy dialogue between cultures. It seemed to me that, to have an impact, development workers would need to understand communities at an intimate, personal level before introducing any solutions.

And who was to choose these "solutions" for communities, if not the community members themselves? It seemed so many outsiders were deciding future strategies for communities without their consent, input, or taking into account the unique histories of various populations. But when a project like

Nkoyet-naiborr's water source was implemented, with the full participation of elders and forward-thinking locals, success was much more likely.

I decided to focus my paper on this disconnect between theory and fieldwork. But to enable me to write it, I had to see such effects in person. As wrong as it might sound to my university dean, I hoped to do my learning without a typical, pre-approved structure. Surely I would learn more about development as a participating observer than as a researcher toting a notepad and a list of pre-written interview questions. For me, it wasn't about methodologies. It wasn't about class time with other American students. It wasn't about lectures. I was looking for a more organic process: drinking tea with new friends, building relationships, learning their language. It was about building trust. The theoretical, academic side would have to come later.

I made plans to travel throughout Kenya to visit some of my fellow students at the sites where they were conducting their own research. Along the way, I hoped to hear about as many different ideas as I could and to see different strategies people were adopting that to help local communities survive. I bid tearful goodbyes to Mama, Faith, my brothers and Samuel, Kokoo and all the mamas I saw every day and prepared for a few weeks away from Nkoyet-naiborr.

My first stop was to visit my friend Linnea, who was staying with a family in a village called Mugombashira in the Kirinyaga District. From Nairobi I rode a typically crowded bus, jammed full of people, bags, mattresses, jerry cans and chickens, headed for Embu, the town closest to where Linnea was staying.

The bus passed through the city's slums and out to small towns curbed into rolling hills, terraced farming and lush rice pads. After several hours' journey, a rusting signboard that read "Karibu Embu" welcomed us to the bustling town of about 50,000. Compared to Nairobi's skyscrapers, Embu's few concrete buildings and wooden, tin-roofed stores seemed modest—yet if Mama, Faith or Kokoo had been there with me, even this small city would have floored them.

As we arrived at the station, I immediately broke free of the mob greeting the bus for a happy reunion with Linnea. We hurried away before any taxi drivers could swarm us, and Linnea led me to her favourite *hoteli* restaurant in town.

We dropped into our chairs and ordered fresh passion fruit juice. Despite our relief and delight in seeing one another, we were both exhausted, and we took our time catching up. I told her about my family, the circumcision and all I'd learned about the community's ever-changing culture. Linnea told me she'd contracted malaria and was only now getting over it: the fatigue was still apparent in her eyes.

She shared some of the history of the area and the development issues she'd found. Due to its arid climate, no people had lived there even twenty years ago. The pressure of expanding populations had meant that even this harsh environment had to support people, and most living in the area were subsistence farmers, meaning they raised enough crops to support themselves, but usually little more. Most plots were about ten acres, and the soil was generally fertile enough to raise maize and beans, used to make a dish called *githeri*, the area's staple food. Other crops included tomatoes, bananas and mangoes, sold for profit or consumed by the farmers' families.

As the community grew, it became obvious much more water was needed than was available. The land was designated as arid and semi-arid land and the lack of rainfall was devastating the local economy. Since farmers were raising many of the same crops, any difficulties plaguing one farmer affected the entire community. That year, many crops—including the main export, french beans—had failed.

The community looked to the nearby Kiye River, with hopes of creating a system of piping that would let people access the river from their homes. They sought funding from the United Nations Development Program; however, in order to qualify for the specific grant they sought, the project was established as a women-only group, called the Kugeria Women's Water Group.

The funding was used to purchase piping. The women carried the pipes on their backs more than fifteen kilometres every day, over and over, to the Kiye River, where a technician connected them one by one. The ambitious project's gruelling schedule meant both women and their families suffered: the women were also required to pay monthly dues, which meant they had to raise added money by hiring themselves out as field hands or finding other extra work. Meanwhile, domestic chores at home went unattended, since they were so busy working on the water system.

But through the women's continued, determined efforts, four years after the first pipe was laid, the project was complete. Each home could then purchase connections from the main line to their own home. If they couldn't afford to buy a direct connection, they could still visit the holding tank and obtain water from a faucet available there.

In the beginning, Linnea told me, only a few women joined the project, so there was more than enough water to sufficiently irrigate all of their fields. Yet as the project thrived, more and more women wanted to join. The demand for water rose, while the supply remained constant. During the dry season, the water would often be depleted before reaching users at the distant end of the pipes. As well, with so much water required for everyday household use—laundry, cooking, cleaning and other needs—there were often insufficient supplies left for irrigating crops.

To try and advance fair access, the area was divided into six regions, each with its own water supply route. In dry seasons, a supervising water technician would manage each area's usage as needed, in order to equally distribute availability. Those areas who had their water shut off often objected, but it helped keep water flowing to where it was needed most.

"It's not a perfect system," Linnea admitted, "But it is very well organized."

In order to maintain their funding from the United Nations Development Programme, the Kugeria Women's Water Group women had to prove the project would be independent and sustainable. Its thirteen-member committee, with the purpose of ensuring sensible rules were established and followed, was comprised of two elected representatives from each of the six regions. Sara, the mother of the family with whom Linnea had been staying, served as the project's chair.

Though the area still faced many struggles, by acting together, these women had made a significant contribution to the survival of the community, and they were a successful demonstration of change and hope.

An afternoon meeting of the Kugeria Women's Water Project.

The reclining sun told us it was time to head back to the village. Linnea and I paid our bill and hopped a matatu back to Linnea's homestay with Sara. She greeted us with open arms, ready with a hug for her two "daughters," as she called us.

Sara's home was excellently kept, with a concrete floor, wooden siding and a tin roof. We gathered for tea in the wooden kitchen, using empty buckets for chairs. Outside chickens scurried throughout the compound, which also housed a large water storage tank; a solar heating system to boil water (unfortunately she explained, it didn't work very well); and a grazing pen for her two large dairy cows. Her sons, she explained, were out working the fields, but would be home soon.

Sara was eager to share more of the area's history, explaining further how the entire region's prosperity revolved around the seasonal harvests. It was an ongoing seesaw of fortune and failure. When one crop flourished, all did. The increase in supply, with demand staying stable, then reduced the value and price. Therefore, the farmers often earned lesser profits, even when crops were doing well.

For example, Sara described how the previous September there was such an overabundance of tomatoes that a crate weighing sixty kilograms sold for only fifty shillings; usually, they sold for 600 shillings. To access other markets, farmers required significant upfront capital. If they could transport the tomatoes themselves to the market in Nairobi without employing a middleman as broker, they could earn a profit of 203 shillings per crate, yet would have to put up a 5,000 shillings transport fee, plus 1,200 shillings to the municipal centre, a 300 shilling distribution fee, plus other costs. In the end, they paid upward of 8,000 shillings just to get their tomatoes to the city's markets.

Other than farming, few income opportunities were available, especially for women. Working on another farm or doing housework for another family might bring in only about 100 to 150 shillings a day, and they still had to find time for maintaining their own households. Most women struggled to save enough money to afford the very basics: sending their children to school, or health care when their families became sick.

When drought struck, money was even scarcer. At these times, more people bought maize and beans, since they were relatively cheap in comparison to other foods. However, this had the adverse effect of raising prices: demand increases, but supplies stay the same. This was the situation in January through June, when maize and beans had to be sent as relief from the United States and distributed by the Kenyan government.

Despite these challenges, Sara said conditions had remarkably improved, compared with even fifteen years before. Previously, there had been no road to the market in Embu. The walk to the main road could have taken anywhere from twenty minutes to more than an hour, depending on conditions, and from the main road to Embu was another three hours. Sara had three children, two of whom had been sick as infants and, with her husband often away working in Nairobi, she would have to make the trip alone.

With our tea finished, Linnea and I began peeling potatoes for dinner while Sara attended to other housework. I tried to process all I had previously read with what was actually occurring here. This village was a prime example of a rural economy in a state of constant crisis. If crops failed, families didn't eat and food prices rose to unaffordable levels. If crops flourished and became widely available, prices plummeted and people earned less money. It was a conundrum that seemed without resolution.

After the potatoes were peeled, Linnea and I headed behind the house and rested on the dry, dusty ground. The soil cracked beneath us, having received no rain in months.

Linnea told me of yet another factor affecting the area. International corporations often visited Embu to purchase goods from farmers. A few years ago, these corporations had offered farmers abundant supplies of french bean seeds, with an arrangement that the company would then return to buy back the vegetables produced. Many farmers took up this offer, and so several times a week trucks arrived from the city to buy crates of beans in bulk.

This provided extra income for the farmers, as well as new income opportunities for women hired as bean pickers, who made as much as 200 shillings (about three dollars) per day. However, the farmers' actual profit margin, after paying for labour, pesticides and other equipment, was incredibly low.

Meanwhile, the beans were hurriedly shipped to the company's headquarters in Nairobi, where workers packed the beans to be flown overnight to Paris, from where the beans were distributed throughout France. The end profits the company yielded were, of course, much higher than that of the farmers who actually raised the crops.

Linnea said many questions still bothered her. There was so much inequality, so many contradictions. Who was to blame? Did it have to be this way? When she'd contracted malaria, 400 shillings (about six dollars) bought her the medicine that helped her recover. But for most poor Africans, such expenses were simply out of reach. Families would have sell twenty-five tins of maize, a chicken or even a cow, if they even had one to sell in the first place. Even if they could afford it, the facilities might simply not be accessible.

We'd both glimpsed Kenya's wealthy elite, driving around in Mercedes-Benzes, surrounding themselves with security guards and hired house girls. Linnea had visited some of these wealthy households. It seemed everyone she'd met who had accumulated any significant wealth had done so, at least to some degree, at the expense of those poorer. One family she'd visited was led by a man who sold cars to rich politicians, the same officials who had helped Kenya earn its reputation of having one of the most corrupt governments in the world. This man, whose wealth came from a system feeding off exploiting the poor, was rich enough to send his son to study overseas at Berkeley—where, ironically, the son was studying international development.

Linnea said she'd had to force herself to accept these frustrating contradictions. She made her peace by working to understand the daily lives of ordinary people, the women and their families. She'd recently spent a day helping a mama haul water from the communal source. Linnea considered herself a strong, fit girl, having played basketball and practising daily yoga. She'd thought she'd be ready for the chore.

"It was so difficult," she told me. "After carrying one container, I thought I was going to collapse. Seriously, I cried. I was sore for days."

These women possessed incredible strength and endurance. Theirs was a world of hard work, dedication and a willingness to do whatever it took for them and their families to survive.

I next travelled to Mau, just north of the large town of Meru, where my friend Sandra was doing her research. In addition to her research with a local widows' group, Sandra was volunteering at the Maua Methodist Hospital, working mainly with AIDS patients. From what Sandra had described to me by email, I knew tough scenes lay ahead. But with all I'd heard about AIDS in Africa, I had to learn the real story.

As my matatu pulled into Maua in the dark of night, all I could make out were littered streets and small stone, tin and wooden structures lining both sides. Though small, Maua was still an urban centre, and urban poverty, I was finding, was quite different from rural poverty.

Sandra quickly found me in the crowd, and soon we were in one of her friend's shops, enjoying a soda while sitting on crates of empty Fanta bottles. After we caught up on the events of the past months, Sandra began to fill me on the situation into which I was headed.

The area's economy was fuelled largely by production of *miraa*: an addictive, hugely popular stimulant made from a flowery plant grown throughout East Africa. Miraa, also called *khat*, had a shelf life of only forty-eight hours, so it had to be transported immediately after being harvested. At a central location off Maua's main street, men packaged several shipments a day to be delivered to major hubs in Mombasa and Nairobi. From there, flights brought the miraa to markets beyond—mostly in the United States, Europe, the Middle East and Somalia.

Every morning women arrived at the site to sell their banana leaves, used for packaging the miraa. What was called "one kilo"—actually a huge bundle weighing much more than one kilogram—sold for somewhere between 3,000 and 4,000 shillings (between forty-five and sixty dollars). This created a significant source of income for poor families, especially since miraa—unlike many other regional crops—could be harvested throughout almost the entire year.

This business also created job opportunities that otherwise would not exist: for men as drivers; for women through the sale of banana leaves; and for young boys hired to pick the miraa. It was a practice deeply entrenched in the culture and livelihoods of the families and community.

But it also created deadly situations for many families, even beyond the health risks of taking the potent stimulant. Men in the miraa trade often travelled to big cities and, while there, they often engaged in extramarital sex. Many contracted HIV, then returned home to pass it on to their wives. When either parent became sick with HIV-AIDS, families suffered a loss of income. Coupled with the added expenses of medical care, this had devastating effects—not only for the infected individuals, but those who depended on them for survival. Responsibilities of home fell on young girls or wives, who were often unprepared and uneducated. In hopes of survival, too often their only option was to exchange sex for food or money—even further increasing their risk of contracting HIV.

My conversation with Sandra continued long after our sodas were done, all through the walk back to her apartment. As she told me about the horrible scenes she'd encountered at the hospital, I was terrified, saddened and intrigued. Late into the night, I was kept up with visions of what I might encounter in the morning light.

The next morning, after a quick breakfast of tea and bread, we headed to the hospital. The staff there were helpful and happy to provide some background history.

The first case of AIDS in Meru District was reported in 1987. By 1993, some 646 cases had been reported, and by the time of our visit thirty-six percent of Meru's people were reported to be infected with HIV. This widespread epidemic had drastically affected the socioeconomic future of the area and permeated all aspects of the people's livelihoods. In poor health, the economy simply couldn't function, furthering already-widespread poverty. Everywhere, parents were dying and children were being left as orphans.

To make matters worse, AIDS bore a devastating social stigma. When a woman contracted the disease, they were often rejected by relatives and denied the opportunity to participate in community affairs. Ostracism and gossip made it incredibly difficult to receive financial, let alone emotional, support. For example, when inheritance rights were being secured following the death of a family member, an infected woman's parenting abilities were questioned. AIDS-infected women were seen as "unclean" and unworthy.

Meanwhile, Kenyan women were usually powerless in influencing their husbands to wear condoms, yet expected to comply with their sexual demands. This widespread denial, along with the inability to afford vaccines, prevented any effective control over the disease's spread.

Through its educational efforts, the Maua Methodist Hospital served as the area's main force against AIDS, striving for new, innovative solutions. With Sandra, I took a walk throughout the hospital grounds, wrestling with the complexities of these problems.

I'd heard the statistics, that over half of the world's HIV-AIDS cases were in Africa, and that millions died annually due to AIDS and related illnesses. It was very difficult to gather reliable information about the reality of AIDS in Africa. The World Bank, the United Nations and other international bodies openly admitted to the difficulties in obtaining accurate data in developing countries.

However, it was one thing to hear about these issues and another entirely for them to truly sink in. Usually, when I began to feel overwhelmed by so much misery and distress, something inside me clicked off. This time I couldn't let that happen. I had to stay focused.

As I passed a room containing several beds, a nurse in a navy blue sweater asked if I wanted to take a look inside the AIDS ward. I was taken aback. *Inside? Why?*

But several patients had noticed my presence, and they awaited my response. I didn't want to let them think I was afraid to approach them, so I followed the nurse inside.

Eyes blinked at me: the watery eyes of people knowing they came here to die, ostracized by their homes, feeling unworthy of care and love. They were scared. They felt alone. They suffered tremendous pain, surrounded by sickness, with no control over their fates. They didn't know what to do, maybe afraid of how their children would eat. The only companionship they found was in understaffed, exhausted nurses and other patients also ravaged by the disease.

I passed lifeless bodies in beds, sometimes two sharing one. Some were so shrunken I almost didn't notice them lying there. Others I couldn't ignore, like a man with such extreme sores around his mouth and throat he clearly was unable to swallow. When he tried to sit up and greet me, he erupted in a coughing fit; unable to swallow the phlegm and saliva streaming from his mouth, he tried to catch it in his hands, until the nurse brought a tissue to help. He was so weak and, likely embarrassed, he collapsed back onto the bed in silence. I went to his side and patted his shoulder as reassuringly as I could before continuing down the corridor.

Leaving the ward, I thanked the young nurse for letting me visit. She explained to me further dilemmas facing her patients. Few people in Maua and its surrounding villages could afford health care. For families living on less than one dollar a day, bringing a sick child to a doctor meant an entire family likely went without food. When someone was perpetually sick, as in the later stages of AIDS, going hungry was obviously not a viable option. So the average patient remained at home, without medicine, without relief. For those few who could afford treatment, they were scarcely better off, facing the grim reality of the hospital's haunting halls.

The next afternoon, Sandra invited me to the meet the widows' group she'd been interviewing for her research. The women, numbering about a hundred, met every other week in a village just outside of Maua. Together they supported one another through their shared struggles. Many earned only about 1,000 shillings per month, or about fifteen dollars for thirty days—barely enough for two meals a day, let alone medicine and other necessities. Worse still, many of these women were widowed from AIDS and would likely require additional medical assistance in the future. So they pooled their resources and fought for their survival together.

The women all knew Sandra and greeted her as one of their own. A group of them leapt to their feet, swaying back and forth and belting out a song until they lost their breath. After our wild applause died down, the gathering's leader turned to Sandra and me, indicating it was now our turn to perform.

I glared at Sandra. *"What are we going to sing?"* I hissed.
The women waited in expectation as Sandra and I racked our brains, gritting our teeth with pained smiles plastered on our faces. Reluctantly, we made our way to the front, whispering to one another.

" 'Good Riddance' by Green Day?" I suggested.

"I don't know the words. 'Row, Row, Row Your Boat'?"

"That's ridiculous. What's something we both know?"

"What about 'The Star-Spangled Banner'?"

"Good one! Ready? 1 . . . 2 . . . 3!"

Our voices rang like children at an assembly. The entire scene was completely absurd, but it didn't matter. We made it through, and the women gave us an enthusiastic standing ovation.

After the meeting, I sat in on an interview between Sandra and some of the women. Many women we spoke with hadn't even heard of the disease and, of those who had, few had been tested. Most feared testing because they'd heard there was no cure, no medicine; all they knew was one would suffer and die. So there was no incentive to get tested, knowing this fate awaited them. This got me thinking: how could any progress be made against AIDS when entire populations didn't even understand what the disease really *was?*

While there were encouraging signs among Kenya's youth population on safe sex, the older generation were still resistant to change. Women told us of husbands reusing condoms and of turning the situation around to accuse their wives themselves of cheating: why else would they want them to wear condoms? Initiating such conversations could lead to beatings, so women felt discouraged from bringing up the subject with their husbands.

The Maua Methodist Hospital had introduced education campaigns through outreach workshops, producing some positive results. Many women were learning more about the disease and how it was spread. But in order to achieve lasting change, men needed to be included in these education campaigns, learning the importance of using condoms and practising monogamy.

While the miraa market was a significant contributor to the area's high prevalence of AIDS, it was certainly not the only factor. Just as the French bean harvest had profound effects on Kirinyaga's economy, every area faced issues requiring drastic changes. I was discovering things were always more complex than they seemed on the surface.

Still trying to understand what a successful development solution would look like, I visited Eva, in an eastern region called Kitui. It had only been a few months since we'd seen one another back in Nairobi, but when we reunited I felt a huge sense of relief. I was losing perspective, grasping at anything to make sense of the complex situations confronting me. I needed some clarity and hoped Eva could provide it.

We walked through Kitui's dry, dusty heat as she told me about the region. Eva had been working in an international office attempting to set up sustainable water projects.

As she explained to me, Kitui was another arid region where drought was a persistent problem. People walked kilometres every day to fetch water from the nearby river; for some people, this took four precious hours out of every day. There was also high animal activity near the river bed, especially that of the donkeys used to help carry water. As a result, Eva said, the water unfortunately tasted strongly of donkey urine.

To help create a more stable water supply, an international non-governmental organization was co-funding a water and agriculture project. Its ultimate mission was to be sustainable throughout and beyond the three years of committed funding. Staying by Eva's side for the next week, I saw a stark difference between the promise of this project, initiated by outsiders based on financial targets, and Kirinyaga's, which was based on community involvement and real-world facts.

This international organization entered the community proclaiming a purpose of increasing water availability. It chose the locations where the projects would be installed, then quickly dug ten boreholes—holes drilled deep into the ground to draw out water below the surface—and constructed storage tanks, meters and faucets. The boreholes were equipped with diesel-fuelled generators, which ran about three hours a day. Each surrounding community was told to form a committee of twelve people, each of whom would appoint an operator and a night watchman to monitor access.

Instead of providing it for free, the water was sold to help the project sustain its costs. The water was sold for two shillings (about four cents) for twenty litres of water. Many women still chose to walk the extra distance to obtain free water from the river beyond. The boreholes' generators required regular fuelling and maintenance and, in order for them to operate during dry seasons, when people would presumably be buying the most water, supplies needed to be stored during periods of rain.

The community simply wasn't motivated to learn about and maintain the project. While the organization futilely tried to host awareness meetings, farmers continued to work their thirsty fields. Once the water committees had been established, their purposes and responsibilities were left unclear. Some people I met said the borehole water required using more soap while washing clothes, or that it tasted salty and made poor tea. Most continued to use the river water, even given the inconvenience.

There were also questions about financial sustainability and the long-term goal of alleviating poverty. For example, there was talk of the NGO creating a pipe extension closer to the market. If kiosk water was available there, it was thought, people would enjoy easier access, and they would therefore buy more, increasing the project's profits. It was thought that particular kiosk would then be able to financially sustain itself when the organization inevitably removed itself from operations.

But when Eva and I chatted with people on the street, they said there was already a sufficient water supply near the market, whereas people farther away from the kiosks and river were in serious need. What should one do: strive for financial stability, or provide the most help to those who needed it? There were even deeper issues here: how could the water committees keep accurate records, when so many adults were illiterate? Should basic education instead be the number one priority?

These types of dilemmas kept Kitui in poverty, and poverty kept distracting community members from buying borehole water. It was a classic dilemma.

Eva and I pondered this challenge throughout the week we spent together, walking in the communities, conversing with mamas, visiting the water stations, sitting in a mango tree for hours or peeling potatoes for supper. We began to realize that maybe it wasn't really as complicated as it seemed. Communities simply needed to be involved in their own development. They had to feel a sense of ownership and empowerment, making decisions for their own benefit. Certainly a plan developed with the help of those who actually lived with these situations every day would make things work better. Who were outsiders to come in and make such decisions, when the locals were the ones with the inside knowledge?

Projects led by outside organizations could only succeed with a full understanding of the community and its issues. This particular organization, while meaning well, had entered Kitui with its own agenda, failing to ask the community what they *really* wanted and needed.

Eva and I weighed the differences between the community-initiated water project in Embu and this outsider-imposed water project in Kitui. Which was more successful? Which would last longer? Which would respond more positively and efficiently to the inevitable obstacles that would arise? What made the most sense?

The discussion took us long into our last night together, and it continued in our minds long after she saw me off the next morning for my ride back to Nairobi.

On the ride home, my matatu stopped at a roadside town for tea. Sipping a steaming cup of chai, I strolled down the roadside, along a row of busy storefronts and shacks.

Then suddenly someone rushed past, bumping my shoulder. My first thought was it was a pickpocket, so as the runner sprinted away I checked to ensure I still had my bag. Thankfully, it was untouched.

Then I saw a crowd forming just ahead, blocking the runner's flight. Shouts rang out and, drawing closer, I saw a mob forming around him, a wall of people closing in. I watched with horror as punches and kicks were thrown. The man fell to his knees, shrinking to protect himself from the torrent of blows.

Somebody help him! Why wasn't anyone helping him? What did he do, to deserve such violence? I wanted to rush to his defence, but felt paralyzed to act. I stopped a man, also watching the chaotic scene unfold, and asked what was happening.

"He robbed a merchant down the street," he told me. "Witnesses called out and alerted the rest of us."

It was mob justice, and I would learn it was perfectly legal in Kenya. If the authorities failed to prevent crime, the people were free to take matters into their own hands. Even in a case like this, before officials had time to intervene.

"But they're kicking him!" I cried. "He'll be *killed!* Shouldn't we call the police?"

I was frantic, but no one else seemed concerned. The crowd only squeezed in tighter and more kicks flew.

The man assured me police were on their way. "If they get here soon, they'll take him to jail and deal with it from there. But if they don't get here soon . . . ."

His voice trailed off, but I knew what would happen. The man would be beaten to death, a victim of mob justice. I'd heard stories of such incidents occurring, but hadn't known whether it actually happened, or was merely a rumour. What could I do? To the Kenyan people, it was their way of standing up to criminals in order to protect their families and their livelihoods.

In stunned silence, I awaited the arrival of police. But none came. Soon the crowd began to disperse on its own. It was over. The man was dead. There was nothing left to do but continue on my way, back to the matatu and wait for the ride to Nairobi.

Back in Nairobi, I stayed with my friend Eva and her host family. We met up with another classmate, Skye, and spent the afternoon weaving through the teeming downtown streets, past the vendors in their makeshift stalls and pleading beggars sprawled on flattened sheets of cardboard.

Later, Skye and Eva wanted to go out for dinner. I debated whether or not to join them; I was working on a long-overdue letter to Erin and was intent on finishing it. But I was so glad to have the company of friends, their pleas were hard to resist. So I caved, yet brought my journal with me, just in case I was further inspired to add to my letter.

After a pleasant dinner of sweet and sour vegetables with fried rice, we strolled leisurely back to the family's home. We were just turning a corner, with Skye a pace or two ahead, when Eva stopped in her tracks.

"Oh, no."

As if in slow motion, three men wielding machetes emerged from the surrounding alleys, encircling Skye, tapping his shoulders and arms with the flats of their blades.

I froze, not knowing what to do. I felt removed from the scene, as if watching from a distance. Then I heard a voice, demanding, "What do you want?"

The men turned. Unbelievably, these words were mine. With all eyes on me, I swallowed and asked the question again. *What do you want?* Behind me, Eva echoed in Swahili: *Unataka nini?*

Two of the men approached me, machetes raised. I raised my hands, saying, "I have nothing. Look, no pockets."

Dressed only in my sarong, I really did have nothing. Eva didn't either. But we both knew Skye was carrying all of his money and his passport. "No pockets," I said again. "All I have is . . . *this.*"

I showed the journal. One of the men nodded, then another plucked it from my hands. Then, just as quickly as they'd surrounded us, the men disappeared into the night. I shouted after them, but knew it was pointless.

Skye, Eva and I joined hands, verifying we were all okay. Nothing else had been taken other than the journal. The only thing we could do was to continue on our way. We came across a policeman, and we warned him three men with machetes were on the prowl. The policeman barely even nodded.

Afterward, Eva was shaken. Skye was barely fazed, and explained he had only crouched in submission to protect his money belt.

As for me, I was upset, mostly at the fact they'd taken my journal. A journal! What would they do with it? Wrap chapattis in it? They'd quickly see it was of no value, then throw it into the trash on Uhuru Street. Yet it contained my most intimate thoughts from the last few months, my heart and soul.

Perhaps it was fate. I'd debated whether to go out and briefly questioned bringing the journal with me. Yet I'd brought it, and it was the only thing taken. Strange. Maybe fate, maybe simply one of life's random twists.

I was reminded of a dream I'd had when I was about ten years old. In the dream, my mother was kidnapped and held hostage. When I attempted to rescue her, the kidnappers made an offer: they would set her free, but only if I took her place. In the dream, I'd immediately refused and run away, leaving my mother behind. Waking afterward, I'd felt incredible guilt. I remembered debating whether or not to tell Mom about the dream, fearing the truth would come out and fearing what it revealed about me. I never did tell her.

When I tried to come to Skye's defence, demanding, *What do you want?* and diverting our attackers' attention, I considered backing off, just like in my dream. But this time, I'd stood my ground.

The next day, I spent the afternoon putting my research together holed up at a recent discovery: Java House, a refuge of ice cream, good coffee, Heinz ketchup, apple pie . . . and a much-needed break from the beggars and hawkers of the city's streets.

I sat back with a mug of coffee and thought about the issues and people I'd seen. *Whew.* It was so much: across Kenya, from drought-prone arid land to lush farmlands, from the coast to the savannah and all points in between, the realities of this world were so overwhelming. In hopes of focusing these ideas, I'd written to my fellow students, who were each doing their own research across Kenya. I fanned through the stack of letters and printouts of emails I'd accumulated, each describing my classmates' unique experiences.

Megan was working on a project where government officials had optimistically constructed a water dam, yet had failed to perform mandatory checks, leaving towns without water and facing breakouts of malaria and other diseases.

Cherri's overbearing host family in Western Kenya de-shelled her eggs for her with manure-covered hands and insisted on escorting her everywhere—even on trips to the bathroom.

Stephanie lived in a mud hut in Malindi, working on reforestation and, in coming months, she would be interning on an ambitious new community agri-forestry project.

Rosa saw four people die of AIDS in three weeks, including people she'd interviewed only days before.

Rajesh said he was receiving more love from the three sisters of the Kamba host family than he'd ever experienced. A dentistry student, by day he pulled teeth in a hospital, the only cure for tooth pain was with removal.

Brenda was working with expecting mothers, also in Kitui— she'd become adept at estimating their delivery dates simply by feeling their stomachs.

Before Katie had come down with malaria in Machakos, she had already been administering shots to patients on only her second day working in a dispensary clinic.

The stories went on and on. In different ways, we were all learning and making mistakes along the way, trying to make sense of these new, complex issues we were facing.

But what was *I* doing? Aside from this half-finished research paper . . . what was I *really* accomplishing? I was facing things I'd never known before, filling notebooks with thoughts and ideas, yet I still couldn't process it all. At home I'd heard terms like "exploitation" and "fair trade." I'd heard how governments and corporations took advantage of impoverished nations so wealthier countries could enjoy cheap produce. Meanwhile, lobbyists and activists accused the international community of unfair treatment. I could almost hear my mother: "Gosh, tomatoes are now $2.39 a pound!"

I'd visited villages where trucks came only every third day, where farmers sold french beans for marginal profits, where workers made next to nothing. Then their crops were on shelves across Europe within forty-eight hours of the harvest. Was *this* exploitation? Who benefited? Was the system totally off-base, or just my perceptions?

Was there a larger process I was missing? It surely couldn't work like this. Or could it?

Never having before studied international development or global economics, these kinds of topics were new to me. I was glad that instead of learning about these problems in a classroom or in a book, I was seeing these conditions first-hand. Afterward, in my personal research, I could explore the terms and theories defining these issues.

Many organizations doing development work in Kenya relied on so-called "white money" aid and "*msaada*." But comparing world population growth rates with the United Nations Millennium Development Goals—a set of goals agreed upon by the international community toward alleviating global poverty—showed this made little lasting difference at the ground level. For any development work to be successful, it seemed it must not only be asset-

My American family.

The busy streets of Nairobi bustle with traffic.

The market town is the hub of activity in rural Kenya, where vendors sell their wares and families stock up on food and supplies every week.

Mama, in the doorway of her home.

Kokoo, in her *manyatta*, adjacent to our family's.

Metengo sweeps up outside Kokoo's home.

Samuel, in front of the home he has struggled his whole life to support.

Fetching firewood has always been my least favourite chore.

Mama Lekishon (Shaila) and I wash clothes behind our home.

Learning from Mama's expertise, I quickly adopted the art of fetching and carrying water.

Mama Samuel and Mama Toti, her daughter, relax in their *manyatta*.

Mama Samuel.

Samuel and his brothers David and Joel show off their traditional Maasai *shukas*.

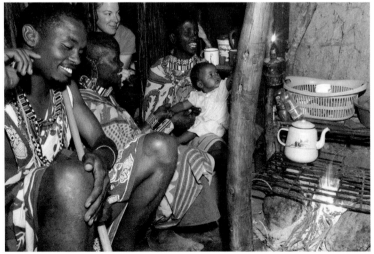

Gathering for mealtimes and a steaming cup of chai tea is a cornerstone of Maasai family life.

While women do the household chores, Maasai men herd livestock—the goats and cattle that are central to the community's economic survival.

Sananga, Samuel's youngest sister.

Samuel and I take a moment to chat in the shade of an acacia tree.

Introducing my American parents to my adoptive homeland was a moment I'd dreamed about for years.

Touring the site of what will soon be their new schoolhouse, children look to the future with hope.

Bringing visitors from abroad to meet the communities where we work is always an exciting experience, and the local children never tire of making new friends from far away.

Samuel, Maasailand . . . and me.

Photo compilation courtesy of V. Tony Hauser

based and sustainable in the long run, but also in equal partnership with the community.

The shining success I'd found among all these efforts was the women's group in Embu. Their success demonstrated how programs could be powerful when designed on a grassroots level. This, to me, seemed the true hope for rural Kenya.

Once again I had to question the complicated realities I was witnessing. What was truly important? What would bring real justice and prosperity? And what could I do, as just one person in this huge, frustrating system?

I visited an internet café, eager to touch base with home. In my travels, I felt disconnected from everyone. To my own surprise, I looked forward to the usual gossip, the ordinary day-to-day chatter of American life.

But I was disappointed but what I found. *No new messages*. I couldn't believe it. *Nothing?* It had been weeks.

I wrote an accusatory emails to my family, telling them I'd felt abandoned by their lack of communication. *Where are you?* I felt disconnected from home, forgotten and ignored by everyone I'd known. With my departure, everybody I'd ever known, all my relationships and friendships, had been reduced to an inbox of emails and a handful of handwritten letters. Spanned over the last four months, it amounted to so little. Did these relationships really mean anything? Was I really alone, or just isolated because I was so far away? Since I wasn't a part of anyone's physical world, could I really expect to remain part of their emotional world? But wasn't this exactly what I was looking for, to flee the world I knew?

I felt the only one I could truly count on was myself. Finally I left Nairobi behind and headed back to Nkoyet-naiborr—back to what really mattered.

9 A Boma of My Own

Returning to daily life in Nkoyet-naiborr was like sliding on a comfortable old shoe. I was again immersed in chores, family and Swahili lessons with Samuel. But upon waking early one morning, I found my body unexpectedly stiff and weak. I'd spent the previous day hard at work helping our neighbour Nalamait build a new manyatta, so I assumed these were just the typical aches and pains after physical labour. I also didn't find it too odd that my mind was working slower than usual, as I'd been preoccupied with distressing news from home: when at market I'd checked my email, only to learn my cousin in the military had just been commissioned to the war in Iraq.

So that morning I went through the regular motions of doing dishes, seeing my brothers and sister off to school, making tea and fetching water. I was sweeping our kitchen's dirt floor when Nalamait stopped by to thank me for yesterday's work. After our greetings, she told me I looked unwell.

"Do you have a headache?" she asked.

"A little one."

"Do you have a fever?"

I put my hand to my head and found it was burning hot. "I guess I do."

"Are you tired?"

"Yes," I conceded.

Mama, working outside over basins of laundry, overheard us.

"You have malaria," she piped in.

Though my arms and legs were perpetually dotted with mosquito bites (malaria is passed to humans through their stings, and the family could not afford the protective mosquito nets over their beds that many wealthier homes had), I had never missed a single day of my anti-malarial pills. I knew they weren't 100 percent effective . . . but, malaria? *Me? How do I tell Mom that I have* malaria?

"No, I don't, Mama. I'm fine, just tired, I think."

I tried to sweep with more vigour to show her I truly was okay. But even this small effort made me dizzy, and I almost fell backward. Mama ordered me to rest and forbade me to do any more chores for the rest of the day.

Not knowing how to fill free time now that I had grown accustomed to daily chores, I went to lie down in the shade of an acacia tree. Watching clouds drift overhead, I could feel my fever rising, my body's strength draining further. Every once in a while I swatted away a fly but then eventually resigned myself to their interminable presence. Mama checked on me throughout the day and, when school was over, Faith kept me company with a fresh cup of tea, laughing at herself as she fought to recall a poem she'd learned that day in English class.

The experience of being ill in rural Kenya was a far cry from how it would be at home. Watching ants parade along a gnarled tree root was different entertainment from watching movies while curled up in a blanket on the couch. Faith's tea was not like the cold Sprite my mother usually served me when I was sick. And when Samuel heard I was unwell, he and Mama Samuel came by with tea made from a special root herb, a Maasai concoction called *enkoibor benek*. She warned it would be bitter, but swore it would make me feel better. I downed the thick brown liquid then fought hard to keep it down.

I told myself I just needed to rest. Perhaps my body was overtired and fighting some small infection or virus; after all, my symptoms were much like those of the flu: headache, fever, fatigue, upset stomach. Against Mama's wishes, I didn't board the truck into the market town the next morning to go to the clinic, thinking my symptoms would pass. But by midday they had only worsened.

I couldn't stand up on my own. The endless throbbing in my head was so loud I could barely concentrate. Any energy I'd had was completely drained from my body—I couldn't even bring myself to shoo away the circling flies. The pain stemmed from my joints through to my bones. What if I did have malaria? Dad's last words echoed in my mind: *Robin*, he had said, *if for whatever reason, you don't come back, if you catch some horrible disease . . .*

Maybe it wouldn't be so bad to go see a doctor.

Cramming into the back of the pickup truck the next morning wasn't exactly at the top of my list of things I wanted to do, but I had no other choice: I had to muster all my energy and get to a clinic in Nairobi. During the hour-long ride into Soko, milk cartons battered my already-aching head as a small child parked himself on my sore, weak legs. A few hours later, I arrived in Nairobi, where for 300 shillings (about five dollars) I was provided a doctor's consultation and a quick blood test.

After a quick wait, my doctor returned. Mama was right: I did indeed have malaria.

As he wrote my prescription, the doctor seemed amused by my reaction. I was strangely proud of my diagnosis—contracting malaria, an infectious disease unknown to most in the West but common throughout Africa and Asia, was almost like a validation of my desire to wholly immerse myself in this other culture. Malaria was one of Mom's biggest fears for me, and why shouldn't it be? My travel doctor had warned me of the dangers, and he prescribed a pill every day to prevent it. I'd read the numbers: every thirty seconds an African child dies of malaria—2,800 children a day, one million a year. Malaria accounts for up to one-third of all hospital admissions and up to one-quarter of all deaths of children under five in Africa. Yet still . . . I could easily afford a doctor visit and the medicine. *But what about the others?* Mama Sawoi, for example, would have to sell a goat to afford it.

I returned to Nkoyet-naiborr and rested while the medication ran its course. Without my daily routine of chores, all I could do was sit and think about my current situation, trying to articulate it in the new journal I'd begun to replace the stolen one.

The intensity of this illness is crazy. My thoughts constantly tumble over one another, when I'm falling asleep, when endlessly swatting flies. Even in lazy afternoon walks, there is a silent intensity that is impossible to unravel.

When I try to make sense of what I'm seeing, what I think most about is the huge disparity in the world, more than I'd ever imagined. I think of my family at home, arguing about who gets to control the TV remote. Then I think of a mother choosing to walk four kilometres to market, just so she can use the money she would have spent on bus fare to buy not one, but two oranges to share among her four children. Meanwhile, back home we eat until we're full, then complain how we've overeaten.

What gives me—educated, clothed and healthy—the right to walk through these impoverished villages, where people wear the same ragged clothes every day and eat the same corn flour and beans at every meal? How can some people be bored from too much free time, when others do manual labour all day, every day, in the equatorial sun? How can some people sit comfortably on the couch, watching a program like Survivor *and call it "reality," when others are truly fighting for survival, wondering which of their children will live the longest? How can such different situations exist in the same world?*

As I recovered, I almost forgot another significant event occurring around this time: my twenty-second birthday. With my mother's birthday on the same day—January 20—our family often went out for a big celebration dinner, often at Red Lobster.

Here in Kenya I spent my birthday alone, still recuperating from malaria. Tea took place of Red Lobster's cheddar biscuits, and ugali took the place of Seafood Fettuccine Alfredo. The significance of the day was lost on my adoptive family. As I'd learned, until only recently the Maasai didn't keep track of birthdates or ages. Since most people in the community didn't know exactly how old they were, they certainly didn't celebrate their birthdays.

But because my birthday is so close to New Year's, I always use it as the date to set my yearly goals, instead of making any new year's resolutions.

This year I thought about how my future as a comfortable, middle-class American was wide open compared to the future of most Kenyans. According to the World Health Organization, the average life expectancy in Kenya was fifty-one, twenty percent less than the world average. Of Kenya's children, 120 in every thousand wouldn't reach the age of five. The growth of about thirty percent of these children is stunted for their age and about twenty percent are underweight.

I was thinking about these health issues the next day during my weekly trip to the Soko market. After spending the morning bargaining for tomatoes and onions, I joined a group of women from the community for a classic "market lunch" of deep-fried potatoes and soda; it's a favourite meal because it's one of the cheaper ones available. Like many North Americans, I'd been taught to avoid fat, salt and sugar, and to try and seek out healthy, nutritious food options. However, women in this community felt the fat gave them strength, and the sugar gave them energy. These foods were seen as nourishing, not junk food.

While the women gossiped in Maa, I again wondered about these differing ideas of nutrition and health. Doing some research for my paper, I'd read that, according to the un's Food and Agriculture Organization, almost a third of all Kenyans are malnourished. Everywhere, I saw people who were hungry, thirsty and weak from lack of proper food resources. Meanwhile, obesity rates in North America skyrocketed. One couldn't help but be frustrated.

Back at home, Faith took on additional household chores as necessary while I recuperated and Mama entertained me with stories about her "merry-go-round."

The merry-go-round was an activity practised by local women's financial cooperatives to help their families meet domestic needs. Each woman participating received a random number, indicating the order in which she would receive the revenues from a collective pot, generated by each woman's equal and regular contributions. The recipient mama could then put this money toward necessities, such as blankets, dishes, goats, tin sheets for creating a roof—any items or costs to help their household. Each woman took a turn reaping the benefits of shared communal wealth, which in turn benefited the greater good of the community as a whole.

I loved it. The merry-go-round was a brilliant, practical way of pooling resources in a place of scarcity. And the women were running it themselves—you could see how empowered and proud that made them feel.

Poverty in Kenya has been on the rise for thirty years. Even though the country enjoys one of the best-developed economies in East Africa, more than half its people still live below the poverty line. The United Nations has called it "one of the most unequal societies in the world," where the country's richest ten percent controls over a third of the economy. My recent trip from Nkoyet-naiborr to visit the doctor in Nairobi definitely showed me how wide this inequality really was. Solutions like the merry-go-round provided desperate women with comfort and hope to provide for their families.

My bout of malaria had made me edgy and weak, and I quickly became annoyed by small things such as my hair: too short to fit into a ponytail, long enough to constantly fall in my face as I worked—I considered shaving it all off, they way many Maasai women did. Another irritation was that my stomach rumbled constantly on a breakfast of only tea. Yet another problem was that the only sunscreen I'd found available in Uchumi, one of Nairobi's grocery store chains, was so greasy it blocked the sweat with a layer of oil, so I chose not to use it; as a result, the weeks of unrelenting sun, aggravated by a sensitivity to sunlight caused by my malaria medication, had created blisters on my nose. Worse, I'd also developed second-degree sunburns on the backs of my hands and the pain affected my ability to fulfill my chores. The endless presence of the flies only aggravated me further.

Worst of all, months of walking barefoot were taking their toll. In recent days my left foot had developed an insatiable itch. I attributed this to the mosquito bites dotting my legs, but after two more weeks of aggravation, scratching away with everything from my fingernails to a rough stick in hopes of relief, the itchiness hadn't let up.

While at market, where there was an internet café with three (extremely slow) computers, I did some research and self-diagnosed my calloused, discoloured skin as a planter's wart. I visited the local chemist and picked up some topical wart cream, hoping that would do the trick.

After applying the cream, I tried to carry on with chores and duties, thinking about what might frustrate me as bitterly back home. Burned toast, maybe. Sibling rivalry. Exams. My parents' nagging. None of these things came close to the aggravations my Maasai family had to put up with here. Like when drought struck, and water simply was not available, so people had to choose between washing their clothes and bathing their children. Or when food became so scarce that parents had to go hungry for days on end just so their children could eat. I tried to look at my petty annoyances in a larger perspective.

The next morning my itch had become serious pain, and the fleshy lump had expanded. The wart cream only seemed to have made it worse. Finally, I found Mama in the kitchen and showed it to her.

She laughed. "You have a jigger."

"I have a . . . ?"

I cleared my throat.

". . . a *what?*"

"A *jigg-er.*" She pronounced it slowly, accentuating each syllable so I heard her correctly.

Nonchalantly, she called for my brothers and sisters to bring matches, a razor blade, a nail and my father's spirits. A chigoe flea, or "jigger"—called a *kiroboto* in Swahili—is a type of parasitic flea that feeds off the blood vessels in a host's skin. They are commonly attracted by walking barefoot on flea-infested soil. A jigger can stay in the skin for weeks, and they even lay eggs there. The very idea horrified me, but Mama seemed unfazed.

The family gathered as Mama instructed me to lie back. She propped up my foot and doused it in the spirits. She struck a match to heat the large razor until its blade became extremely hot, then she did the same with the nail. With both in hand, she turned her attentions to my ankle.

"Whoa!" I cried, instinctively shrinking away. "What are you going to do?"

Mama was blunt. "We have to cut it out."

I asked Faith to hold my hand as Mama began her surgery, using the razor to scrape away layers of skin while using the nail like a needle to pick out the intruder. As she squeezed and pushed on the skin surrounding the jigger, I willed myself to not cry. After witnessing the girl's fearless display at the circumcision, I thought it best to put on a brave face.

Meanwhile, Baba, appearing at the door, was delighted. "Where's your camera, Naserian?" he said. "Let's take a picture!"

Eventually Mama's efforts were successful. Working her thumbs, she squeezed a wormlike mass of green goo from my foot, leaving a hole a centimetre deep and a centimetre wide. I had to endure the additional pain of cleaning the wound with hydrogen peroxide and then had to hop everywhere to keep the wound clean, but by the third day my ankle had pretty much healed. That was the end of the jigger.

The next week, Mama gave me permission to attend her women's group meeting. She had never before allowed me to take part, saying someone needed to stay at home to take care of chores while she was away. But finally, after I pestered her incessantly to take part, she allowed me to observe a "merry-go-round" in action.

The meeting took place in the manyatta of one of the women who were participating from a nearby boma. The meeting opened with a prayer; then all the women joined together in song and a choreographed dance. Each woman took a turn dancing forward with her contribution, dropping her share in a collective pot as the others applauded and shouted. Each mama danced without reservation, singing at the top of her lungs with her head tossed back, smiling at the others as they sang. Brilliantly coloured shukas jingling with Maasai beads were raised in the air. The mamas danced as individuals, yet they were unified in pure joy. Together, they were strong.

But the moment the proceedings began, my stomach began to flip-flop violently. The feeling consumed me so suddenly, I almost forgot where I was.

I needed a bathroom . . . and *fast*.

Hoping no one would notice, I made a speedy exit. In a panic, I scanned this unfamiliar boma for a pit toilet. A child watched as I doubled over, clutching my stomach. When I asked him for a toilet, he shook his head and told me in broken Swahili that this boma didn't have one.

Barely able to contain myself, I ran toward a small cluster of oleleshwa trees; the plant's soft leaves, I'd been taught, could be a passable substitute for toilet paper. I made it just in time and squatted among the bushes for almost ten minutes.

En route back to the meeting, I again felt another cramp and had to return to the bushes. Then again. Twice, thrice, again and again. By the eighth attempt, I resigned myself to remaining at the secluded spot I'd found. My stomach was holding me hostage. When I finally felt strong enough to walk, carefully placing one foot before the other, I headed back to the women's meeting.

Along the way I encountered Mama on her way to find me. She asked why I hadn't stayed for the meeting, after begging to attend. When I explained my reasons, the look on her face went from annoyance to sympathy. She told me I must have contracted typhoid.

Typhoid? How could I have typhoid? I'd been immunized against it just eight months before coming to Kenya. I told Mama she must be wrong.

"Wait," she said. "You'll see."

Over the following days, I completely lost my appetite. My skin became pale and clammy. My trips to the pit toilet increased from eight times a day to upward of twenty. The one roll of toilet paper meant to last a full week for our entire family disappeared quickly, with no market day coming for several days to stock up on replacements. I came to know every branch of every oleleshwa tree in our boma.

I didn't want to leave for the clinic in Nairobi, as the coming Saturday was the wedding date for Baba and a twenty-two-year-old woman named Shaila, who was to become his second wife. I had only been introduced to her briefly a month before, but there was no way I could miss such an important day, my first Maasai wedding. I ordered myself to suck it up, reported only half of my symptoms to Mama and waited for the long days to pass.

By Friday I had barely eaten in days and was rapidly losing strength, but fought to keep a brave face. That night, our family hosted an all-night cooking party with our volunteer wedding committee of thirty-five mamas. I did my best to keep the mamas company, and we were up all night, them cooking chapattis and rice and preparing beans and me readying the household for the festivities. By the time we'd completed all the many preparations, I could barely stand upright. I was completely, utterly exhausted.

It was strange for me, anticipating another woman joining our family. But polygamy, or the practice of keeping more than one wife, is a longstanding part of Maasai family tradition. It is a practice that is both cultural and historically practical—given the high infant mortality rate, widespread rates of disease and the many hardships families faced; a large, sprawling family with many able-bodied offspring can be a valuable economic asset.

While multiple marriages remain common throughout Kenya, the inevitable effect of increased Western influence has made them controversial. Yet communities such as the Maasai still regard polygamy as a cornerstone of their society. As with the ceremonies surrounding circumcision, a marriage is an opportunity for people to join together and mark significant milestones in life.

To my surprise, I learned that Shaila had just given birth to a new son, Lemite, late Friday night. I found that Maasai women often kept pregnancy a secret as long as possible. To me the idea was strange, as in my world women were quick to announce their pregnancies, with showers and celebrations of gifts while they were expecting. But in a place where complications in childbirth are very common, and infant mortality rates are high, new mothers are often wary. They wore loose clothing and tried to hide their expanding bellies as long as possible, and they spoke of their pregnancy to only the most trusted few.

Since Baba and Shaila's wedding took place early on Saturday, the new Mama Lekishon was unable to attend her own wedding. Instead, she recovered in Kokoo's manyatta, cradling the bundled baby boy while 300 guests from adjoining communities, all dressed in traditional Maasai outfits, gathered outside.

An elder stood before the crowd and spoke on behalf of all elders, advising the couple on how they were to live together under traditional Maasai customs. Others rose to praise the couple and lavish them with gifts of blankets, dishes, livestock, gourds of milk and money, confirming the bond that would now exist between the couple.

An old mama spoke on behalf of the community's women elders, also describing how their lives together will be led. "You must treat each of your two wives fairly, with equal attention and resources," she declared.

Baba's father then addressed the attendees. He turned to his son, saying, "You have chosen to unite two communities. This is not just a union between you and Mama Lemite. It is not only a union between our two families. It is a union between our two communities. If for any reason, you choose to end this union, it is not a decision you will make on your own. Together we all decide the fate of this union."

Finally, Baba stood. In my time living with the family, I still felt I didn't know him very well. This was partly because he travelled often and partly because of the respectful distance Maasai families gave their fathers. I knew him to be a strong-minded, intelligent man, a capable provider and an important figure in the Nkoyet-naiborr community. But I'd never seen him assume the spotlight in this way. I was proud of him, as if he were my own father.

Baba gave an elaborate speech of gratitude for the support of friends and family, expressing his appreciation for their welcoming Mama Lemite. He voiced his admiration to her home community for the woman they had brought up and now offered to him. Baba promised everyone in attendance he would take care of Mama Lemite, said she would have her own manyatta and kitchen in our boma, and he invited everyone from her community to come stay with him at any time. Everyone cheered their approval.

This was the end of the ceremony and of my energy. *Whew.* I returned inside, excusing myself from the celebration of drinking, dancing, singing and laughter that went on just outside my window long into the night as I collapsed in sleep.

On Sunday morning, as the many people who had slept over at our boma slowly made their way back to their homes, I began the long trip back to the clinic in Nairobi. There I was met by the same doctor who had treated me for malaria. Three hundred shillings (about four dollars), a stool test and forty-five minutes later, the doctor returned with the results. He said if I'd been happy about contracting malaria, he had even better news for me this time.

"You have typhoid," he said. "As well as a stomach amoeba."

Mama was right again. While I watched him write out a prescription, I could only think how fortunate I was to be in a position where I could actually pay for necessary medicine. I had only recently learned Samuel's persistent, years-long illness had gotten worse. He revealed he'd been coughing up blood for the past two months. His family had been forced to sell two chickens to pay for a doctor visit. Finally, after many consultations and much precious money spent, his condition had still not been properly diagnosed.

There is a stark difference between the health status of poor countries like Kenya and wealthy countries like the United States. In rich countries, the main causes of death chronic diseases—like cardiovascular disease, lung disease, cancers or diabetes. In sub-Saharan Africa, infectious diseases are a much greater problem. The number one cause of death is from infectious diseases such as malaria, tuberculosis and diarrhoeal diseases, followed by respiratory infections—like the one Morio suffered from. These are all hazards that could actually be prevented, if only the necessary education and medical resources were in place.

It would take a change in priorities on a global scale for things to change in Kenya. But most of the world simply didn't seem to be aware of these realities.

With my departure date looming in about six weeks, I often daydreamed about what it would be like to live in Nkoyet-naiborr free of a determined end date. I imagined keeping my own manyatta, starting a family and living here for the rest of my life.

When I shared this idea with Mama one day over washing dishes, she nodded knowingly.

"The time has come for you to have a place to call your own," she said. "You are old enough to be your own mama."

Mama saw how I always wanted to test myself, to learn more, to be challenged. She could see how I wanted to prove I could manage my own home and all the duties that entailed: to find the best firewood without getting lost in the bush, to haggle for vegetables in the market, to speak in Swahili well enough to be able to host visitors on my own.

Even though I was still facing my imminent departure, plans began to help me construct my very own manyatta.

Constructing the family's mud hut home is generally women's work. Here Kokoo helps a neighbour build her manyatta.

We formed a small committee with Mama, Baba, Samuel and Mama Samuel, and between us set out to determine exactly what I would need to do before I could live on my own. Samuel suggested a small plot of his family's land, and Mama Samuel offered to assist me in building my new home—the ultimate sign of a mother's love for her daughter. However, Mama warned about the cultural implications of such a plan. Others in the community might perceive the bond between Samuel and me as something more than it was—a little more permanent than either of us were ready to commit to yet. Instead, we selected another available tract of land, near the local school.

Building a manyatta is typically a woman's job, so Mama and I set out on this enormous task. But just as construction began, we hit a snag: the section of land we'd selected had recently become densely populated by prowling hyenas, which were not only annoying pests, but also potentially dangerous. Recently one of our neighbours had left a few donkeys out overnight, only to find nothing but bones in the morning.

Our next option was to build in an area named Seu Seu, next to the dam where our cattle were brought to drink. Gazing on the beautiful rock outcroppings and clusters of acacia trees overlooking the water, I knew it was the perfect location.

With the location settled, we began construction. Toiling under the blazing sun, we first laid a foundation of large logs planted into the ground to create the outside walls. Smaller twigs were then interwoven horizontally to connect these pillars. A concoction of mud and cow dung formed the walls, smeared about five centimetres thick on both sides of the twigs. Other more modern manyattas I'd seen included sheets of plastic on the roof between the twigs and the mud to serve as a waterproof membrane.

Inside the manyatta, rooms could be created by building walls in the same way as the outer walls, covered by mud or not, depending on personal preference. In my manyatta, I chose to separate the "bedroom" from the sitting room and kitchen with an interior wall. Maasai manyattas are typically only one-and-a-half metres tall; people spend so little time actually indoors, there is little need to waste extra materials building houses larger than necessary.

When my sister Erin had moved into her first apartment after university, my parents helped her get settled in and stock up on all necessary supplies. My situation was no different. Just as Mom had helped Erin with groceries and other necessities, Mama wanted to help me choose everything.

We made a shopping list together and headed to the market in hopes of finding everything I'd need to get started. We debated fiercely over whether I should buy a more durable, yet more expensive, yellow mitungi or the thinner, cheaper black one. For a difference of thirty-five shillings (forty-five cents), I opted for the yellow one. Mama also helped me pick out a machete for chopping firewood, along with all the bowls and cups I'd need for hosting meals, plus a basin for washing my clothes and dishes. Best of all, Mama bought me a much-appreciated housewarming gift: a beautiful new pot in which to cook all my food.

And just as my dad had assisted Erin in thoroughly cleaning her place and arranging all the furniture, Faith helped me in setting up my new home. Together we fetched the stones that would form my fire and decided where I'd store my dishes, basins and supplies.

"Naserian, I'm going to come every day and help you cook your dinner," Faith said.

"Thank you," I said. "You're a good sister. But you have so much of your own homework to do."

She eyed the pile of firewood we'd just collected. "Then I'll come by every second day and help you collect firewood," she offered.

I could see what she was implying. "Faith, I'll be able to do it myself. You don't have to take care of me anymore."

We both laughed, already missing each other. We'd become so used to being with each other every morning and evening, and she'd been such an important part of my life in Nkoyet-naiborr, it was hard to imagine daily life without Faith. Nonetheless, she promised to always bring a jerry can of water for me every time she visited.

When Mama paid her first visit to my new home, she was impressed by how meticulously I'd set up my modest household. But really, I'd just done exactly as she and Faith had shown me. To repay Mama for all her help, I happily cooked for her the very same meal as she'd cooked for me when I first joined the family: lentils and white rice—an extra-special dish, as it requires two pots for cooking instead of all in one pot, as most of our usual meals were prepared.

Having my own manyatta meant a lot more freedom, but also greater responsibility. Though I had fewer daily chores to perform, I hadn't anticipated the constant stream of visitors. Hospitality is a cornerstone of Maasai culture, and everyone throughout the community I'd ever visited now returned the favour. My brothers came often, usually staying overnight, and Samuel visited almost every day. Every mama in the community, men from other families, anyone passing through the hills—all stopped by unannounced.

Proper etiquette as a mama dictated one should always be ready to serve visitors, at any time. If someone stopped by in the early afternoon, I was expected to cook lunch for them. If they came by in the night-time, I was to provide dinner. If guests arrived at any other time, I was to rouse the fire and serve tea. While I appreciated the friendly gestures, the constant visits from unexpected visitors dropping by at all hours often became exhausting.

Despite the frequent visitors, I still enjoyed more time for myself than when I'd lived with Mama and the family. Washing laundry for one person rather than ten, or fetching water only once or twice as needed opposed to multiple trips, gave me more time to reflect on my experiences.

I often whiled away afternoons relaxing on the rock outcrops by the dam, piecing together my research project and writing in my journal in the shade of acacia trees while watching my Maasai neighbours leading their cattle to the water. My journal was truly my closest confidant, the only way I could let my thoughts truly wander freely.

Somehow things have gone from attempting to explain everything to an abstract understanding that refuses to be articulated. I'm laughing, I'm learning, I'm living. I'm being. There are so many things that make me cry and yearn and burn and fill me with wonder, hope and despair. Life is just life, no matter where we are. You could be in Nkoyet-naiborr, or sitting at a desk in front of a computer, cooking at a kitchen sink, waiting at a bank or at a traffic light, in a farm or a city, in America or on Mars ... and there are things that make our hearts race and things that make us hurt others and things that make us love others . . . enough things to make your head spin.

The view from my manyatta—one I could call my very own.

10 "Go with Peace"

I wasn't ready to leave Kenya, not yet. But the date on my return airline ticket was about to interrupt my life here. While at market I called the airline from a payphone, hoping to extend my stay, I learned the ticket expired exactly one year after it had been issued. This had been the first time I'd booked my own international flight, and I hadn't known this policy. I definitely couldn't afford to buy another ticket: flights from Nairobi to the United States are astronomically expensive.

I'm not ready! I hadn't achieved the closure I'd hoped for. Was I really going to leave? I'd be back in the States in . . . *dare I even think it?* . . . four weeks. It was so soon. Soon it would be only two weeks, then two days, then I'd be at O'Hare Airport, surrounded by people clutching their Styrofoam Starbucks cups with Uno's Pizza sauce dripping down their shirts. I pictured myself there amid the chaos, like a kid who'd lost her mommy. Then I would really know I was back.

I could still picture things back home as clear as day. My room, my closet, my bed. The worn carpet and the TV, the back deck and swimming pool lined with pine trees, the white siding of our house. Efficient, wealthy

Schaumburg, with its traffic lights and impressive library and grocery stores, the lawns of freshly cut grass. After I returned home, would my mind drift back to Kenya, recalling it only as a memory? Would I still know which routes to take through Nairobi to avoid being hassled by hordes of street children? Which places sell the cheapest and best chips? The best internet cafés and matatu routes, how to fend off inane marriage proposals from strangers on the street?

And in Nkoyet-naiborr, there were so many things I wanted to preserve. Mama Samuel's smiles and loving questions, always welcome and never probing. The challenges of learning Swahili, the monotonous meals of ugali and cabbage I'd grown to appreciate, the peace and tranquility of daily life. The most beautiful trees en route from my boma to the school. Flies and sweat, the lowing of cattle, the weary chore of lugging water. Steaming tea in darkened, smoky manyattas, listening to the wise words of old mamas. Understanding one another, even when speaking in different languages. All this and so much more. Scrawling in my journal, I filled pages and pages. There were things I couldn't even find words to explain, no matter how hard I tried. I shared a million secrets with no one but myself.

To walk away from this year meant telling myself things were "wrapped up." But things were far from concluded, summarized, finished, *over*. Would they ever be? You can never say you know everything there is to know about a place, just as your heart will never be through with a place you call "home."

During my year in Kenya, I'd done things I'd never done before. I'd found myself in situations I'd never imagined. I'd played so many roles. The explorer and the tourist. The strong mama and the clumsy child. The calm spirit and the impatient thrill-seeker. Gracious and flustered. Courageous and nervous. An apathetic pretender and a convincing defender. A determined minimalist and an obedient daughter. Humble, yet opinionated. Selfish, yet selfless.

Throughout it all I was becoming a new person: the person I needed to be in order to survive in a new, much more complicated, world.

Even as I reflected on the ups and downs of this emotional journey, I was under pressure to finish my research paper and submit it to Professor Jama in Nairobi. From my travels, I had collected many stories and interviews about the development solutions I'd seen, and I'd read many articles and books about this field—there was so much to learn, my research had only really cracked the surface. But I'd witnessed with my own eyes what many academics had only debated in classrooms. Personal experience, I felt, was my unique perspective on the topic of development aid.

Obviously I didn't have a computer in Nkoyet-naiborr, only small notebooks packed with my drafts and notes. I described the scenarios I'd witnessed in Mugombashira, in Kitui, in Meru, in Nkoyet-naiborr . . . trying to come up with a coherent sense of what making real, significant change in Kenya would actually entail.

Across the world, I wrote, *people seem to have the same needs and desires: food, water, shelter, health, schooling for children and social acceptance. Different generations will seek new priorities.*

Over weeks I wrote by long-hand, seated under an acacia while swatting away flies, my notes and stacks of research books fanned around me, was far from an ideal scenario for writing my thesis. I imagined the luxury of working in a quiet, air-conditioned library at a comfortable desk, a world of research at my fingertips, being able to concentrate rather than just fitting in a few minutes here and there between fetching firewood and water.

Finally, with my backpack stuffed with notebooks, I boarded a matatu for Nairobi, where I holed myself up in an internet café for hours and furiously typed out all that I had amassed. When I came to the end, I looked over what I'd created: an eighty-eight page paper titled "Honesty from the Field: The Reality and Sum of Development—Disorder Between Theory and Fieldwork Case Studies in Kenya."

Whew. The paper encapsulated as best I could all my eye-opening experiences here, using my own research as well as a heap of outside sources to seek potential solutions to the dilemmas of development in this region. It was the most intense, in-depth thing I'd ever written and, looking at the end result, my heart swelled with pride. I printed off a copy for myself, then emailed it to Professor Jama and to my department back home, relieved to have gotten it done and even on time. Then I went back to Nkoyet-naiborr where other, less academic, responsibilities awaited me.

With my departure date creeping ever closer, the reality that I was actually leaving set in. We decided as a family that in our final weeks we should spend as much time together as possible. Despite my affection for the manyatta we'd built, the family came first. With little hesitation, I moved back home for the last few days leading up to my departure.

As we arranged for our weekly market shopping that Saturday, I noticed Mama had added ten kilograms of sugar to the list—five times the usual amount. When I asked her the reason for such extravagance, she was cagey about the answer. When pressed, she revealed that the family was planning a blessing ceremony for me on our last day together.

I was honoured and touched to know they would miss me too. More than ever, I longed to share this experience with my family back home. On a whim, I tried calling my parents' house from a payphone while at market.

"Hello?"

I could picture Mom standing in the kitchen, the phone tucked against her ear, the country blue cord twirled around her fingers.

"Ma!"

"*Robin?*" Hearing her animated voice lifted my heart. But her voice sounded less delighted when I asked her to take a spontaneous leap of faith and come visit me in Kenya.

"It would mean so much to me, Mom. For you to meet everyone and attend the blessing ceremony . . . to see all the passion and love. Then we could return home together! Mom, it would be so *great!*"

She didn't say anything. Was she even considering it?

"Please, Mom," I begged.

But she could not be convinced.

"Please . . . please don't ask me to do this," she said, her voice wavering with emotion.

I dropped the subject. I still held out hope that one day my parents would get to experience this country I had come to love so much. But for the time being, I would focus on enjoying as much as possible what time I had left.

In the following weeks, I made a conscious effort to capture every second in my memory and in my journal. Every groggy morning's chores, every laugh shared with Faith, every late-night conversation with Samuel, every whisper of wind through the acacias . . . I had to preserve these moments forever, so I would never really leave.

Then, Monday, September 1: the fateful day. My flight out of Nairobi was late at night, so I could still enjoy most of my final day with family and friends. I woke up as on any normal day and performed my usual slate of chores. But my heart was heavy as I went for water, cooked tea, swept the kitchen and took a quick bucket bath, all for the last time. I was torn between looking forward to seeing everyone back home and the sadness of saying goodbye— potentially forever—to my beloved friends and family here.

Later in the morning, Faith began shredding cabbage for lunch while I cooked ugali over the fire. As various neighbours began to stop by to bid me farewell, Faith and I put our biggest pots on the fire to cook a huge vat of tea.

Mama called me into our house, and together we sat on the bed to share our last moments alone together. I had no words, nor did she. Instead, we simply held hands in our laps and cried: tears of love, and tears of fear at not knowing if we'd see one another again. Tears of overwhelming emotion, and tears of understanding.

Wiping her nose, Mama revealed she'd been going into the bush every day for the last month to secretly work on a parting gift to me: a hand-sewn traditional Maasai ceremonial outfit. As she presented it, I gasped at its beauty. It was a deep blue skirt like her own, sewn with red and white beadwork and adorned with jingling bells. Mama helped me put it on, wrapping a new shuka around my shoulders as a final touch. The shuka had Swahili text inscribed across the bottom. "*Watu wa amani.*" People of peace.

"Naserian, your name means 'person of peace,'" she said, choking on tears. "The Maasai are also people of peace. You are our daughter, whether you are far away in America or here in Nkoyet-naiborr. When you leave tonight, go with peace. Take our greetings to your family in America, and tell them they have family here waiting in our community. We love you and always will.

"Our world is changing so fast," she continued. "One day you are here, yet tomorrow you will be gone. One day Morio was born, and suddenly now he is five. Some changes are good, and others are not. I want my children, all of my children, to have everything they need to enjoy a better life than the one I had growing up. The world is an unstable place. Thieves can take away our material things. The only thing that I can give my children that cannot be stolen, lost or destroyed, is education. Thank you for helping my children learn to speak English. Education is the best gift we can give them."

We cried final private tears together, then headed back outside, both in our ceremonial Maasai dresses.

I was stunned by what met us. By now visitors had poured in from all over the community to wish me farewell. Under the bright afternoon sun, they formed two long rows, parting to allow Mama and me to pass through the centre. High-pitched voices sang out as the gatherers danced in unison, gyrating their shoulders back and forth, bending forward, then raising their faces to the sky, following behind us in a parade of continuous song. With my eyes clouded with tears, I clung to Mama, counting on her to guide me toward the gathering's head under a large acacia tree. *All of these people gathered, for* me?

Baba served as master of ceremonies, introducing various community members as they came forward to speak. A community elder rose and spoke on behalf of the elders; then an aging woman spoke for the mamas. Each voiced their love, telling me I would always remain a member of their community, whether near or far, and that I always had a home with them. They told me to take this love back to America and spread it to my family. The elders spat at me, a Maasai gesture representing affection and respect. The old Robin would have recoiled, horrified at being spat upon, but the new me—Naserian, a Maasai mama—was honoured by this blessing.

Then I was given a chance to speak. I was so overwhelmed—what could I possibly say? How could I thank them for how much they'd taught me? How could I explain, in a way they'd understand, just how meaningful they have impacted my life? Stumbling on my words, I thanked those who directed me when I was lost, those who first taught me how to tie my mitungi rope, those who came to visit me in my manyatta. I was simply unable to fully express my gratitude, stammering and making little sense. My words were just as confused as my clouded vision. It was just like the time long ago when I'd lost my stream of consciousness, shouting nonsensical words in anger at my parents—except this time, my lack of control came not out of anger, but from gratitude and love.

Baba then offered an opportunity for any parting gifts. All the mamas I met every day—Damaris, Leah, Linda, Mama Toti, Mama Naomi, Nalotuesha, Nalamayi, Shosho, Mama Skola, Mama Sawoi—approached to slide their handmade beaded bracelets on my forearms.

The line stretched longer and longer as more women came forward to bestow their handmade jewellery upon me, filling my arms and piling around my neck. They even remembered everyone in my family and made special gifts for them. One mama gave me a beaded bracelet for my brother in his school colours of red and white, and another did the same for my sister's university. They gave me bracelets in America's red, white and blue to take home to my mom and dad. By the time all the mamas were done, both my arms were covered with bracelets and the stacks of leather and beaded necklaces on my chest rose all the way to my chin. Two large bags were needed to hold the heaps of gifts I couldn't manage to wear.

I had never experienced such an outpouring of love and affection. Tears streamed down my face. In this moment, I found a new definition of generosity. These people, many of whom rarely had enough to eat every day, had used their little money to buy beads and taken days of their busy schedules to craft these elaborate pieces of jewellery . . . for *me*.

The singing began anew, echoing off the hills. Samuel emerged to guide me back toward my house, where we gathered my things, then piled the bags into a truck waiting to take me to the airport. We had rented two pickups from the market town, and a representative from each neighbouring household was to accompany me to the airport. At least forty of us, most of us dressed from head to toe in Maasai ceremonial clothing and beadwork, crammed into the trucks and drove down the dirty road toward the market town, singing all the way.

Taking a last look at the joyful gathering, I took my spot on the lead truck, pulling Morio closer in my lap. His toothless gaping smile never faded as he squealed once again: *Naserian! Ao! Sopa! Ipa!* This game of endless greetings never ceased to amuse him, but for me in the course of a typical day it became tiresome. But at that moment, I could have gladly greeted him a hundred times over.

The road smoothed out as we drew closer to Nairobi. Most of my Maasai friends were seeing the big city for the first time and, by the time we arrived at the airport, the cheerful noise had dwindled to an awed hush. Men and women who had never experienced a hint of city life gazed in astonishment at the tall buildings, sprawling shopping complexes and traffic jams.

But as we unloaded, our group again broke into song and danced all the way to the airport entrance. It must have been quite a sight for the other travellers: a gang of traditional Maasai piled into a truck, clustered around one awestruck white girl.

We had to say our goodbyes outside, since only passengers were permitted inside the departure gate. I hugged each of my brothers, making them promise to study hard and take care of our mama. Overcome by emotion, Faith and I were barely able to make eye contact, but hugged tightly. Mama Samuel and Kokoo each kissed me and spat on me for an additional blessing. Mama and I hugged one last time and waved a final goodbye.

Samuel had been given permission from a security guard to walk me inside, through the security checkpoint and up to the check-in counter. As Samuel and I stood together in line, time seemed to stop. I couldn't believe it: here, amid airport chaos, check-in lines separated by "Economy" and "First Class" labels, harsh fluorescent lighting and busy European men in business suits, Samuel and I were sharing what might be our final goodbyes.

"Naserian," he said, tears welling in his eyes, "wherever you go, whatever you do, remember me. Wherever I go, whatever I do, I will remember you."

"*Next!*" an attendant called.

As Samuel and I moved forward, the gum-cracking attendant eyed us blankly. "Where to?"

"Chicago, via Brussels."

As she tapped keys on her computer, I tried to relax. Everything felt unreal.

Then the attendant sighed. "The flight is overbooked."

Since I'd arrived early, I could still take a seat, but they offered to switch my flight to another, leaving tomorrow. I'd also be put up in a five-star hotel near the airport. Would I mind staying in Kenya an extra day?

Without a moment's hesitation, I accepted the offer with a quick signature. Samuel headed back toward the entrance, his face brightened with the prospect of me staying another day. But when he turned to ensure I was following behind, I was still lingering at the counter.

In that instant I realized how selfish I'd been toward my parents. All along I'd acted in my own best interests, or in the interests of the people in Kenya with whom I'd become close. But I'd neglected to think about my first family back home and how much they missed me. After having waited a year, one more day for them would seem like forever. I couldn't torture them by making them wait any longer.

Unfortunately, when I tried to renegotiate with the airline agent and reverse my decision, she stubbornly refused to help me out. I pleaded my case as best I could, but with no luck. I had to find a payphone to call home and endure a tearful conversation with my mother, explaining I'd arrive a day later than expected, apologizing for my selfishness. Thankfully, she understood my situation. One more day wouldn't be the end of the world.

Samuel and I whispered our final goodbyes, then parted ways. I turned back one last time to see him wiping tears from his face. Was this the last time we'd ever see one another? Would I ever see his smiling face again? My heart ached as I watched Samuel heave a deep sigh and head back to rejoin the community members waiting anxiously outside.

In a flurry of activity, I was whisked away by an airline employee, and the next thing I knew I was in a swanky hotel room, waiting for the next morning's flight. The queen-sized bed with fluffy pillows and luxurious, freshly laundered blankets was too much for me, when I was used to sleeping in a tiny manyatta.

I curled up in a corner on the floor with the thinnest blanket I could find, trying to sleep while waiting for the return home.

11 Back in America

With the trans-Atlantic flight came more tears. I was overwhelmed, by both joy and fear. My feelings were so overpowering, so complex, I found it impossible to even fully identify what I was feeling.

As we ascended through the clouds, I replayed the last year in my mind. So much had happened. I couldn't deceive myself into thinking the resentment and yearning that had driven me all the way to Kenya was now gone. But I felt I had gained new perspective on what really mattered, what was truly important: life, love, generosity, people taking care of one another. It wasn't needing to get the last word in, watching what I wanted on TV or getting my way.

It wasn't about me. It was about people, community and family.

I caught sight of my parents immediately as I emerged from the arrivals gate at O'Hare airport; they were practically jumping up and down (in the most non-Maasai way), excitedly clicking away with a disposable camera. I couldn't help but break into a wide smile. Mom's warm tears wetted my face as Dad eagerly snapped pictures. Just like when I'd left over a year ago, the three of us shared huge hugs before heading for home.

The disorientation and culture shock hit me immediately. Coming from different locations, my parents had each driven a different car for the hour's round-trip to the airport: Dad in his beloved Lexus, Mom in her red Camry. This alone was strange to me. *Two cars?* It seemed so incredibly wasteful, even extravagant.

I slid into the front passenger's seat of Mom's car. It was amazing: the dashboard and windshield, so impeccably clean, with no dust or bugs; the windshield wipers working perfectly; the stereo playing soothing pop music that wasn't distorted and deafening; the automatic windows that actually functioned.

After a year of hopping matatus and riding crammed in the backs of pickups, I felt so refined in the car, so alien. If I'd been in a matatu, three people would be squished into one of these cushioned, roomy seats. Here I reclined comfortably, protected in a sanitized environment.

Mom chatted constantly, asking how I was, how the flight went, saying that our neighbours looked forward to hearing about my trip, how excited Fluffy was to see me. But she quickly switched to describing household details: the weekend plans for a family brunch with my grandmother, how they had yet to store the picnic tables away for winter, how excited she was for the sale at Kohl's tomorrow and the errands we'd have to run on the way home.

It was truly bizarre. These concerns were, broadly speaking, the same as those my other family dealt with on a daily basis: family, community, meals, preparations for the home. But it was all on such a radically different scale.

We joined the line to pay for parking on our way out of the airport. "Honey," she asked, "will you grab some money from my wallet for me?"

Rummaging through her wallet, I found three twenty-dollar bills. In times past, this amount would have been nothing out of the ordinary. But looking at the money, I hesitated. All I could think was how this could pay for a month of groceries for Samuel's entire household. Dozens of ugali dinners, heaps of cabbages.

"Robin?" Mom gave me a confused look and plucked the bill from my fingers, snapping me out of my daze. We continued on.

The drive home was a complete blur. With oldies playing on the radio, I gazed out the window at the city passing by. Everything was both familiar yet perplexing. The roads were so smooth and well-maintained. No suffocating diesel fumes; no overstuffed minibuses veering wildly and peeling onto the road's shoulder. And yet despite the prevailing sense of order, I saw drivers visibly consumed with road rage and anxiety, unlike the cool, impassive faces of the matatu drivers.

I noted how the streetlights were so close together—barely feet apart, in some places. I tried to imagine what it would have been like if there had been streetlights when I'd first taken the road from Soko to Nkoyet-naiborr. The idea was unthinkable; even if they'd existed, the access to electricity for powering them wouldn't even have existed.

On the way home, we stopped by the same enormous supermarket where my family had shopped for years. But now it seemed so unfamiliar: its automated doors, the gush of huge fans.

Moving air? I thought. *What a waste!*

That was nothing compared to the incredible abundance found inside. There were heaps and heaps of produce, packaged foods, enormous loaves of bread in the bakery. Giant slabs of meat in the butchery. Stacks of shining oranges lined in perfect rows. Boxes of Cinnamon Toast Crunch cereal that looked as much like toys as the plastic surprise packaged inside. The place seemed so fake and artificial, like a cartoon world.

Where did this food even *come* from? It was a question no one, including me, ever seemed to ask. In Kenya, I knew where my meat came from. I knew which cow had been slaughtered and which farmer had raised it. I even knew what grass it ate. I knew where our cabbages were grown—they'd come straight from the mama who'd picked them from her own garden.

Then I thought about all the steps that had brought this food here to the supermarket, the hours of transit and fuel required. And the food just sat here, sprayed with pesticides and artificially coloured, heaped in crates and waiting to expire on shelves.

I was beginning to feel like Samuel on his first visit to Nairobi, overwhelmed by everything I saw. I just wanted to curl up and shrink inside myself.

In the weeks that followed, I tried to readjust to life in America.

I was so excited to share my stories and pictures, to tell everyone all about Mama, Faith and Samuel, about daily life in the household and about Maasai customs. I hosted my entire extended family aunts and uncles with a traditional Kenyan dinner of ugali and *sukuma waki*: fried cabbage and spinach.

Yet even among these well-wishers, I found myself feeling inhibited, not knowing what to say, how to describe my experiences. Neighbours came to visit, asking, *How was Africa?* I was dumbfounded, not knowing how to even begin to answer such a question. They'd ask, *Did you see any lions? Did you climb Mount Kilimanjaro?* Or, having seen a program on the Discovery Channel, *Do they really . . . stretch their lips like that?* They wanted me to answer their questions simply, then move on to some other topic of gossip or pop culture, leaving me out of the loop.

When I tried to show my photos to my brother and sister, explaining the stories behind the images, they only gave them a cursory glance then moved on, flipping ahead.

"Oh! And that's our kitchen, see how we put the rocks so the ..." But they had flipped the page to the next photo.

"See! That's Faith, she's Mama's sis- . . . ." But they flipped the page.

"Oh! This one! This is Samuel. He's my . . . ." But they flipped the page.

I tried to describe to them the kitchen and the boma, my friends and siblings, the harsh but beautiful landscape. But they just kept flipping forward.

Then I gave my brother and sister the bracelets the mamas had crafted especially for them, in special colours. They thanked me, but in their most polite terms said there was no point, since they wouldn't wear them. *Of course, that's not the point. You don't have to actually* wear *the bracelet. You just have to* appreciate *it.* But saying this just reinforced how they really didn't understand what I was trying to share. Eventually I stopped trying. It simply hurt too much.

At one point I tried to show my father my pictures. Again, I tried to tell him people's names and explained the complicated intergenerational family structure.

He just frowned. "Why are so many Africans so promiscuous? Don't they know that's how they contract AIDS?"

I was furious: how dare they spoke of the people of Nkoyet-naiborr, or of Kenyans, as if they knew them! No one understood. I knew others had their own concerns, but what I'd experienced in Africa felt so vital, so *real*, I wanted my family to understand. But they just couldn't.

I stopped trying to share my stories and photos. I was so hurt. *Why can't anyone just open themselves up to let me share what I saw? Why do they have to negate my feelings and experiences with generalizations? Do they not care about what had been my whole world for the last year?* No one understood, but moreover, no one seemed to even want to understand. I felt so alone.

I stashed the pictures and notes in a Zip-Loc baggie and stored them away in my bedroom closet. There they would stay, untouched, for over two years.

Over the next few weeks I awoke most mornings in tears, desperately missing everyone in Kenya. They had no home phone, no real postal service, so there was no way to keep in touch with them. I worried incessantly: *are they safe? Are the kids keeping up with their studies? Is Samuel still sick?* Did they miss me at all . . . or had they forgotten me already?

Meanwhile, I struggled to get back into the feel of my "home" culture. Visiting Woodfield Mall, I was horrified by the exorbitant price tags, the latest fashions and hit songs I didn't recognize, the displays of luxurious king-sized beds and gleaming appliances. Everywhere I went, I felt foreign in my own homeland.

Increasingly, I found myself alone. I simply didn't know how to be around people. In Africa, I'd learned the importance of spending time with family and friends, stopping by to pay friendly visits, to amiably greet strangers on the street and welcome guests to the home with tea and openness. But the expectations were different back here. The only person open to impromptu visits was my grandma, who welcomed me graciously for afternoon tea.

I walked barefoot everywhere, unable to reacquaint myself with wearing shoes. I spent entire mornings walking nearly ten kilometres to and from Mom's office just to say hello, carrying sandals with me—I knew any stores I visited along the way wouldn't allow me in without them.

Visiting the dentist, I found out I had six cavities; I'd never had one before in my life. He asked if I'd at all altered my hygiene habits recently. I stayed mum on that one. How could I explain it?

Coming home was much harder than building a manyatta, or having a jigger extracted from my ankle, or shouldering the heavy weight of morning water. I couldn't bring myself to speculate about my next steps for the long run; all I did was dwell on the past. I often laid out all the colourful, lovingly crafted gifts I'd been given, remembering the incredible blessing ceremony and that day's outpouring of love.

Every day I imagined a reunion with my family in Nkoyet-naiborr, but with my parents included in the daydream. It would mean everything to me for my two sets of parents to meet one another, for my mom and dad to experience the love and sense of community in Nkoyet-naiborr. It seemed the only way I could reconcile my American upbringing with my new Maasai identity. I begged my parents to consider a trip to Kenya, but the subject was always roundly dropped.

One day, we were driving down the highway in my father's Lexus, he and Mom in the front, me in the back. It'd been almost a month since my return, but I was still amazed by the flutter of streetlights, the hulking concrete medians, the whooshing traffic. Once again I sat in silence, my thoughts a confused mush.

Finally my father blurted out, "Robin, when are you going to get over this?"

It felt like I had been punched in the stomach; my air stalled in my throat. It took everything I could not get angry or cry. *Get over this? I don't want to* get over *any of it!*

I snapped back, "Dad, you don't *understand!*"

"What don't I understand? You've been back for over a month, and you've just been moping around the house, not doing anything with yourself."

I couldn't even respond. That was what he thought; maybe he was right. But I just went deeper inside myself. I knew the time had come: I had to leave Chicago again.

I first went to stay with Adam at university in Indiana, hoping to gain some clarity and composure. But crashing on the couch in his tiny dorm was painful for both of us and seeing ambitious groups of students, enthralled in their studies and hunched over books in the university's gigantic libraries, only deepened my all-consuming resentment. In Kenya I'd had to struggle to find a spare moment to read a book under a tree, interrupted every few minutes to do washing or cook tea or to swat away the pestering buzz of flies. Seeing young people walking around with iPods and cell phones, focused on their bright futures, only underlined how I no longer related to this society of isolation.

Next, I visited friends at my alma mater—the University of Illinois. But they weren't exactly pleased at having a freeloading guest hanging around, sleeping on the couch, while they struggled with their own daily lives as students.

In Madison, I checked in with some former classmates from Nairobi. I hoped that being with them would feel like being home, as they knew for themselves what I'd seen and experienced. That plan too fell flat after a few days. They were all moving forward with their plans, while I had none.

I had no place to belong. Yet returning to Schaumberg meant the same banal routine and extravagance that only reminded me of the scarcity throughout the rest of the world. Huge wasteful, overpriced family dinners. Thoughtless waste of water, flushing the toilet so many times every day. When I started limiting my flushes, my father was outraged, saying that while in Africa I'd become primitive, forgetting how to use even a toilet. Though my family's concerns were out of worry and love, they were driving me crazy. The wedge between us grew and grew.

As an incentive to stick around, my parents gave me the family's twelve-year-old minivan, thinking it would provide me with more freedom to get around and enjoy my time at home more. Their plan backfired. I withdrew the remainder of my meagre savings, filled the van's gas tank and removed the back seats. I loaded it with practically everything I owned, especially lots of blankets; it was one of the coldest winters in recent memory.

I called up Brenda, who was back from Kenya and also trying to figure out what she was doing with her life. We had kept in touch, and she'd become a close friend. I didn't even ask; I just told her she and I were going on a road trip.

"Where are we going?" she asked.

I laughed. "Who cares?"

We embarked on a wild road trip, headed for the east coast. If I was going to be stuck in America, I needed to see it in all its ugliness and beauty. Along the way we slept in the van at rest stops and in Wal-Mart parking lots, living on Little Debbie snacks from gas stations. We hit Pittsburgh, Philadelphia, Boston, Hartford and New York, awestruck at these American cities in all their excess, yet excited by the freedom of the open road.

At the end of the trip, Brenda hopped a train back to Wisconsin for the second semester of her senior year, while I stopped to visit my sister Erin for a couple of days in Buffalo, where she was working at the university. Before I knew it, those "couple of days" in Buffalo turned into six months of crashing on Erin's couch.

I quickly became miserable again. I had no money, no life. The only friends I made came through a Kenyan group on campus. Meeting them was initially comforting, as they provided a reminder of home. I could brush up on my Swahili and talk about Kenyan culture.

But I soon found these students represented what I'd liked least about many Kenyans, particularly in Nairobi: a relentless impulse for Westernization and a blind attraction to modern consumer culture. They'd fled their homeland and come to America seeking what I loathed most, hoping to escape the very way of life I was craving.

My sister grew impatient with me. Rightfully so; I was broke and contributing nothing to the household. But unemployment was high in Buffalo. On top of it all, my van, my only possession worth caring about, was dying a slow death.

After a frustrating search, I landed an office job through a temp agency, working on a mortgage project. It was a grim scene: no gratuitous conversation between co-workers, a rigid lunch schedule, five-minute breaks allotted only for those who smoked, mandatory overtime and a tyrannical boss constantly barking at us. I quickly became the typical disgruntled employee.

I still felt there was something more valuable I could be giving back to the world. What I'd seen in Africa had stirred a way of caring that I'd never felt here at home. Yet I was sinking back into a system where no one cared, where all the lessons I'd tried so hard to learn meant nothing. This passion for life was the very thing I'd been striving for all my life, and I was losing it, day by day, minute by minute.

The most valuable lesson I'd learned in Kenya was the power of community. In those miserable weeks, even crowded with my sister in her tiny one-bedroom apartment, I never felt more isolated. And yet those who loved me thought I was simply struggling to "adjust." I even stopped writing in my journal. I had no idea what the future held.

Suffering this daily slog, I did my best to keep focused. I sought other solutions, searching out ways I could escape my current situation.

I began scanning jobs in international development. Thinking back on the successes and failures I'd witnessed in my travels, I thought the varied insights I'd gained and the places I'd visited could be put to good use.

But I quickly realized I was far under-qualified for most of the jobs that intrigued me. Working for a credible international development organization typically required fluency in two out of five official UN languages, seven years of certified field experience—usually in a supervisory capacity—and a master's degree, if not a doctorate. All things I didn't have. The first-hand education I'd received in Africa was unofficial, uncertified, undocumented . . . useless.

Considering overseas volunteer positions, I found many of them required a large financial investment upfront: flights, meals, accommodations, health insurance. Sometimes even a hefty "placement fee," just so you could volunteer your time and energy to a cause. Meanwhile, I was broke.

There was such a huge gap there, between the good work across the world that needed to be done . . . and those like me: energetic, ambitious young people who simply wanted to make a real, positive difference throughout the world, but lacked any assets to channel into philanthropic ends. Since I'd left for Kenya, I'd come to know many people in their early twenties who wanted to reach out to other cultures, to work toward meaningful ways of resolving the world's inequalities, to seek the greater global good.

After sitting idle so long, I was compelled to take matters into my own hands. I wrote letters to newspapers and media outlets, everything from Oprah Winfrey to the *New York Times*, countless newspapers and magazines, trying to articulate this helplessness, these obstacles I'd come up against. Not one responded, except the local newspaper from my hometown: the *Schaumberg Review*, who offered me a potential column to share my experiences. They requested writing samples, which I sent immediately. That was the last I heard from them.

Still undeterred, I contacted universities and high schools, offering to come, free of charge, and conduct information sessions with students on working in developing nations. I thought young people might be interested to hear what it was like to work in the field. Maybe some would be inspired to do the same thing. Again, no one responded.

Everywhere I ran into brick walls. It felt like I was being prohibited from living out the ideals and beliefs I'd cultivated. I became more and more disheartened.

Months passed. Before I knew it, it had been a year since my return. I'd been hunting for a job in international development, yet came up against the same obstacles over and over: I was under-qualified for the most intriguing positions, and most volunteer opportunities carried some sort of catch. The most frustrating thing was that young people in America are so often told they are apathetic, lazy, narrow-minded. Yet when we want to get involved and change the world, so few trustworthy avenues are available to do so. It just didn't make sense.

Then I received a promising email from a friend, Melanie. She told me she'd found an organization working out of Toronto called Free The Children. It had an interesting story of how it began, and they facilitated short three-week volunteer trips to Kenya. I said I'd investigate, expecting just another disappointment, one of a thousand leads producing the same depressing results.

But this organization was impressive, and there didn't seem to be any suspicious hook. With a youth-oriented focus, they organized motivational speaking tours, leadership education and volunteer training trips to Africa. *I don't want to* go on *one of those trips*, I thought. *I want to* lead *one!* I used the contact information provided and fired off a somewhat frenzied email. I needed to get involved. I was ready.

A week went by, a month. Nothing came of it. The possibility fell off my radar, and I was back in my doldrums.

Then one day, I received a response.

Hi, Robin! Sorry it's taken a long time to get back to you. We're pretty busy over here. Tell us more about yourself, along with a CV. Thanks, Ed.

Yes! But I didn't even know what a cv, or curriculum vitae, even really was. I rushed to Barnes & Noble and bought a guide on how to write a proper cv and cover letter. A busy afternoon of writing later, I sent my meticulously honed reply, explaining who I was, what I'd done and how I was the perfect fit for their organization. My life's mission statement, I said, was synonymous with theirs. I described everything I'd ever done that would make me seem the ideal candidate, from public speaking training in school to lugging water in Kenya.

Ed responded promptly. I was floored. He was on the way to give a speech at the Jane Goodall Foundation. He asked if I was still interested.

"Heck, yeah!" I said, fighting to maintain composure.

Later that day, I received a call from a guy named Marc Kielburger. Marc, I would later learn, was the organization's co-founder and chief executive director. But he was so young and friendly, he didn't sound like the intimidating executive type. We chatted for about twenty minutes as I sat perched on the edge of my sister's bed, a huge, goofy grin plastered on my face. He asked if I'd be able to travel to Toronto and meet everyone in the organization. Of course, I agreed.

It was an incredible weekend, meeting everyone on Free The Children's small but committed staff and seeing the tremendous work they were doing. On Monday, I was asked to join the team as a leadership facilitator. My role would be to work with high school students in the Toronto area, teaching the benefits of volunteerism and community action. Everyone I'd be working with was so warm and open, and the organization seemed so full of possibility and optimism.

I called my mom. "Guess where I'm going?"

"Oh, Robin! You're coming home! Tony, Robin's coming home!"

Once again, I had to disappoint her.

"Uh, no . . . I'm moving to Toronto!"

Free The Children was founded in 1995 by Marc's brother Craig Kielburger. Driven to action when learning about the murder of Pakistani child labour activist Iqbal Masih, Craig had started Free The Children when only twelve years old.

It began as a small group of students drawing attention to unethical child labour practices around the world. But with Craig—a gifted, charismatic speaker, even at an early age—as its spokesperson, Free The Children grew exponentially, gaining international media attention and inspiring kids to start Youth in Action groups of their own. Their philosophy was to show young people at home how they could positively affect the lives of their peers in places like sub-Saharan Africa, South America and Southeast Asia.

With Free The Children's youth membership eventually topping 100,000, they began hearing pleas from young people that they lacked the practical skills, direction and training to accomplish their goals. Activist kids were continually ignored or dismissed for their lack of experience.

In response, Marc and Craig founded Free The Children's sister organization Leaders Today (which later evolved into a network of further social enterprises called Me to We), with the principal idea being that young people don't have to wait to get involved; they can be leaders today. They began developing ambitious programs to encourage youth leadership and activism, including public speaking, negotiation strategies and fundraising techniques. It proved wildly successful. Within a year, Free The Children–Leaders Today facilitators were giving seminars throughout Canada, the United States and Europe.

As Free The Children began to shift toward increasingly ambitious development projects, the next step was to actually lead young people—and like-minded adults—on volunteer training trips overseas. One of its most successful contacts had been with members of the Maasai community, and Kenya become one of its main hubs of activity internationally. My first-hand knowledge of the region was one of the reasons I'd been an appealing candidate for the job.

I was impressed by its grassroots, youth-driven approach. Its core values of sustainability and partnering with communities—rather than simply throwing money at a problem, as I'd seen many charities misguidedly do—made perfect sense, in light of what I'd discovered during my travels.

The moment at which I joined the team was to coincide with a pivotal moment for the organization. With the hard work of all its impassioned members, Free The Children was blossoming from just a few enthusiastic young people working out of the Kielburgers' suburban home into a truly international network and respected Faith organization. A week after I arrived in Toronto, we moved into an office building in a downtown neighbourhood called Cabbagetown. We were still painting the walls ourselves and sleeping in the office, but there was a tremendous energy driving us. It was incredibly inspiring and just what I'd been seeking for so long.

One day, while lugging boxes during the move, I was told I had a call waiting for me. The phones had only just been installed, so I assumed this either a mistake or I was being set up for a prank.

Neither was the case. It was Marc, with whom I'd barely had a chance to speak since our quick phone interview; he was often on the road, giving speeches and representing the organization.

"Robin," he said. "When you were in Kenya, how long did you live with the Maasai?"

I wasn't sure where this was going. "About a year. Why?"

"We need someone to help facilitate three weeks of trips to Kenya. Are you interested?"

Of course, I told him, straining to maintain a professional tone. I asked when the trip would be taking place.

"You'll have to be at the airport at two o'clock. *Tomorrow.*"

I was stunned. There were still a few minor logistics to be worked out, he said. But in the meantime, I was to hurriedly prepare myself, getting any necessary shots and making sure my passport was up to date. I couldn't believe it!

I called my mom. "Guess where I'm going?"

By now, she'd learned to not get her hopes up. "Where now?"

"Back to Kenya!"

But this time, my parents were more supportive. They'd seen my frustration and disenchantment during these months back home, and they saw how passionately I felt about my adopted country. It was an incredible opportunity: to show the place I loved to a group of keen-minded, socially aware students.

Mom and Dad gave their blessing and, after almost a year away, I was suddenly headed back to Kenya. Back to my home.

12 Return to Kenya

Often in life we are tossed around against our will, desperate TO find our footing. But then sometimes we are thrown opportunities, those defining moments that help us seek our true character and challenge our integrity. These moments shape how our lives' journeys are going to unravel— those precious moments when fate and opportunity converge to open new pathways.

For me, this new position with Free The Children was a golden opportunity. I could have kept stagnating and wallowing in self-pity, thinking "nobody gets me" and that I was doomed to never realize my potential. Or I could choose to take advantage of this incredible prospect being offered to me.

So the same way I threw myself into the experience of life with the Maasai community, I invested myself wholeheartedly into facilitating this trip. I was honoured with the chance to lead young people into a rural Kenya village, and I vowed to give them my entire heart and do everything in my power to offer them as full an experience as I'd had in Kenya.

The night before leaving, I barely slept. I stayed up thinking about these twenty students I was about to lead, heading to a place where they'd be thrown completely out of their comfort zone. I wanted these young people to have their preconceived notions of comfort and safety challenged to the core, just as had happened to me.

By the time the entire group had assembled the next day at the airport, I felt ready to jump out of my skin with anticipation. Throughout the flight, I showed each of the students every change in the landscape below, making sure they didn't miss a thing. *Look!* I cried, pointing out the window. *We're almost there!*

As the ocean's blue gradually shifted to sandy brown, the Mediterranean cascading to African dunes, we knew there was no turning back.

On the taxi ride from the airport through the city, I gazed out the window, fascinated by what I saw. Much had noticeably changed since I'd last been in Nairobi. The new government had instituted sweeping changes. Neon-coloured logos and billboards had overtaken the streets, commerce was visibly flourishing and public sanitation had brought cleaner streets. Many of the illegal flower vendors, charcoal salesmen and food kiosks had been bulldozed in city-wide renovation efforts.

Yet the city still maintained its characteristic smells of burning garbage and diesel, and the chaos of traffic was as frenetic as ever. After our first day's quick tour of the city markets and craft vendors, I returned to the guest house where our group was staying to find I already had black build-up in my nostrils from inhaling polluted air.

But the excitement and impact of facilitating these educated, active young minds set on taking action on social issues never faded. The students were amazing, their curiosity and passion leading every step of the journey.

Every day was a new adventure for these students. We practised Swahili and learned about local customs and social issues in fun workshops in the brilliant sun. We visited families, lugged buckets of water from the Mara River with mamas and embarked on long, fascinating nature walks through tall savannah grass and acacia trees. In the villages, the kids had the chance to meet children not much younger than them, but who certainly led much different lives.

We took the students on a day-long safari in a rugged lorry, chugging over the rough terrain through the valley. Seeing giraffes and zebras running free across the flatlands, even a pride of lions in the distance under a cloud-rippled sky, their faces lit up with excitement. In their young, exuberant faces, I saw a trace of my younger self, when I'd first seen these sights myself.

Every night around the campfire we would learn about AIDS in Africa, female circumcision and women's rights, and the power of education in stopping the spread of poverty. We discussed the realities behind often-cited facts and issues, like what did it mean when we said "half of the world's population lives on less than two dollars a day"? They were shocked to hear that 30,000 children die every day due to poverty-related reasons, or that 1.2 billion people worldwide lack adequate water and sanitation facilities. But I encouraged them to not just take these facts at face value but to do their own research on the issues they cared about.

Over meals we brainstormed how they can make a real difference in the lives of children overseas by bringing these lessons back to their own communities, their own schools and their own families. We'd watch the sun set while journaling about our life goals, future education and relationships at home. I was honoured to be the one to guide them on this once-in-a-lifetime trip, and I was thrilled that my new position with Free The Children promised many future trips just like this.

As time passed, it had proven difficult to keep in touch with my Maasai family or Samuel. The postal service in Maasailand was unreliable, and the family certainly had no internet access, so it had been an excruciatingly long time since I'd communicated with anyone from the community. After my time back in North America and several months with Free The Children, almost two years had passed. I returned to Kenya with more trips, but each time my schedule was so demanding and my responsibilities so extensive, I never found an opportunity to schedule a visit. But never did a day pass without my mind turning to the boma, Mama, Samuel, the children, the stars over the savannah at night.

Finally I found a break between two rounds of student trips, and I headed east to Nkoyet-naiborr for the weekend. No one would be expecting me, and I wasn't sure what I'd find when I got there.

That familiar bumpy matatu ride took me from Nairobi to the market town of Soko. Suddenly I was back among the crowds, the dusty roads, the Maasai men and women in their trademark combinations of handcrafted traditional garb and cast-off American clothes. It was so strange to be back after so long, like the experiences of the past were just fragments of a long-lost dream. Trying to reacquaint myself with the scene, I scanned the bustling market stalls for a glimpse of any familiar face. Seeing none, I headed uphill toward the intersection at the town's centre, fighting to exude confidence despite the calls of onlookers and almost tripping on the rubble-littered terrain.

"*Mzungu!* Let me shine your shoes!"

"*Mzungu!* Where from?"

To my shock, I spotted a familiar face in the crowd: Baba, my host father! My heart instantly hammered with expectation. What would he say, seeing me again after so much time had passed? No one had any idea I was coming. For a moment, I worried that he might not even remember me.

"*Naserian!*"

He ran toward me, his eyes wild with excitement. Clearly, I didn't have to worry about him recognizing me.

"No!" he cried. "I don't believe it! Is it really you?"

He squeezed me by the shoulders, hugging me first to the left, then to the right. Then he held me at arm's length, eyeing me up and down with amazement.

"Does Mama know you're coming? She'll be so happy! Oh, my goodness!"

Baba pulled me close and again squeezed me tightly. I still hadn't uttered a single word; an appreciative smile was my only communication.

He led me all through town, enthusiastically greeting other men in market for the day. Soko had grown, and I was stunned to see how much construction had taken root: new stores, new restaurants, even an apartment building! After much anticipation, we joined others in the old familiar rusted white pickup truck for the ride down the valley to Nkoyet-naiborr, taking seats on piles of old milk cartons.

The ride was just as beautiful as the first time I'd travelled there. Past the dam where our cattle were brought to drink . . . the small brick schoolhouse where my brothers and sisters attended classes . . . the familiar turn-off to Samuel's boma. Every scene stirred another memory.

Finally the truck reached the same church where Mama had first greeted me; it was so long ago, but felt like it could have been yesterday. Baba and I hopped off and started up the winding path. When we arrived at the boma, Baba went first, while I waited outside. My stomach was a knot of butterflies with anticipation.

"Mama!" he called out. "We have a visitor!"

"Who?"

My heart skipped a beat at the sound of Mama's voice.

"Come and see," Baba said.

I huddled behind the fence of thick tree branches, hiding as Mama emerged from the manyatta, her figure as tall and slender as I'd remembered.

"*Naserian!*" she shrieked, the emotion apparent in her voice even before seeing me. *How did she know it was me?*

"Mama!" I cried back.

"Naserian!"

Then all my brothers appeared, surging forward to greet me. I threw down my bags and let them tackle me with a barrage of hugs, kisses and laughter. I was astonished by how much they'd all grown, yet they met me with the same warmth as ever. The feeling of being among them again was pure bliss. Faith lingered in the background, waiting to share our own personal reunion. She was beautiful: a bit taller, a bit more grown up, proudly dressed in her school uniform.

"Faith!"

"Naserian!" We flung our arms around one another. Holding hands, we ran into the kitchen giggling, eager to spend time catching up while preparing dinner.

Dinner was ugali and vegetables, a modest meal, but to me it was delicious. After the kids had gone to bed, Mama and I talked privately in the quiet of the night's fire. By the flickering flames we caught up on the past two years, sharing news and the current status of both our lives.

I was surprised to hear about all the changes that had occurred in their standard of living in the last year, mostly improvements to the boma: thanks to Mama and Baba's hard work and smart money management, they now had a concrete floor, wooden siding and a rain catchment system. I was pleased to hear how much my brothers had grown, not just physically but intellectually, improving their English and succeeding in school.

To my surprise, in the middle of our conversation, a strange, high-pitched sound rang out. Mama reached into the pocket of her shirt and produced something I didn't expect: a cellular phone! It was one of her neighbours, sending her a text message about their upcoming merry-go-round meeting. I was astonished; it seemed so improbable and out of place. But in recent months, Mama told me, many people in the community had purchased cheap cell phones, which were taking Kenya by storm. Even Samuel had one. Reception wasn't ideal, with major gaps between reception towers throughout the Great Rift Valley and, with no electricity at home, they could only charge their batteries on weekly visits to Soko's markets. But the phones had become an integral part of their lives, allowing them to share information about climate and cattle herding, as well as make money transfers. Now we could keep in touch, and I wouldn't have to live in constant worry for their well-being.

It warmed my heart to know that the entire family had missed me just as much as I'd missed them. Mama told me of her fears that she would never see me again. Many nights she awoke calling out my name. She would toss and turn, waiting for sleep to take away the longing. Once, she had actually risen from bed and drifted outside into the night, certain I was calling to her from the trees. Then, realizing it was only a dream, she cried herself back to sleep. *All those nights I was dreaming of her . . . and she was dreaming of me, too!* Now I'd returned, and her worries could disappear.

Suddenly, it was like the past two years hadn't even happened. The next day we resumed our usual duties: Faith off to market, Mama to her women's group meeting, Saigilu to herd cattle, Kipulel and Parsinte to compete in a soccer match at school. Metengo and Morio, now five and six years old, respectively, remained behind with me. Both had begun school and were learning to speak Swahili. Now Morio and I could actually communicate! It turned out his personality was just as mischievous when equipped with words. Even better, with improved medical treatment his persistent health woes had eased, and I was delighted to hear him breathe freely.

After preparing chai, peeling potatoes, carrying firewood and washing clothes, I went with the same old jerry can and rope to fetch water.

How could it still all feel so natural? I walked along the footpath, careful to avoid catching my skirt on the acacia thorns, but scratched my calf anyway while stepping over the fence of dried branches. Some things never changed. Approaching the water source, I hid behind the nearest bushes. All of the regular women I knew were there—Mama Toti, Nalamait, Mama Sawoi, all the others—lined up with their water cans, engaged in animated conversation.

"*Endasopa!*" I called out. Hi, everyone!

It was a greeting that always caught attention, and they automatically shouted back: "*Ipa!*" But then I could hear their obvious disbelief at hearing my voice.

"Naserian?" one mama called out.

"*Ao!*"

I stepped out from behind the bush, and the women erupted in laughter. Bursting forward with my mitungi dangling, I lowered my head to be met by each in turn, and we allowed ourselves a break for conversation as they filled me in on the recent news. Births, funerals, circumcisions, weddings, migrations—so much had changed in their lives, yet so much remained the same.

But the day's work had to continue, so we filled our water cans and went our separate ways. Mama Toti and I left together, stopping first at her home to pick up her laundry so we could do our washing together. She tied the laundry into a large shuka, heaving it up onto her back to balance the load. Then she assisted me in hoisting the water on my back, loading her can on top of mine. I was afraid that I wouldn't be able to manage the tremendous weight, nearly fifty kilos, being so out of practice. But I remained steady and, after a moment to adjust, I followed her down the red soil footpath toward home.

Mama Toti asked if Samuel knew I was back. I hadn't told anyone I was coming, so it would be a surprise to him too. Trying to contain my excitement, I asked if she knew where he was right now.

"Alienda Suswa." He'd gone to Suswa.

I almost dropped the water as my heart sank at this news. Suswa was a town far across the Great Rift Valley, a full day's journey away. I likely wouldn't see him at least until Monday, even if I hurried there right now. And I couldn't stay to wait—back in the city, preparations were underway for an upcoming visit of twenty-five enthusiastic volunteers.

Mama Toti told me Samuel was still in school, attending classes in Standard 8 from Monday to Friday, then working at a country club in Suswa on the weekends. I tried to compose myself, but in truth I was devastated. I'd imagined our reunion every day for the past two years. *What would we say? Would his English be stronger, or would he have forgotten it entirely? What would he look like? Would he be thinner, fatter, healthier, weaker? Would he have gotten married?*

Returning to the boma, Mama Toti and I washed clothes in our buckets—my knees and back groaned from bending; my flexibility needed a refresher course—while she filled me in on some further developments. She told me about neighbours who had new babies and about how big her eighteen-month-old son Emmanuel, now being looked after by Mama Samuel, was getting. Two families had migrated to new tracts of land on Nkoyet-naiborr's outskirts, and the local leadership had evolved, and the government had increased its supplies of food aid in response to a long drought, now six months in. Throughout the morning, gossip spread the news throughout the village that I'd returned, and people flocked to visit.

On Sunday we celebrated with the slaughter of a goat. Community members flocked in droves, the men preparing a slaughter, the children playing in the fields, the women gathering by the fire. Mamas came bearing gifts of beadwork and handicrafts for me and my family back home. I hadn't expected *them* to be giving *me* gifts—I was the one who owed them so much. But as always, their generosity knew no bounds.

Many people filled me in on dreams they'd had, just like mine, hoping for my eventual return. They'd wondered: what would we say? How would I look? Apparently, they all assumed I'd have gotten big and fat!

All around were signs of time's passing. When I'd left two years ago, Baba's other wife's son Lekishon was just six months old. Now he was talking, walking and laughing! Kokoo had always been old and wrinkled, and still was . . . but she remained vibrant with life. Some people had fattened up—a good sign—but too many had obviously lost weight from sickness and drought. Though the joy and love of the community remained strong, people's survival was still at the mercy of this tough environment.

I fell asleep Sunday night with Morio on a new bed with a wooden frame, a cozy cotton blanket, fresh-washed sheets and a thicker, more comfortable mattress: another recent upgrade. I couldn't remember a time when I felt so satisfied and happy.

Monday morning brought more of the usual chores: water, milk, cooking and tea, dishes from the night before, seeing everyone off to school. Then, machete in hand, I headed off to the bush to collect firewood.

An hour and a half later, when passing Kokoo's house through the empty cow pen, I dropped the bundle of firewood and began splintering it into smaller pieces. *Whew!* I'd almost forgotten how heavy firewood was. I'd rather fetch water ten times than deal with one bundle of firewood. Sweating under the hot sun, I was drenched in minutes. I'd forgotten to wear a hat and could already feel burns forming on my nose and neck. My shirt was covered with dust and shreds of bark and twigs. I was in desperate need of a cold bucket bath.

But I had to laugh to myself. *This is exactly what I needed!*

I was brushing myself off when I noticed Ben, baba of a neighbouring family I'd just met for the first time at the previous day's feast, entering the compound.

"Naserian!"

I wiped sweat from my brow and we exchanged the customary greetings and handshake.

"Have you seen Samuel yet?" he asked.

"Not yet. He's away at work."

"No, he's here now."

My hopes rose for an instant, before I realized this must be a mistake, or a joke. "No, he's in Suswa. Don't tease me like that."

"Naserian, I am serious," Ben said, laughing. "He's in your kitchen."

There was only one way to end this. I left the firewood and continued on to the kitchen. Squinting through the smoke, I peered in to find an empty, dark room.

"I told you, he's not . . ."

And then I caught a glimpse of a figure in the corner wearing a white shirt, his head buried in his knees.

"Samuel?" The air was heavy with hesitation.

I crept into the dark hut. The figure began to rise, still shielding his face with two hands. Recognizing him, I lost all composure.

"*Samuel!*" I cried.

His movements remained guarded as he very deliberately removed his hands from his eyes. Seeing me there in the flesh, he fell back onto the bench, stunned.

"*Sam-u-el!*" I yelled, like a child tugging at his mother for attention.

He jumped to his feet and embraced me tightly, hugging me first to the left, then to the right. Then he backed off and held me by my shoulders at arms' length so he could gaze into my eyes.

"Naserian? Is it really you?"

We hugged and both fell back onto the wooden bench, laughing together, simply amazed to be together again. Samuel began speaking so quickly, I could barely follow what he was saying.

"Oh, Naserian. I always knew you would come back. One time, I dreamed you and I were walking back along the hills from Soko. I went ahead for a minute and when I turned back, you were gone. I kept calling out your name, but couldn't find you. I looked for you back up in the hills, but you weren't there. I ran all the way down the hills, but you weren't there. It was becoming night and the hyenas were prowling, but I couldn't find you!"

My heart pounded as he gushed with words. I was surprised at how much Swahili I was remembering.

"I had to go all the way back to your house and tell your Baba I couldn't find you. He sent me away, telling me not to return until I'd found you. Then I heard you! You were screaming out my name, '*Samuel! Samuel!*' But Naserian . . ."

His voice became slow and soft, barely a whisper.

". . . I never found you. I wondered if we'd ever see one another again."

He paused, collected himself with a breath, then continued.

"Joel came to Suswa on Saturday night to tell me you had returned. I didn't believe him, but he swore it was true. Last night I came as fast as I could, wondering: is it true? But I couldn't believe it. What if it wasn't true? It only became real for me when Mama said, yes, you were back.

"She said she had seen you collecting water. But Naserian . . . I still couldn't believe it. I hid myself here in the kitchen as soon as I returned, saying if you would return, then I should first hear your voice, to determine if it was really you."

He lowered his head. Then he looked back up and said what we were both thinking: "I just can't believe we're here."

Just then, Mama's voice roused me from my elated daze.

"Naserian! You have a visitor?"

"Yes, Mama! Samuel's here!" Mama understood how important Samuel and I were to one another.

"So have you cooked tea for your visitor?"

Oh, gosh! How could I have forgotten the first rule of maintaining a Maasai household? Flustered and embarrassed at my forgetfulness, I quickly grabbed a pot from the top of our firewood pile and filled it with water from the morning's collection.

For the first time I realized how dishevelled I must have appeared, still dirty and sweaty from chores, now hunched on the kitchen floor, face to the ground, hurriedly blowing ashes to restart the fire. I hadn't seen Samuel in so long, and this was how I greeted him? But he patiently helped me, handing me small pieces of dried bark for me to build the tripod, and soon the fire was going.

When I ran off to the to retrieve some milk from the cattle shed, Mama stopped me with her arm, eyeing the pile of firewood I'd left still scattered on the ground by the kitchen.

"Mama, I . . . ," I started, but she cut off my explanation with an understanding smile. She told me instead to gather food from the kitchen's shelves—some cabbage, potatoes, vegetables and corn flour—to start making lunch. As I began chopping, I felt weak with these sudden waves of emotion. My hands were so jittery and sweaty, I kept dropping the gathered food.

What is coming over me? This strange euphoria was unprecedented. Seeing Samuel again had shaken me in a way that I hadn't expected and that I didn't quite understand. Clearly I'd missed him more than I'd even imagined. I rejoined Mama and Samuel in the kitchen, my arms full of supplies. Mama brewed tea while I settled back on the wooden bench to peel potatoes. I tried to relax, but I was so flustered, the knife kept slipping from my grip.

Never breaking from conversation with Mama, Samuel reached over, took the knife from my hands and picked up a potato to peel, relieving me of my duties. I left the kitchen and went outside for a moment, hoping to recollect my thoughts and let loose some excess energy. I hadn't expected my reunion with Samuel to be so powerful, so overwhelming.

When we found a spare moment, Samuel and I went for a long walk through the hills, just as we had many times before. As we followed our usual path, he updated me on his situation. He was still in school, attending classes during the week and working in the kitchen at the country club on the weekends. It was a two-hour walk from home, and he earned a paltry 150 shillings per day (about two dollars), working from half past seven in the morning till well past midnight. They didn't provide him food, so he had to buy his own lunch, which reduced his daily earnings to fifty shillings. And yet this was currently his family's only source of income. Sunday nights after work, he made the long journey home, arriving late at night to get in a few hours of sleep before rising early for school.

All for less than a dollar a day. To me it sounded like hell, but the job was actually respectable work for a young Maasai, and he spoke of it with pride. Yet he had hopeful plans for the future. That night he, Mama Samuel and I

Samuel, Mama Samuel and me in front of Mama Samuel's home with her grandchildren.

sat and discussed plans for a better career. After debating many options, we decided Samuel would enrol in a driver's and mechanic's school in Machakos, a large town southeast of Nairobi. It would mean time away from his family, but it offered hope of a true, lasting career that would support the entire family. I said I would help him with the enrolment fees; it was the very least I could do to pay him back for being my guide to the Maasai world.

Samuel's life had always been full of such ups and downs. He never fully understood why he was continually sick and fatigued until a recent visit to Nairobi, where a new physician gave him a proper diagnosis: it turned out he'd been suffering from pneumonia and tuberculosis for the past twelve years. A gruelling twenty-eight-day regimen of daily injections and weeks of pills followed before Samuel was healthy again. But Samuel—probably the most optimistic, hard-working, respectful person I've ever known—only looked at this as a positive development.

"All my life, I never knew why I'd felt down," he told me with a smile. "Now I know why: I was sick. This is a fresh beginning for me, a new start!".

I couldn't believe how easy it was to slip back into my role in the community. Yet at the same time, I was surprised by how different everything was. Everywhere I looked, things were changing, evolving, brimming with new challenges. The Maasai's struggles were never-ending, but so was their capacity for hope.

At the end of my visit, I bid everyone farewell and headed back to the city, where another trip facilitation awaited me. Leaving this time was only bittersweet, as I hoped my new job would bring me back to Kenya for repeated trips. I pledged to return again and as soon as I could.

Back in Nairobi, I immediately called my parents and once again pleaded with them to reconsider and come to Kenya. I wanted them to really understand how big of a part of my life, my identity, this country and these people had become. I wanted them to be proud of my accomplishments here and to take seriously this life I'd chosen. And I wanted them to change their thinking about Africa, about the world, and to see their own lifestyles and attitudes in a different light. The young trip participants I'd led told me with breathless excitement how they would return home with a new way of thinking and acting. I longed for my parents to have the same experience.

But in our hasty call, I could tell they were still resistant. *I don't know*, my mother said. *It sounds so difficult.*

It was, I could see, still too much to expect them to make that leap. For now, things for them would continue as always for them. For me, I began spending half the year in Kenya leading volunteer trips full-time, guiding hundreds of visitors through three-week volunteer experiences. My other six months were spent motivational speaking throughout North America, calling youth to action. This allowed me to stay in touch with my Kenyan family and to keep my Schaumburg family at a loving distance—close enough to keep the peace, without being *too* close that we would be at each others' throats.

13 Faith

In early 2006, severe drought raged throughout East Africa.
Climate researchers had predicted that during the three-month rainy season
Central Africa would face a thirty-three percent increase in rainfall, increasing
each subsequent season. The result would be widespread flooding and topsoil
erosion. Populations would be displaced and crops would be threatened. After
the heavy rains, a dry season would follow, lasting indefinitely. Many people
feared the worst. Back in North America between facilitating trips, I stayed
glued to the international news, worrying about the safety of everyone in
Nkoyet-naiborr.

Unfortunately, these dire predictions came true. Kenya's rainy
season in Maasailand typically extended from January to March, with another
brief wet period again around October. This year, that second rainy season
found barely any rain at all. The land lay barren and dry, and most crop
harvests proved disastrous. As a result, markets were bare and shelves
were empty. Without rain, crops don't grow. When crops don't grow, there
was no food to sell at the market and thus no food. The prices of the little food
remaining at the market rise, as supplies go down. But demand remains the

same: people need to eat.

Once again, basic supply and demand economics ravaged the lives of an already-impoverished population, just as Linnea and I had seen in Mugombashira. As prices increased—first doubling, then tripling—basic food staples simply became unaffordable for most families in East Africa.

In many communities in times like these, there is only one place young people can find reliable sources of food: school lunch programs. But these were also in jeopardy, due to widespread shortages. The United Nations World Food Programme announced they'd be forced to cut aid to lunch programs throughout the region, unless they could secure additional funding. Unfortunately, the international community failed to provide an adequate response, so shortly thereafter the area's district education officers received word that food supplies would be discontinued.

With no food at home or in schools, classrooms emptied. Children had to work extra jobs to help their families survive. Large numbers of boys dropped out of school to herd their starving cattle to grazable land. Many cattle, too emaciated and sick to be sold for meat, were slaughtered to sell skins, a huge loss of earnings: skins only reaped about 100 shillings per kilogram, meaning a cow that was once worth 50,000 shillings in meat was sold for little over a thousand.

All across sub-Saharan Africa, people were malnourished and bankrupt. To make matters worse, water scarcity brought on by the drought meant water sources were overshared. This led to an abrupt rise in waterborne diseases, such as cholera.

After almost two years of facilitating trips, my time was increasingly spent working with these communities on behalf of Free The Children, helping implement their development model called Adopt a Village. The philosophy behind Adopt a Village came from our direct interaction with these communities, recognizing that finding solutions to poverty wasn't going to be simple. It was going to take a holistic, multifaceted approach.

The model involved several strategies: school building and educational programming, clean water and sanitation projects, income-generating activities and kitchen gardens, mobile health clinics and lunch programs. The idea was to empower local communities to become sustainable and durable with that basic building block of success: education. With knowledge came power. But making sure people in these impoverished areas could gain an education meant supporting them through the process, making sure they were healthy, safe and able to survive financially.

I'd seen the effects at work. The volunteer groups I facilitated often joined in construction of Free The Children schools and water projects. Along with the satisfaction the kids found in dirtying their hands with tough but productive work, we'd seen the transformations that took place in these communities. From my experiences in Nkoyet-naiborr, Kitui, Embu, Maua and Kilifi I'd learned first-hand that for any development to work in the long run, it needed to be owned and maintained by the community. Adopt a Village took exactly this approach.

For example, at Emorijoi Primary School, near the Free The Children centre in the Ololunga Division of Narok South District, enrolment rates were on the rise and grades were steadily improving. Students were even requesting additional classes. Teachers were dedicated and daily attendance increased. Their resources were quite different from those of a typical primary school in America, where students enjoyed sports teams, teeming shelves of textbooks and bright decorations on every wall. But these Kenyan children had more enthusiasm for learning than I'd ever witnessed in kids back home.

Yet with the crippling effects of the drought, attendance was plummeting. In response, Free The Children implemented a food assistance program of its own, delivering sacks of maize and beans gathered together from the meagre supplies from several nearby markets.

On the day of the first shipment, I steered a Land Cruiser loaded with supplies into the schoolyard. I hopped out and hurried up to Joseph, the headmaster of the school.

"Joseph!" I told him, "We've brought more food. The children will be able to eat!"

Word quickly spread to the students that they would be provided with lunch that day. Whispers of excitement filled the air and children's faces lit up with eager anticipation.

"Food has arrived!"

"We're going to eat today!"

"Oh, I'm so excited to *eat!*"

As the trucks began to arrive in the schoolyard, the students rushed to help move the massive ninety kilo sacks of maize and beans into storage. The entire Grade 8 class was called to help unload the under their teachers' supervision. Bag after bag emptied from the Land Cruiser and filled their kitchen. A group of boys went to the back of the white truck and began hauling a bag from the trunk. They tugged . . . pulled . . . and finally got it out.

But the bottom of the sack had snagged on the trunk's edge. The more the boys pulled at it, the wider the hole ripped. With one final pull, the beans and maize spilled out all over the ground. Everyone gasped with dismay at the wasted food.

A teacher, Ruto, broke the silence.

"*Kila mwanafunzi uchukue maharagwe mia mbili,*" he commanded. Every student must gather 200 beans—don't let a single one go to waste!

And they did. Every student got down on their hands and knees and picked up 200 pieces of beans and maize, shifting through the small dirt piles until they'd found every last piece. The collected food was then gathered and readied to be cleaned.

It took less than half an hour for word to spread through the village that food had arrived for the children. Mamas volunteered to cook for all the students, more than 400 of them. Fires were lit, and some boys from seventh grade came forward to help serve younger students. Soon all the students, who had dedicated so much of their energy and effort to their lessons, were enjoying a hot cooked meal.

Over the next two days, the school again began to fill up, and classes began as before. Despite harsh times, people still remained optimistic.

My work at Emorijoi and several other schools and construction projects throughout southern Kenya had kept me busy for months, and I was afraid to go to Nkoyet-naiborr and check in on how my family was holding up. The news was reporting the region was one of the most affected areas across the country. I knew the horrors I saw happening on television—starvation, disease, desperation—would be even worse in the cracked earth Mama walked on in Nkoyet-naiborr. When I finally found a break in my schedule, I took the opportunity to visit. I was terrified, imagining I'd arrive to find my family sick, all skin and bones, their paltry finances utterly wiped out.

But when I arrived, I was relieved to find the family appearing relatively healthy, though everyone had obviously lost some weight. All of the cows were accounted for, and only a few goats had been lost. There was still the same laughter, cheer, fire. Everyone was there . . . except Faith.

I asked Mama where she was.

"We'll talk about it later," she said.

"Mama, where is she?"

"We will talk about it. Later."

I backed off, and we continued with dinner and chores, and the usual post-dinner singing and stories. But after the brothers had gone to bed, Mama and I stayed up by the fire. Now that we were alone, I asked again what had happened to Faith.

She told me Faith, only fifteen years old, had become pregnant. The family had only been made aware recently, and she was expecting any day now. She had gone to stay with her grandmother in Orpurlkel, a faraway village, to deliver the baby. Her grandmother would serve as midwife.

I was shocked. I'd heard the statistics: apparently twenty-five percent of Kenyan girls and women ages fifteen to nineteen were either pregnant or already had children, and eighty-five percent of women did not use contraceptives. There was a serious lack of sex education in Kenya, as well as longstanding traditions that curtailed women and girls from learning more about sex, and so they were often at the mercy of the boys and men who pursued them. But still—this was *Faith!* Even though she was Mama's sister, she was closer to me in age and she had become like a sister to me. Mama told me their father had decided to remove Faith from school and planned to marry her off to one of the many suitors now visiting him. Mama asked me to make the journey with her to Orpurlkel, in hopes of convincing the grandfather to allow Faith to remain in school.

I'd seen the destruction early marriage had on the lives of many young girls. Starting a family at such a young age meant sealing their future forever. Faith would be a mother at fifteen, bear two or three children at the age at which I'd graduated high school, and become the fourth wife of a sixty-year-old man. Starting a family at such a young age meant sealing her future forever. I didn't want this to be Faith's fate. Of course, I agreed to go, and we left for Orpurlkel the next day.

The news of our visit to Orpurlkel preceded us and, upon our arrival, we were quickly ushered into a small hut to visit Faith and her baby girl, born one week ago today.

Faith sat on a bed, calm before a glowing fire. The proud mother showed off her tiny child, who had been delivered on the very bed she sat upon. As my eyes adjusted to the smoke and darkness, I joined her on the bed. At first I was speechless, overwhelmed at the sight of this beautiful newborn. Then Faith handed me her baby girl, and I marvelled at the small body I held in my hands, wrapped in a blanket: her tiny ears, narrow eyes and gorgeous little nose.

Mama sat across the fire on another hide. "What did you name her, Faith?"

A smile came over Faith's face. She looked at me.

"'Robin.' She will be called Baby Robin."

I was still thinking of that moment the next day as we readied ourselves for our meeting with Mzee, the baby's grandfather. The prospect was daunting; I was about to make a plea for understanding that could decide Faith's future. If she was to be married, she would likely become the second, third or fourth wife to an elder, eliminating her chances of returning to school and shaping the rest of her days. I'd seen Faith's intelligence, her wit, her ability to take on tough challenges. I knew with the right encouragement, she could go a long way.

What do I say? What words of wisdom could I use to secure Faith's education? What if I came up empty? Mzee had every reason to question my arguments, as the Maasai had only begun receiving education in his own lifetime; his daughter, my Mama, was among one of the first generations of Maasai to receive a modern education. And, of course, for all that I'd been accepted by my Maasai family in spirit, I would forever be an outsider. Who was I to dare defy another culture's traditions?

He was waiting for me outside his manyatta, idly sitting on a pile of dried cow manure. Around him, other family members lingered, observing this meeting at a distance. Images of Faith in school, looking forward to a long future and success of her own design, reeled through my imagination.

As I approached, I removed the red bandana from my head in a show of respect. Slowly, I lowered my head for him to touch in the traditional Maasai greeting. His face was weathered and stern, and around him others hushed their voices. Clearly here was a well-regarded man, a father figure to at least thirty others.

"*Sopa entito*," Mzee began. Greetings, my child.

"*Iba Mzee*," I replied. I receive your greetings, respectful elder.

I had to remember: conversations in Maasai culture are an art unto themselves. They typically begin with customary greetings, then gestures of appreciation, then affirmation, eventually segueing into the topic at hand. First, one speaker began and spoke for a few minutes. Then, after a long pause, roles switched places as the other person took a turn for several minutes of speaking. Intermittent responses by the listener were placed after every few words to confirm understanding with that characteristic sound: "*ayyy.*"

I began our long-awaited conversation, working to make sure my Swahili was very precise. Though I'd become practically fluent, I still had to choose my words with care.

"Thank you for welcoming me into your home. I have been given tea, food and then more tea again. Your home has been very generous to me, and I appreciate this."

His dark eyes were fixed on me, his expression unchanging. I took a deep breath and paused.

"I have been living with your daughter now for a long time, and I feel very much at home with her. I love your family, and Faith has become a sister to me. She helps out so much at home. She knows how to care for her family and do her chores. She will make a great mama some day."

Mzee nodded. "*Ay.*"

I paused and took another deep breath. Here was where it got tricky.

"But she also is an excellent student. She has gone far in school and has a bright future within education. She tries very hard and has quite an intellect. As you know, the future of Maasai is changing from how it has been with your ancestors. Education has now begun to empower the people, and Faith is one of the benefactors.

"I know you care very much for the future of your children. If she enters an arranged marriage, we all know exactly where she will be in two years, and in twenty. You know her fate. She will be one of several wives and a mama to many children. This is a fine life, but there are also many other opportunities for her. But if Faith stays in school, we don't know where she will be in ten years. She could be a teacher, a pilot, a doctor. She could be the leader of her community, able to assist others in their struggles, and help Nkoyet-naiborr find prosperity. She could do anything she desires.

"I have travelled far to see you today, all the way from Narok District. More and more families in that region are sending their children, many of them girls, to school. Maasai everywhere are deciding that education is indeed an investment in their children and their communities' future. I have come to you today to request Faith remains in school."

Mzee paused for a good thirty seconds as he considered his words. Then he began, and I took my turn listening, offering the periodic utterance: *ayyy.*

"Thank you for your journey and sharing your words with me. I will respect and remember them as I continue in making my decision. Entering my homestead today, you have seen how many children I must take care of. Sending children to school is expensive, both directly with school fees, uniforms, pens and paper, and also indirectly in hiring others to tend our cattle when my children are too busy to perform this chore themselves.

"You can see that I have many children's futures to consider. You also have noticed this terrible drought we are currently experiencing, the worst in many years. We have lost 300 goats to this drought, and it is not yet over. The sky tells me the rains will not come for some weeks.

"I have many things and people to consider while deciding Faith's fate. I will indeed remember your words and appreciate your journey to share your thoughts."

A moment passed as we sat there on the manure pile, noting the straw-like grass and dusty earth, dried and burning in the sun, the gaunt frames of nearby villagers. His true feelings were impossible to read. *Am I getting through to him . . . or making things worse?*

Then I offered my response.

"You have spoken the truth, respected one. Yes, I see the drought has caused much destruction across Kenya, and I am sorry for your family's loss. We will continue to hope for rain to visit soon."

I took a deep breath, then continued.

"Faith is indeed like a sister to me, and I could not turn my back on her. You know I come from America. I had never left my home country myself until I had gone to school. It was only through school that I was able to first come to Kenya, a country I have come to cherish. If Faith continues with her education, she could be anywhere within ten years. This would provide for her, and your family, more than early marriage. We are all in this together, respected one. I appreciate our conversation, so we can decide together how to best take care of Faith."

He thought this over. I looked at Mama, and she gave me a slight nod that told me I had chosen my words well. "Faith's body needs time to heal before any decision can be made," he said. "In this time, this drought will also not find its end."

His eyes returned to the sky, his gaze slowly and methodically passing over the land surrounding us before he carefully chose his final words.

"*Wache tungojee mwezi moja ingine.*" Let us wait another month before making our decision. "Return to see me in one month's time, and we will continue this conversation. No decision will be made before then. His voice was authoritative, but the care in his eyes gave away an inner tenderness.

My heart wished more girls had the chance to continue in school. Whether pregnant or not, many girls were forced to marry at an early age, whether directly by parents' choice or by peer pressure to choose marriage over education.

Many girls in rural Kenya—not only Maasai—are married off at a young age. Looking at school registrars, one found many girls enrolled between first and fifth grades. The numbers began decreasing in sixth grade, with even fewer in seventh. By eighth grade rates were at their lowest. This was due to the fact that free primary education hadn't been introduced until early 2003, and it was also in part attributable to the handfuls of girls dropping out of school to be wed in early marriages.

In the culture in which I grew up, few women married younger than twenty-two, most in their mid-to-late twenties, but some well into their forties, or even later. My culture also allowed me the freedom to never marry at all, marry and divorce several times or to wait until a ripe old age, if that was the direction my life's path took. While more freedom existed in Kenya's cities, and different regions each held their own varied wedding traditions, it was generally typical for girls in rural Kenya to marry between fifteen and eighteen, therefore reaching marrying age while still in elementary school, putting a halt to their education.

In North America, adults enjoy many opportunities to learn: adult education courses, library seminars, book clubs, bookstores full of stacks upon stacks of knowledge on any subject, websites, even educational cable TV—the list was endless. Here, it wasn't as available. Your day was full of tremendous responsibility, not leisure time to devote to learning. There were few libraries, no television or internet access, no classes to attend and no free time to enjoy them. Expanding one's mind was a luxury rarely enjoyed.

This need fuelled Free The Children's work in adult education. We began to mobilize women's groups and develop strategies within communities throughout the communities where we worked, trying to fill this need. The women who entered the programs did so with incredible passion, quickly acquiring skills and striving for literacy.

I had the privilege of meeting and working with many amazing women who were resisting outdated cultural pressures and waiting to start families until they had established livelihoods of their own. Rather than surrendering to patriarchal traditions, they were creating their own lives. This was how I saw Faith, not shackled in a relationship that would keep her from fulfilling her destiny.

Three weeks later, I returned to Orpurlkel. A cyclone emerging from Mozambique had brought three days of heavy rain to southern Kenya and its surrounding areas, spurring nearby farming communities to plant their seeds in preparation for the farming season. The rains came quick and fierce; within hours dry, crumbling ground was transformed into gushing rivers, washing away precious topsoil and seeds. The few remaining cows at Mzee's boma huddled together under a sheet of tin, their malnourished diarrhoea in splattered piles everywhere.

This is where I found Mzee, shovelling last night's manure, later to be sold as fertilizer for a small profit. I joined him in shovelling, and we exchanged news of our respective communities: the state of everyone's health, the effects of the rain and what gossip we'd heard along the way. I brought news from Nairobi on recent politics and reported on the status of food aid in other areas of Maasailand.

The situation in Mzee's homestead was grim. His three remaining cattle could no longer stand, not having eaten for the last three weeks. He'd heard earlier that morning that Kiserian, their market town, had received some bales of hay for sale. It was urgent that he organize plans for community members to visit there soon, so he had little time for further discussion. For my part, I was also anxious to cut to the chase.

Finally, he presented his decree.

"Faith may return to school . . ."

My heart jumped.

". . . on the following two conditions."

Mzee took his time, scanning the surrounding land, undoubtedly noting the direction of the wind, noises of animals in the distance and the knots in my stomach. I prayed my racing breath was unnoticeable.

"First, Faith must be sponsored 100 percent. We do not have the money to finance Faith's education, and if she is to be given this chance it will require more than what we have to give her."

Paying for secondary school required several hundred dollars per year, and it was a four-year commitment. These pricey fees were the number one reason most parents didn't send their children to school. Was I absolutely sure I could secure that money? It didn't matter—whatever I had to do, I'd do it. Money wouldn't prevent Faith from realizing her future.

"Be at peace," I told him. "Faith will be taken care of. I will make sure the costs for everything is provided, from travel fare to tea and food. Rest assured knowing this condition will be met fully."

I braced myself for the next condition.

"Second," he said, "this must be Faith's decision. She has shamed our family deeply by birthing a child out of marriage. For us to give her this second chance, then have a second baby, would shame us more than we care to bear. She cannot have another child until she is finished school and married. Faith has to recognize this and agree."

This was a fair request, I told him, and I would tell Faith of these conditions. Parting ways, I immediately located Faith in the quiet of her Mama's manyatta and joined her before the crackling fire. The other women present immediately vacated, taking baby Robin with them, leaving us to have our discussion in private.

Faith was a tough girl and always a dutiful worker at home. Most North American teenagers would have been floored by the amount of work and responsibility she tackled. Returning from a long school day and the walk home, she'd help in retrieving water from the spring, where she'd meet other girlfriends from school with their water pails. Exchanging giggles and gossip from home, she'd then rush back home to begin preparing the evening's chai and dinner for the family. Cleaning followed, plus any other chores that needed attending. After a half-hour of studying, she'd retire to bed only to wake up at the next crack of dawn to do it all over again. Never did she complain or shirk her duties. Even on the day of her circumcision, she didn't shed a tear. Actually, I'd never seen Faith cry.

Yet, despite her toughness, now that she was a mother and faced an uncertain future, her fear was apparent.

I looked her firmly in the eyes. "Faith, you know that I have been returning here to talk with Mzee about the possibility of you returning to school."

"Yes."

"However, this is not a decision Mzee or I can make for you. This is your decision, as it will shape the rest of your life. If you choose to marry, it will be your time to begin a family. You'll have a new household to care for. You'll bear more children and begin your life as a mama. Do you understand?"

Faith nodded.

"If you instead choose to return to school, you will do just that. You will wake up early every morning and think of school. You will focus on school in your classes, all day and every day. When you return home in the afternoon, you will care for baby Robin Naserian. But you will also have to study. You will not enjoy any boyfriends. You will concentrate fully on your studies. School will be your life."

I couldn't believe the strict authority I heard in my own voice. I'd never spoken to Faith before with such conviction. I don't think I'd ever spoken to *anyone* with such conviction.

"Do you understand the choice you must make?"

Faith nodded again. I thought I saw her eyes began to water. Must be the glare from the fire, I thought—Faith wouldn't cry.

"This choice will never be presented to you again. This is a once-in-a-lifetime opportunity. Are you ready to make this choice?"

Faith nodded once again, a tear falling from her left eye.

"What is your decision?"

She broke into a huge smile. "I want to go to school, Naserian!"

"And how far will you go in school?" I pressed on, maintaining my strict focus.

"Until I finish Form 4, Naserian!"

I laughed, and she hugged me close. Form 4 was the final year of high school.

"Congratulations, Faith," I said.

The other women, who'd been waiting and listening from the manyatta's door suddenly burst inside, cheering. Ten women, fifteen women, twenty women all crammed inside the hut, squishing together around the fire. Laughter and tears of joy filled the home. Faith wept openly with relief and pride at her decision, cradling her newborn in her arms. I'd seen how Maasai families rallied to help one another. I knew among Mama, Mama Samuel, Faith's mother and myself, baby Robin would be just fine.

I made my way out of the manyatta's smoky air and back into the dry, sunny afternoon, heaving a sigh of relief. In the distance, I saw Mzee, perched in his usual seat atop the dried dung heap. From afar, he gave me a nod of understanding.

Faith: Like many Maasai women, her life faces challenges. But I am hopeful that she will enjoy a promising future.

14 Lives in the Balance

My days had become a constant balancing act. One day I'd be hosting volunteers to our centre, making sure they were comfortable, well-fed and ready to help; in addition to the regular youth trips, we'd begun hosting politicians, corporate donors, members of the charity's executive board—all who needed to feel welcome and fully exposed to the local culture. Then the next day I'd be meeting mamas in remote communities, hearing about their many struggles, but also witnessing their many successes.

It was an exciting time for Free The Children. What was once an idealistic youth awareness movement had evolved into a significant force in community development. The first year I'd joined, we'd built six schools in Kenya; only two years later we had increased to twenty-four schools, and we continued to double our schools every two years from then on.

We were also helping to organize women's co-op groups, helping mamas discover alternative ways of bringing in income for their families. Running their own businesses—everything from bee keeping and handicrafts to small animals for milking and breeding—not only brought much-needed money to their families, but also showed women that by working together

The Adopt a Village model empowers communities through alternative income, health care and education.

they could steer their own destinies, and that they might support one another through domestic violence, female circumcision and early marriage.

The community women loved the idea of the merry-go-round—just like Mama had done in Nkoyet-naiborr. The first year we were able to organize five women groups; a year later, we had twenty. Word spread throughout the region, and before you knew it there were fifty groups, then more than a hundred! And with this added financial support, their children wouldn't have to work and were thus free to go to school.

It was also great to know that Free The Children's school-building projects were financed by the efforts of youth groups in North America. Whether it was elementary school classes organizing bake sales or car washes and sending in checks for a thousand dollars, or nine-year-olds sending in their weekly allowance, seeing how hard they worked for kids their own age, but an ocean away, truly warmed my heart.

The Adopt a Village model empowers women by helping them start their own small businesses and achieve sustainable income.

My role was changing so much that I eventually switched from the Me to We side of our organization (at the time called Leaders Today) of regularly facilitating volunteer experiences to become Free The Children's Kenya Program Director working directly with the communities, which entailed me moving to Kenya full-time. It was amazing: not only was I able to live in the country I loved, but now I could make a career out of it.

Every day brought new challenges, and I often became frustrated, continually humbled by the reality in the communities. Poverty ran rampant; homes with children who had fallen in the fire but didn't know how to treat the burns. Girls who desperately wanted to go to secondary school, but government education only went through Grade 8. Low harvests which gave food lasting only four months instead of twelve.

Yet the moments where I felt the rewards of our hard work—like the opening ceremony of the primary school we'd built in Motony, several hours south-west of Nairobi—reminded me how important the work we were doing really was.

It was a brilliant, sunny afternoon as more than 600 parents, elders, classmates and teachers gathered in the grassy schoolyard. A group of high school students from Canada, here on a volunteer trip I was facilitating, were also among the large crowd there to usher in the newly constructed buildings that would replace their old, dilapidated schoolhouse. The adults sat on wooden benches, while across from them the children of Motony sat obediently, facing them in rows sorted by grades. Everyone waited in expectation, dressed in their new school uniforms with polished shoes, ready with their notebooks and pens.

First, the headmistress stood and welcomed everyone. Speaking on behalf of the community, she turned directly toward us, the Free The Children staff and trip participants, and expressed the gratitude and appreciation of the community.

"The children of Motony," she said, "send their love to the children of Canada, who helped create our school. This love is what helps us all to achieve the basic human right of education."

Next, speeches came from the area chief, followed by the school's chairman, headmistress and deputy head teacher. Then a mama, and a father.

Each spoke briefly, praising all who had helped to realize this dream. Their sincerity and grace brought tears to my eyes and sent shivers down my spine. Each ended their speech with that same plea: that we should tell the children of Canada, who raised the funds for the school's construction, of their happiness and eternal gratitude.

The ceremony continued with joyful singing and dancing. A group of gleeful schoolchildren raced from one classroom to another, taking turns to scissor the ribbon at each new doorway. Afterward, the crowd dispersed and we all roamed freely throughout the school compound. Small groups of girls danced, weaving their way with glee through the classrooms.

Then I noticed a group of older boys, each about fifteen years old, standing together and eyeing one of these new buildings. With folded arms and defiant eyes, their aloof posture stood in contrast to the surrounding joy.

As I approached, they stood to attention, bristling in my presence.

"*Mko kwa standardi gani?*" I asked, inquiring what standard, or school grade, they were in.

They looked at me with scepticism. "Standard 7," one tall, square-shouldered boy answered. He told me his name was Bennard, and he was his class's prefect.

"Have you seen your new school yet?"

He shook his head, and his feet were firmly planted in the ground.

"Do you want to go inside?" I prompted.

"Yes!" they shouted in unison. I pointed to the classroom, and we began walking there as a group. The boys in the back ran to the front of the pack, then the next boys did the same thing. They began jogging, racing one another in an all-out sprint to the door.

But just as we approached the door, they stopped on a dime. I didn't understand their hesitancy and coached along the next step.

"Who here will open the door to their new classroom?" I asked.

No one answered directly. Instead they initiated a debate among themselves about who should have the honour of opening their door. Bennard was elected. Positioning himself before the door, Bennard paused and cleared his throat as his classmates looked on, everyone taut with expectation. Then, heaving a deep breath, he slowly pushed the door open. A moment passed, then, as if a gush of water had been loosed, the boys rushed into the school. Their laughter and screams rang out as they surged into the new classroom, and—almost as if the act of opening the door had created a vacuum—children of all ages came running from all across the compound. Mamas bounded through the door. The Canadian high school volunteers skipped in hand-in-hand with the children, joining the inside crowd. Everyone marvelled at the sturdy construction, running their fingers along the concrete walls, and they gazed in awe at the large windows, the fresh chalkboard at the head of the class, the clean, uncracked floor.

On one wall was a sign with the Motony Primary School motto; showing off their English for their new North American friends, the children carefully sounded it out: *Together we can achieve our goals.* Over a hundred voices read these words, the children's voices echoing off the bare walls, repeating it over and over, until the entire class was shouting these words in unison.

Yes! I thought. Together, as Kenyans, as North Americans, with the contributions of mamas, elders, everyone, and especially the children . . . together, yes, we can achieve our goals. That was the true reward.

Meanwhile, even as we fought to help these communities gain their footing, Samuel's own struggles for his family's survival continued.

At the mechanic's school in Machakos, he'd thrown himself wholeheartedly into his studies, but the school didn't provide nearly the level of support it had promised. Two students shared one bed. No tea was served in the mornings or afternoons, and both lunch and dinner were meagre portions of half-boiled beans and maize. Underfed, malnourished and exposed to Machakos's colder climate, Samuel lost weight and his long-lasting health issues resurfaced, first with a bout of malaria, then pneumonia. Yet he fought to keep up his classes despite the challenges.

Upon graduation, Samuel looked for employment as a mechanic or driver, hoping to apply his schooling into work. He looked everywhere, but the job market offered nothing. Even his fellow classmates were also still unemployed even after extensive networking and filing applications. They constantly called one another, asking if they'd found any work. But the answer was always no.

With a family to care for, and his baba having long given up buying medicine, clothing or food for his family, Samuel couldn't afford to sit around and wait. We began to look for other options on how he could provide for his family. We decided that if what he was after was food, then he should go after the food directly: he'd try his hand at farming. It seemed like a great idea, so together he and I rented five acres of land in a plot about a seven-hour walk away from his boma where rain is more plentiful, and Samuel found six mamas to employ and work the farm. On the first rainfall everyone planted maize, including us.

The number one lesson Free The Children had learned was that helping communities and families achieve sustainable, long-term security often only took small investments. If applied wisely and with the right focus, they can reap large rewards. Our women's groups, which helped women start home-based micro-businesses, only required minimal start-up costs—along with the energy and care from the women who participated.

In a similar way, I thought I could invest in Samuel to help his family succeed. Yes, the plan for him to become a mechanic had failed. But that didn't mean I was prepared to give up on him. No one said it would be easy. I was happy to provide a small financial investment—only a few hundred dollars for me, but a huge amount for Samuel's family—to help them get started, hoping they'd soon be able to support themselves.

Unfortunately, the ravages of drought in Kenya's inhospitable semi-arid lands again had their way, and the season's harvest was disappointing. At season's end the land had reaped only seventeen bags of maize, scarcely enough to justify the investment. Samuel and I were devastated; we put so much hope into those 5 acres of land. We knew there could be more profitable business opportunities.

Together, we discussed a few options. We considered some more farming possibilities, specifically trying again with wheat instead of maize. But we'd seen how vulnerable farms were to the unpredictable weather and spells of drought. It was just too risky. Starting a farm elsewhere, where the soil and weather might be more conducive to raising crops, would mean him travelling to remote areas, leaving Mama Samuel and the rest of his family alone. Nobody wanted that.

On one of our market visits to Soko, we sat over tea and discussed the situation. Samuel said he had a plan.

"I want to start my own business, Naserian."

I had been thinking along the same lines. With Kenyan wages being so low, earning a salary at his limited skill level would never be enough to care for all of his family. Starting his own business was the way to go.

I nodded. "Okay, Samuel. But the maize didn't quite work out."

He shook his head. "Yeah," he gave a small laugh. "Not that kind of business."

Samuel told me how had gone door to door, visiting every small business he knew, talking to every shop owner or proprietor, picking their brains for ideas on business opportunities. It was a world he knew nothing about, recordkeeping and basic business practices. Yet he was determined to learn. From his research and collecting the opinions of every successful man he trusted, he'd settled on a simple but possibly manageable prospect: starting a bar.

A bar? It was such a strange notion, and one that concerned me: from his Baba and brother Joel, Samuel knew all too well how alcohol and the vices of town had negatively affected his fellow Maasai men. But he pledged to run a responsible business, and the idea was actually a pretty good idea. The costs to start it up would be minimal, and the hours would still allow him to stay on top of his family responsibilities at home.

Over the next few weeks, the plan came together. We looked at shop spaces in Soko, but many were too expensive for our small business. There were possibilities in towns farther north, but we knew the plan would only work if the pub was close to home. Then Samuel found an appropriate rental space in Duka Moja—a pretty modest place, and a far cry from the Hard Rock Café in

Chicago, but perfect for our purposes.

When we met with the landlord, however, I had some reservations. Along with the monthly rent, he asked for a further advance for some necessary renovations to the building. As he described the arrangement, the small, wiry man refused to look me squarely in the eyes.

I began to say something to Samuel, to suggest that we should reconsider. But when I turned to him, I saw such hope and optimism in his eyes, I bit my tongue. We would just have to trust that it would all work out. In the next few days we gathered some simple wooden tables and chairs, and together we worked out a reasonable budget, taking into account rent and delivery of a basic inventory of Tusker, the popular Kenyan beer, and others. Hunched over a simple ledger, Samuel fought to balance the finances. Enlivened by the prospect of running his own establishment, Samuel seemed happier than he'd been in a long time.

When the time came for me to supply the investment I'd promised, a total of 25,000 shillings (about $340), I met Samuel at the pub to give him the money.

But when I gave him the heavy envelope I felt slightly awkward. As long as Samuel and I'd known one another, I was either a student—and thus assumed to not yet have a job or assets—or staying with Mama's family, who while they were better off than Samuel and his family, were still struggling to get by.

Thumbing through the stack of bills, Samuel looked petrified.

"What's wrong, Samuel?" I asked.

He looked up at me, his eyes quivering with emotion.

"Naserian," he said. "This is more money than I've ever had . . . in my life. I won't let you down."

I went back to work at our projects in southwest Kenya while Samuel spent the next few months getting our simple place up and running. It turned out to be a somewhat successful source of revenue, and suddenly Samuel's family had a reliable income that didn't require him to do back-breaking work. It was something in which he could genuinely take pride. But Samuel knew that while the bar was a great opportunity, it was also a tremendous responsibility.

He put in long hours and fought to keep the place clean and organized. For the time being, his family was hopeful that things would work out.

Even with this good fortune, Samuel's health complications again re-emerged. After being diagnosed with pneumonia and tuberculosis for the third time in a single year, we began to worry these symptoms were an indication of something graver: AIDS. It took some convincing to get him to take the test. Thankfully, the results were negative. Life for Samuel continued on, with all of these lingering concerns and frustrations.

One Sunday afternoon, with the bar closed for the day, Samuel's Baba came to his boma, asking for his son to join him under an acacia tree. It was the first time they had spoken privately in a long time. And as they sat there together, Samuel heard his father offer encouraging words for the first time in his life.

"My son, you have done well, taking care of the family. You have taken the baggage from my shoulders and hoisted it on to your own. Buying all the medicine for the cows, food for the family, clothes for the children—you have grown into a strong man. You have also made a strong choice in choosing education over becoming a Maasai moran or marriage. If you had become a moran, or married early, you would not have been so prepared to care for our family as you have been.

"My son, your work now is to provide encouragement to your younger brothers and sisters, your nieces and nephews, for them to also follow in your footsteps and pursue an education. I trust you, my son. You have made me proud."

Moved by this unexpected display of affection, Samuel returned his father's appreciation, thanking him for the chance to choose his own path in life. He told his father that he'd also seen an improvement in his treatment of Mama Samuel. The old man's temperament had warmed in old age, and he could now place trust in his son's judgment—even if Samuel wasn't certain he could do the same in return.

They sat in silence for a moment. But Samuel, emboldened by this unexpected intimacy, had more to say.

"Our family is suffering," he told his Baba. "You are older now, and the burden of managing our livestock and land has become too great. I love Joel, my eldest brother, but he is distracted by the vices of town. My sisters are married, and are facing their own struggles. My younger brother Daniel and step-brother Jacob need guidance they now lack. The time has come, it seems to me, to pass on management of our boma and all our assets."

It seemed Baba Samuel was expecting these words. He agreed and, from that moment on, all that Samuel had fought to maintain would be his own. For better or for worse, Samuel was now the head of the family.

I told Samuel I was amazed he could forgive his father, after all the sadness and pain of the past. But to Samuel, the family bond was far greater than his own pride.

"He is my father," was all he said. There seemed nothing else to say.

I began to think more and more about the future of my relationship with Samuel. Our lives had become inextricably linked. He'd been my helping hand for learning the language and customs of this culture, and I'd done my best to help open his eyes to experiences and ideas outside of this close-knit community. To me, Samuel *was* Kenya: traditional values met with a desire to change, generosity and kindness in the face of staggering odds.

One day, hanging up after one of our regular long calls between Nairobi and Nkoyet-naiborr by cell phone, a strange thought struck me: one day Samuel and I could get married. *Married?* In the back of my mind, I suppose I'd always thought Samuel and I would be together. But what would that really mean? To have the thought of taking things further in the back of my mind was one thing; articulating that out loud to Samuel and thinking pragmatically of how it might work were other things entirely.

The kind of multicultural relationship Samuel and I might attempt would face many barriers. He barely spoke English. Until then, he'd only travelled to the city with my accompaniment. He hadn't started school until he was eighteen years old, after spending his childhood labouring as a goat herder In his world, females cooked, cleaned, did all the chores, undergo circumcision and are assumed to be subservient to men for their entire lives.

And even on the most basic level, I had to be realistic: even though I'd immersed myself in Maasai culture and been adopted by this family, I was still very much shaped by Western attitudes and culture. If a pop song I loved came on the radio, or I wanted to just spend an evening curled up on the sofa to watch a Hollywood movie, it was an experience Samuel would never fully enjoy, or at least not in the same way. On the other hand, if I chose to fully embrace another lifestyle, was I *really* prepared to live in a manyatta forever? Could Samuel ever live in a modern Western house? I'd fought accepting that comfortable life, but there were some aspects to it that I still wanted, such as being close to my family, or having opportunities open for any children I might have. Life with Samuel would be totally different. And the prospect of telling my parents that I'd become involved with a Maasai man . . . my father would have a heart attack!

Yet compared to many Maasai men, Samuel's beliefs were quite progressive. On one of our long walks over the scorched savannah to visit a neighbouring boma, I told him about my issues with female circumcision. To my surprise, he said he understood my viewpoint. My off hand remark resulted in a long conversation about the issue, and the differences of belief between my American world and those of the Maasai. He agreed with my belief that education, opportunity and family are the most important things in life.

Samuel had the purest heart of any human being I'd ever met. His values, morals, ethics and integrity encouraged me to be a better person every day. *And he had killed a lion!* If that wasn't bravery, I didn't know what was. We were both trying to reconcile the values of our upbringing with finding a new way of seeing the world.

But in so many ways, our cultural differences decided so much. Where did the boundaries lie? Or were they only in our heads?

Samuel had faced so many trials and tribulations throughout his life. Then things truly spun out of control.

I was at Kichwa Tembo, a luxury safari lodge in southwest Kenya, hosting some adult guests on safari game drives, when I received a call from Samuel. His voice sounded frantic.

"Blind," he said. "She's gone blind." I excused myself from my well-dressed company, leaving the gourmet, candlelit dinner. It took a moment for me to refocus and put myself in Nkoyet-naiborr.

"It's okay, Samuel. What happened?"

Mama Toti, Samuel's sister, had awoken to find she'd completely lost her sight, totally out of the blue. I told Samuel to immediately get her to the closest hospital. With it being evening and near impossible to escort a blind Mama Toti the four hours up and over the hills, we agreed he would take her in the pickup truck the next morning. Without access to internet, just a Blackberry, I sent a message to my friend Louise back in Toronto to ask her to cut and paste information on glaucoma. Knowing many Maasai suffer from this eye condition, I guessed Mama Toti's sight would have something to do with it. I fell asleep listening to elephants trumpet in the background, my Blackberry the only light in my tent as I fell asleep learning about glaucoma—until I was woken up at midnight by Samuel.

A mischievous group of young men no one recognized from the

community had unexpectedly arrived at Samuel's boma, demanding to take Sananga, Samuel's fourteen-year-old sister. When Samuel and his brothers resisted, these invaders set fire to several manyattas. Mama Toti couldn't see what was happening, but could tell the danger. She had begun screaming out the danger—calling for neighbours to come and help. Samuel's brother Daniel and neighbour Jacob rushed to help, bringing their *rungus*—wooden clubs that many Maasai men carry. A massive brawl ensued as the brothers fought to defend their home. Each was brutally beaten with the solid wooden clubs and the fist fighting. Samuel had his neck viciously torn by an attacker's fingernails. The brothers managed to fend off their attackers and extinguish the flames, but discovered that in the chaos the unthinkable had occurred: Sananga had been abducted.

The story quickly roused me out of my sleep. I told him he had to immediately call the chief and enlist every able-bodied man he knew; there were all sorts of awful things the young boys might do to Sananga, and he had to use every means necessary to get her back.

I hung up, too stunned to move. The night lay still. Hyenas howled in the distance as the full moon beamed through my tent's mesh windows. I was several hours away from Nkoyet-naiborr, but knew I couldn't really do anything about it even if I was there. I lay awake that night, reading articles about glaucoma treatments on my Blackberry, praying Sananga was okay.

The next day, Samuel called at dawn.

"We have her," he said. "We're back at home."

I heaved a sigh of relief. *Thank God.*

Samuel described how he, his brothers and two area chiefs had gone in pursuit of Sananga's abductors. They'd trekked all night long, finally locating the young men at a boma a few hours away and intimidated them into handing over Sananga. The chiefs hauled the young men to the police, Samuel brought Sananga back home, where she recovered from the traumatic incident in the comfort of their manyatta with Mama Samuel and Mama Toti, whose vision still hadn't returned. I worried what had actually happened during her capture, and I implored Samuel to get her examined.

"How is she?"

"Stunned and shaken, of course, but she seems to be okay."

"What about you? How are you? How are Daniel and Jacob?"

He'd been viciously attacked with a wooden club and his wounds had not been looked at. *What if he's been hit on his head? He could have a concussion and not even know it.*

"I'm fine," Samuel said. "Let's take care of Sananga and Mama Toti."

I had heard of the trouble idle young boys get in. With Nairobi's unemployment rate at forty percent, and even higher in rural communities, boys without an education often found themselves getting into trouble—alcohol, petty theft, violence, the list went on. I'd heard such stories time and again, but you never think it's going to happen to you. We made plans for both Sananga and Mama Toti to get medical attention. Again, I felt so helpless hearing about these incidents from a distance. Why is all this happening, all of a sudden?

That evening we checked in again, and it seems everyone had been distracted from their woes throughout the day by a herd of elephants. A herd of 160 elephants, wandering north from the lower valley, unexpectedly arrived in Nkoyet-naiborr. These massive herds walked right through Nkoyet-naiborr, dangerously close to homesteads, groups of playing children and young boys herding their cattle. One enraged bull had gone wild, tearing off homes' iron-sheet roofing and throwing people aside with its trunk.

Kenya Wildlife Services had to be called in. Samuel described with wonder the sight of the kws helicopters swooping over the plain, the officers firing shotguns from above. It took nine bullets to stop the enraged elephant's rampage. As it landed with a thud, kws Land Cruisers rushed in immediately and hacked off the tusks and a foot, and left.

The next day, Samuel and Daniel brought Mama Toti and Sananga to hospitals in Nairobi—Mama Toti to an eye clinic for her emergency surgery, Sananga to the Nairobi Women's Hospital. Sananga was given a morning-after pill, but nothing could be done for potential sexually transmitted diseases, so future appointments for tests were set for the coming months. They then returned to pick up Mama Toti from the other hospital, who was thankfully making a speedy recovery after a specialist had drained her eyes. Her vision was returning, but she would have to wear glasses.

The next day I was busy preparing for a major meeting where our staff would be hosting parent committee members from the many Free The Children schools across Kenya. It was a massive, day-long event, with visitors arriving from hours away. Even as I was discussing our ambitious, optimistic plans for future community development, I knew Samuel and his family were at the same time undergoing turmoil. Two days later I made a quick visit to Nkoyet-naiborr to check on how everyone was doing. I was repulsed to see the elephant carcass left rotting out in the open, but grateful to find everyone was generally okay.

I found Samuel at his boma and we discussed the recent events. He was going to check and ensure his attackers from earlier that week were still in captivity. I had to return to Nairobi, but made him promise to check in with me as soon as he had news.

A few hours later, he still hadn't called, and I grew worried. When my phone rang that night, my fears were confirmed.

"Naserian," Samuel said, "I'm in jail."

He was making his one permitted call to me, leaning out the window of his cell, straining to get reception on his cell phone. When he'd visited the jail, the local police had locked him up, demanding a bribe of 1,500 shillings ($23) for his release. He actually had the money on him, left over from the amount he'd taken to pay for Mama Toti's surgery. But even then the police hadn't released him, demanding he cough up another thousand shillings.

The jail was a horrific place. When the inmates weren't being beaten by the cops, they were fighting each other. There were no proper toilets and prisoners were left thirsty and unfed.

I was alarmed, but not entirely surprised. I'd heard stories about the widespread corruption among Kenya's police. It was too late in the day for me to head to Soko to bail him out. I tried phoning Baba, but with no luck. No one I knew was currently in town. In all that had happened, I couldn't think straight enough to find a solution.

Finally, an area chief who knew Samuel was able to bail him out. It was unsafe to walk back home in the dark—there had still been more elephant sightings in the valley—so Samuel couldn't get home until the next day, a Sunday. When he finally called from his boma, we both breathed sighs of relief, thinking these troubles were over for now.

The next day, Samuel called, once again frantic. I could barely believe it: he was back in jail.

He'd gone to ensure justice was finally being served to the young men who had kidnapped Sananga, only to again be thrown in jail himself. Incredibly, the jailed youths had accused Samuel of stealing their food! The audacious accusation was actually partially true, as when they'd set the boma's houses on fire with their torches, Samuel had used some flour they'd been carrying to douse out the flames. Now, they wanted payment for their lost flour. Clearly these young men had bribed the policemen to win them over their side, and Samuel was forced to use the money intended for Mama Toti's glasses to get out of jail. When Samuel told me all this, I was speechless.

Again, we thought this dark period was over. Yet only five days later, troubles began anew. Samuel's older sister, Tupesi, who lived far away in Kajiado, a remote Maasai region farther south than Nkoyet-naiborr, was giving birth at home. Over half of births in Kenya happen at home—opposed to at the clinic. Tupesi was having complications; the blood loss was too much. The baby was lost, and now Tupesi's life was also in jeopardy. Her husband rushed her to the hospital. Samuel was the first person they called.

While Tupesi was on an IV drip in a dirty hospital bed, her husband and Samuel made arrangements for the casket and funeral of the infant. Tupesi's husband was forced to sell one of their only two cows at market for 15,000 shillings ($210) to care for his wife's hospital bills; then he and Samuel headed to the hospital where the sister was being treated.

But on their way to Kajiado, they were accosted on the road by a group of marauding youths who had followed them from the market. Wielding metal bars, they mercilessly beat both Samuel and his brother-in-law, stealing their money, identification, phones . . . everything. Tupesi's husband's arm was broken, so Samuel rushed him to the hospital, then after the funeral a day later, went home to rest, feeling as if his own ribs were broken. There wasn't enough money in Nkoyet-naiborr to send Samuel to a doctor after having been beaten too many times.

Luckily, I was kept in the loop throughout these terrible events by phone with one of Samuel's younger brothers, Daniel. Stuck at the Free The Children centre, I had no way to send money to him, and I pleaded with both Daniel and Samuel to try to find any kind of money to get Samuel to the hospital, but everyone in the community was too poor.

I didn't know what to do in such situations. It was so hard, jumping from one reality to the next. One moment I'd be hosting volunteer guests, giving talks about clean water and social issues in Kenya. The next I'd be talking to mamas, hearing their mournful stories and working with them to help stabilize their households. Then back at the Free The Children centre we'd be munching hors d'oeuvres and sipping wine with our VIP guests. Yet all the time, I'd be worrying about Samuel and his family as they suffered these continued perils and setbacks. I couldn't let him down—we'd pledged to always help each other in times of need. So I just tried to hide one world from the other. Once again, I felt trapped between two worlds I could never unite, separated by incredible disparity.

After a couple of days recuperating at home, Samuel went to go see the bar's landlord in Duka Moja. This shady character was *way* behind on holding up his end of the deal on the building renovations, and I'd had several increasingly hostile conversations with him about it, demanding our deposit back. The last time we'd spoken I'd threatened that if he didn't cough it up soon, I would get the police involved (even though I knew how helpful the police would actually be was hard to predict). Samuel was going to offer him a final chance to make good on his end.

The man had no intention of making good on his end of the deal. When Samuel arrived at the man's home, three large men were there to meet him. Again, he was assaulted with metal rods and wooden clubs.

Thankfully, the police soon arrived and broke it up. All involved were rounded up, and once again Samuel found himself crammed in a small prison cell, again using his one permitted call to contact me. With the help of Samuel's younger brother Daniel, we were able to bail him out after only a few hours. But by then, Samuel was in extremely rough shape. Even over the phone, I could hear the fear and concern in Daniel's voice. Samuel had been beaten head to toe and nearly strangled to death. He was coughing and throwing up blood, and he was so dizzy he could barely stand. He'd lost his voice and was too weak to do anything. He couldn't think straight. He told Daniel he thought he was going to die.

My heart was breaking for him. *Why?* Why did these awful things keep happening—one after another? We can barely heal from the pain before being overtaken by the next catastrophe. *How does Samuel keep his cool in front of his family, to keep them calm? How do I keep mine, to keep Samuel calm?*

Daniel arranged for a motorcycle to pick up Samuel and bring him to the market town, from where they could come to my place in Nairobi, where I'd just returned from work obligations in the field.

While I waited for them to arrive, I described the circumstances of the attacks to my co-worker, Ken, who had worked in security in Soko and remained well-connected to the area. Based on what I told him, Ken strongly suggested all of these incidences—Sananga's kidnapping, the attacks on the road, the violence at the bar—were all linked, the same people in each incident trying to intimidate Samuel. The landlord was likely the one behind it all.

Of course! It all made sense. But we agreed it was best to wait until Samuel had recovered before taking any legal action; these recent run-ins with the police showed us not to place our trust in the authorities.

Daniel and Samuel arrived at my apartment shortly after nine o'clock that night. I was afraid to see Samuel. He'd been through such awful experiences. How would he look? Would he even recognize me? Would I see a change in his eyes? How badly was his body hurt? His *mind?*

When they arrived at my small apartment in the dark, I ushered them inside. At first glance, Samuel seemed okay.

And at that moment, seeing him so defeated, I really didn't know how to care for him. I didn't know what was appropriate between us. Should I hold his head in my lap? Could I hold his hand to reassure him? When he went to the bathroom to throw up, I hesitated at the door—this could be seen as a disrespectful move. I didn't even know what to say; every time I began to say anything resembling condolence or expressing sympathy, he interrupted, saying, 'I know, I know.'

We only had a couple of minutes of privacy, seated together on the sofa while Daniel cooked porridge in the kitchen. I held Samuel's hand and gazed into his eyes. With my most gentle touch, I helped him remove his shirt so he could show me his injuries, the bruises and broken skin where the metal rods had struck his back and ribs.

Barely able to speak, Samuel said, "I know you love me . . ."

I averted my eyes, overcome by the emotion I saw in his face.

". . . and I love you, too."

His eyes then rolled back into his head, and he turned away to lie back on the couch. Throughout the night, he rose several times, stumble to the bathroom to cough up blood. Again, I didn't know how to care for him, and when I tried to help he shunned my efforts.

Something had changed between us in that moment, with our emotions laid bare. It wasn't just that we'd spoken our feelings aloud. I wondered, was this love genuine, or just a response to these recent crises? My thoughts were awhirl, and I lay awake all night.

We went to the doctor the next morning, discovering Samuel had only soft tissue damage. The appropriate medication and instructions of rest were given and, with that, Daniel took Samuel back home to Nkoyet-naiborr to rest. We parted ways on a busy street. Daniel herded Samuel into an already overcrowded matatu to head back toward home. I stood there on the street, left alone. Loud R&B blasted from a street corner. Hustlers selling bandanas came up to me; they mistook my hesitation as interest in their product. I shook them off and started back toward my apartment, trying to get away from the noise.

15 My Maasai Life

Years before I'd written in my journal how I wanted to be cut down, sliced up, bashed and thrown this way and that. I'd said I wanted rebuild myself into a shape that I dictated on my own terms, to incorporate new meanings and existence into my world. *Until then*, I'd written, *I am living someone else's decisions, thoughts and beliefs. I am ready to start living my own.*

Had I accomplished this? A fire still burned within me, one that never seemed to dim. But in this new life I'd found a new focus, a new purpose, for that burning desire. I could see that even when I was rebelling against my parents, I was always, in a way, seeking their approval. And I felt that until they fully understood, they'd never truly be proud of me.

By this time they'd come to realize that my attachment to Kenya wasn't just a phase. Yet they still couldn't understand why I was so dedicated to my adoptive homeland. Their mindset boiled down to, "Robin is helping poor Africans." They didn't understand the impact of our work and the real effect it was having. Every time I tried to explain it to them, it went right over their heads. I tried to show them Free The Children promotional videos or send pictures of the schools and building projects, but they'd be easily distracted and pay little attention.

My dad is a big thinker and loves the possibility of adventure. He has a deep appreciation for challenging ideas and learning, and he is always interested in expanding his world-view—but is happy to do so from the comfort of home. My mother also enjoys having a solid, reliable routine: work, home, errands, preparing dinner, falling in bed by eight o'clock for a bit of television until curling up to sleep. The last thing they'd want to do would be to sit on a plane for eighteen hours for Africa, where they'd be completely thrown from their safe routine.

Nonetheless, I still persisted in trying to convince them to visit me in Kenya, asking countless times, over and over. Not just to appease me, but to show that after all this time they really did support me in the life I'd chosen. Them sharing in my life, my career, my life passion here in Kenya was worth more to me than anything I've ever asked of them—more than any field trip fee in school, any pair of jeans, or tickets to see a live performance of *Grease* for a birthday gift. This was by far the biggest thing I had ever asked of them.

That January I called home on my birthday, which was also my mother's. From Mom's cautious tone of voice, I could tell right away something was up.

"We have a surprise for you," Mom said.

As a birthday present for me, Mom and Dad had actually gone and applied for passports. *Passports?* That meant they were actually considering it.

"Dad and I want to come and visit you in Kenya this year," she said. "We just have to figure out when."

Tears stung in my eyes. I was so excited, I almost hung up on her. I had played the moment hundreds of times in my head, waiting to introduce my Maasai family to my Chicago family. For them to come to Nkoyet-naiborr, to sit in our kitchen and drink tea, to walk the footpaths—what would the two families' conversations be like? What would they say to one another? Would my parents be respectful and patient? What would they say when they met Mama Samuel and saw her tiny manyatta? *Will they understand?*

And what would they think when they saw my work at the schools, the development projects? Would they allow themselves to be moved, or even fall in love with this land like I had? Or would they just worry about applying sanitizer after shaking a child's hand, or fret about getting their shoes muddy? Could they see the bigger picture of alleviating poverty, or would they just count the hours before heading back home?

Preparations happened very quickly. For them, making the trip was an enormous leap. They'd never been outside of the country. The most adventurous trip they'd ever taken was a drive to Florida years before. I had to explain to them how to go through "customs," or the logistics of obtaining a travel visa. Getting travel shots, with the possibility of being exposed to diseases like typhoid or tuberculosis, horrified them. All I could was reassure them that everything would be okay. I'd take care of everything.

Every day I spent living in Kenya I felt closer to my adopted home. Yet at the same time I grew further frustrated by the forces keeping the country from realizing its potential. Corruption existed everywhere, even in places beset with deep poverty.

Kenya's political climate completely shifted with the 2007 December election between incumbent Mwai Kibaki from PNU (Party of National Kenya, the former NARC) and Raila Odinga of ODM (Orange Democratic Movement). Results claimed Kibaki won by a narrow margin, but allegations of corruption flew immediately. Odinga refused to accept the official results, and many agreed.

It was just as I'd seen back home during the Florida vote recount after the 2000 election. But unlike in the United States, Kenya's streets erupted with a wave of civil violence.

Feeding the chaos was a complicated web of ethnic conflicts. Luos fought Kikuyus, Odinga supporters swore vengeance against Kibaki's followers, the Kalenjin people joined in from their historical views against Kikuyus —the whole situation made your head spin. And everywhere police were reacting to the fighting and looting with swift retaliation. Shootings and riots were reported on television nightly.

To escape this widespread violence, people were forced to flee from their homes, taking only what they could manage. Trucks were arranged to deliver people to Internally Displaced Persons (IDP) camps, most of which were established by the Red Cross, but also by churches and other organizations. Police stations also became sites housing hundreds, then thousands. Conditions at the IDP camps were often times miserable, and the amount of food, mattresses and blankets needed was overwhelming.

But bound together in their outrage over the violence, many Kenyans also showed outstanding hope and support for their fellow countrymen. Mass campaigns for peace emerged from individuals, radio and other media, corporations and some politicians. Graffiti calling for peace was spray-painted everywhere, from business sectors to the poorest slums. Yet the violence still continued to erupt.

News stations were prevented by law to broadcast live coverage, as it was believed footage of riots and looting would only incite further violence. International reporters arrived, but in small numbers, who packaged and sold their limited coverage to broadcasters. The same stories were recycled over and over in the international news,

In the meantime, Kibaki and Odinga were too busy fighting for their claim on the presidency to address the violence, the torching of neighbourhoods, the mobs of people being burned and stoned to death. The death toll rose daily, but the two leaders refused to offer any statements on the violence, or welcome any negotiations.

Luckily, for the time being all seemed safe in Nkoyet-naiborr and the communities where Free The Children had its projects. For myself and my team members, life continued pretty much as normal. Volunteers and NGOs scrambled TO HELP THE IDPS, AND PEACE TALKS LED BY KOFI ANNAN, FORMER SECRETARY-GENERAL of the United Nations, were initiated. All of us held out hope that the country could regain its sanity.

Hoping to help relief efforts in the region, Free The Children established a special fund, encouraged its donors to consider giving to help the IDPs. I paid a visit to an IDP camp in Limuru operated by the Red Cross, where we'd be contributing funds and food aid. I was staggered by what I found there.

There were about 4,000 IDPs living in Limuru's three camps. In one camp, they'd constructed a kitchen and latrines, as well as several large plastic water tanks. There was a tiny, one-room wooden structure acting as a health dispensary. The IDPS did the cooking, and mamas used the water for their individual cleaning. People arrived from all over the country, literally climbing into a moving lorry while being chased by mobs wielding machetes and torches, with nothing but the clothes on their backs. The lorry brought them here, to this camp. They arrived hungry, confused and afraid. Sometimes they arrived with their families, sometimes without.

Red Cross ran the camp amid organizing other relief efforts nationwide, providing supplies and channelling cash donations as they came in. They were also working to register each individual as they came in, but the numbers were overwhelming. Two days before I visited, seventy-five displaced people had arrived. Some days forty people might arrive; other days the camp might find 400, all looking for refuge. Each was provided with a mattress, blanket and food for a week.

In a room barely double the size of our family room back home, more than 300 women and their children slept on the dirt floor or on mattresses. This same room doubled by day as a dining hall for about 3,000 people. Many people in this camp were orphans, or had been separated from relatives, or were parents missing their children. Staff onsite had trouble keeping up with the growing numbers of displaced people, an estimated 250,000 and rising.

These camps required enormous amounts of food. Four or five gigantic potato sacks stuffed with piles of french beans were poured onto a tarp, with a dozen women preparing for the afternoon meal. I imagined feeding 4,000 people—*for just one lunch, how many cabbages would be needed?* And this would be repeated multiple times a day, not only at the five camps across Limuru, but at camps housing the estimated 250,000 IDPS across the country.

I spoke with the Red Cross volunteer coordinator and asked her what was needed, as far as volunteer help. The volunteers she mainly dealt with were trained individuals, but we discussed how Free The Children could play an active role, from offering our staff as volunteers to helping distribute resources between other camps.

A church just outside of Limuru had a gathering crowd and quickly developed an efficient system and philosophy around running their camp. The mission of their camp wasn't to make residents comfortable for long-term living; their purpose was to help inhabitants feel secure for the time being and empower them for when conditions were safe enough to leave. Massive amounts of food were needed, yes, but food isn't always the best thing to offer. Counselling was needed for the children, or support for the schools nearby the camps so the thousands now out of school still could attend classes and have some sense of normalcy. The adults needed to start thinking about "what's next?" as opposed to just sitting idle around the camps; therefore we invited micro-finance organizations to come into the camps to give workshops on savings and how to re-build or start a business. Camps moved from centralized communal eating and living to sleeping and eating in family units for empowerment, and they used techniques such as calling their inhabitants "visitors" to specifically avoid creating a sense of home, instead a feeling of urgency to be ready to leave as soon as it would be safe. Opposed to sitting around idly while violence raged outside, during these tough days, people began taking steps to ensure a safer future.

No one knew how long the camps would remain. Ever since the elections, people like myself who initially felt surprised and shocked at the tremendous wave of violence were beginning to realize this wasn't a short incident that would wrap up quickly. Government spokespeople were throwing out accusations of ethnic cleansing and even genocide.

I had never dreamed the country could come to such a state. Most Kenyans were extremely upset and discouraged that their countrymen had lashed out in such violence. Everyone I spoke with still maintained their belief that they were a peaceful people, and the instigators of the violence were not representative of the population as a whole. Yet this crisis had revealed a darkness in the country's soul that worried us all.

Amid all of this chaos, I realized I hadn't spoken to Samuel in almost a month. We'd gotten in habit of staying in touch by phone at least once a week. But when I tried to contact him to check on how he was doing, I had no luck. After the conflict with the landlord, the future of the bar was in doubt. We'd never really talked about his attack, or the unarticulated feelings still left unsaid.

I called Mama and asked if she'd seen Samuel lately. She gave it a thought, then realized that, as a matter of fact, she hadn't.

After another week of trying to call Samuel daily, I couldn't get a hold of him. Sometimes it takes a few days, as he can only charge his phone when he goes to the market town, but he would have had the chance after another week. I started to get worried. *What if something had happened to him?*

To talk to anyone in his home, I'd have to go to Nkoyet-naiborr. I arrived at Mama Samuel's home and we went inside her manyatta to drink tea.

"Oh, Naserian!" she said, smiling brightly to cover her distress. "He hasn't come home in over a month."

A few of us took the lead in organizing a search party. Mama Samuel, Daniel, Jacob, Mama Toti and I discussed our next steps. We decided to wait another week, then take action. Meanwhile, the political violence was continuing sporadically throughout Kenya. I feared that Samuel might have gotten caught up in something, maybe defending Maasai in some ethnic clash. In my worst nightmares I saw him in a hospital, or in jail. Or in a morgue.

After six weeks, someone had heard a rumour that Samuel had gone Narok, nearly 250 kilometres south of Nkoyet-naiborr. Even though this made no sense, it was my only lead, so I headed to Narok by matatu and began asking around, waving a picture of Samuel to everyone in sight. I spread the word as widely as I could, basically issuing an all-points bulletin. But nothing came of it.

For weeks I cried myself to sleep every night, fearing the worst but trying to keep up hope. *Why would he have left?* I imagined what my first words to him would be if he were to call me. My emotions were in a tug-of-war, yanked on one end by despair of possibly losing Samuel into the unknown forever, held on the other side by disbelief that my parents were coming in less than two months. Meanwhile, the date of my parents' arrival crept closer. I prayed Samuel would return before they came.

Seven weeks turned to nine weeks.

Mama Samuel, Mama Toti and I sat down, along with Samuel's two brothers, to discuss our strategy. We agreed a widespread search was needed. A week-long search party across Maasailand was conducted.

Still Samuel was nowhere to be found. I cried until I had no more tears.

Speaking to my parents back home, they echoed the same perceptions much of the world held about Kenya: that the country was so backward, so "primitive," it wasn't worth considering a visit. All they knew about Africa was misguided stereotypes. I worried the sensational images in the media about the political violence only confirmed their worries.

Gradually, however, the country was beginning to settle down through Annan's peace negotiations. A Grand Coalition was formed, naming Odinga the Prime Minister and dividing all ministries between the two parties in equal number. It looked like there was hope for the country, even as I clung to my hopes that Samuel would return unharmed.

The week before my parents arrived, I meditated to put myself in the right frame of mind. My heart was continually filled with fresh fear over Samuel's disappearance during the political violence. Yet, after five and a half years of *begging* my parents to come, within twenty-four hours they would be here. *Finally*, my parents would visit me, sharing my world, my friends and family, my career, my "home," with my parents. I wanted them to feel safe, cared for and inspired. I called them every day, walking them through the visa process within the airport, their lay-over in London, reminding them everything would be safe and that I'd be there at the airport to pick them up.

Yet, they were fine. They didn't need reassuring. They weren't stressed, overwhelmed, have last-minute questions. They were only talking about whether or not they were going to pack everything into one suitcase or two. Mom was excited about the gifts she had brought for people in Nkoyet-naiborr. Dad was excited to meet everyone and get his chance to try and herd goats! Soon we hung up the phone, to see one another next in the Nairobi airport.

When I picked up Mom and Dad, they were so much more relaxed than I'd anticipated. I was surprised, and grateful, at how willing they were to go with the flow. While I drove them past the city toward my apartment, they seemed more tired than overwhelmed ... and certainly excited to be here. The next morning at breakfast, we were going over our itinerary.

"When do we get to see Mama?" my mom asked. "I hope she likes the purse I brought for her."

"We'll definitely get to see Mama. You'll meet the whole family. I have some pretty interesting stuff planned for us."

"What about Samuel?" Dad asked. "Do we get to see him? You spoke about him so much."

I hadn't told them Samuel had gone missing; I had held on to the idea that he would reappear before Mom and Dad got here.

I turned my head to look for the waiter to refill my coffee cup, averting my instantly tearing eyes. Here was probably the only opportunity in our lives for him to meet my birth parents. For five years I'd waited for this moment, through all our trials and tribulations together, but it seemed not meant to be.

"What's wrong, sweetie?" Mom asked.

I simply stood and left the table. It was too difficult to talk about. I hadn't spoken his disappearance with anyone outside of Nkoyet-naiborr, and couldn't do so now. But I compelled myself to pull it together; while my parents were here, we had more important things to do than sit around shedding tears over what may or may not have happened.

We headed out the next day in one of the organization's Land Cruisers. Mom and Dad gazed in awe at the rolling savannah. In his excitement Dad couldn't stop snapping pictures of everything they saw. Even when our truck blew a tire on the bumpy roads, my parents took it in stride.

Our first stop was Enelerai, where Free The Children had recently helped construct a new primary school. They were greeted by the teachers and elders working there and were swarmed by excited students in a wave of bright blue uniforms. The two of them in their large safari hats stood in the middle of a crowd of little bodies in blue school uniforms, climbing on my parents as if they were a jungle gym. All of the students wanted to touch them, try and rub the white off of their skin, or were startled by the hair on my parents arms.

Mom and Dad were initially taken aback by the kids' open affection, but they quickly warmed to the outpouring of hospitality. All 400 voices broke out in unison, singing in practised English for my parents:

> *Our visitors, we really love you!*
> *We are happy to be with you!*
> *To be with you in our Enelerai!*

Mom and Dad stood arm in arm in front of the assembled student body, clapping along, their faces beaming.

The next day we walked through another community, Emori Joi. We met a mama named Jane from one of the women's groups we worked with. Jane took my mom and dad to her home and introduced us to her neighbours, ensuring my parents understood we all had been able to accomplish together in the past few years: the schools we'd built, the lowered female circumcision and early marriage rates, the fewer typhoid cases due to lessons on boiling water. More and more women from the community heard my mom and dad were around and came running from all corners. Before long, we were a parade of more than twenty women, each carrying young babies wrapped on their backs. Everyone wanted to hug my parents, thank them for coming and share what impact they'd experienced by Free The Children.

"You're her mother? You look just like her!" Jane said, laughing. "After six years of her talking about you, we didn't think Robin even *had* parents!"

The women laughed at every comment as we walked toward their water source, the Mara River. Jane had brought an extra mitungi with her to pick up water for her home, and Mom offered to carry it back for her on her back.

I took Mom aside for a moment. "Mom," I whispered to her, knowing full well the other women wouldn't understand our English anyway, "you don't have to carry the water. It's really heavy."

"Let me try it," she begged. "If I can't handle it, you can carry it for me!"

When he saw a mama hoisted a massive log for firewood across her shoulders, Dad approached and through some awkward body language indicated he would carry it for her. So soon, there my parents were: Mom carrying water on her back, Dad prepped with firewood as the women kept a watchful eye to ensure nothing went wrong.

A day of joyful work: Mom hauls water while Dad carries firewood as local women look on.

As we passed by the school on the way back, word had evidently spread of these strange guests from away, and a crowd had gathered to greet my parents. Children sat in rows on the grass while elders and other adults sat in rows of desks, clapping their hands, intermittently yelling out "Welcome!" in English.

Mom and Dad, ailing under the weight of their cargo, did their best to smile for the growing crowd. When we arrived at the head of the gathering, women relieved them of their loads and Mom and Dad brushed themselves off, stretching their aching backs. Arm in arm, they followed me through the receiving line, greeting all who had gathered in attendance along the way.

Villagers burst into dance and song, calling Mom and Dad forward to join them. A group of women crowded around Mom to bestow gifts of jewellery upon her, while Dad was given an elder walking stick by a group of old men. Dad, still a natural public speaker, addressed the community at large—through my translation—to express his appreciation for the warm welcome.

Mom is used to Dad speaking on both of their behalf, so she was unprepared when the women began chanting her name.

I nudged her. "They want to hear your voice, too, Mom!"

I could see the anxiety in her face as everyone waited on the edges of their seats. The children on the ground crept closer and closer until the teacher had to tell everyone to scoot backward.

"Oh, Robin!" she said under her breath. "You'll be with me, right?"

"I'll be right next to you. Just speak one sentence at a time and I'll translate." Mom stood in front of the crowd, holding my hand. "It's so difficult to watch a child grow up," she began. "First you carry your baby in your stomach. Then you carry them in your arms. Then you watch them scamper across the floor, then learn to walk and then learn to run.

"My baby girl ran away. She ran all the way here, to Kenya. I never understood why, until I saw she had family like you. Now I can leave, knowing she's being well taken care of."

The crowd cheered, and Mom and I joined Dad on the desk chairs. "Did we do okay?" Dad asked. I sat in between them and squeezed their hands.

For weeks Dad had been glued to the *National Geographic* channel, studying every animal he hoped to see. So when we headed off on safari through the Great Rift Valley, he breathlessly spouted off facts about the giraffes, lions, zebras, crocodiles and other animals native to the region we were able to see. His camera never stopped clicking.

But for me the true highlight of their trip was when we went to Nkoyet-naiborr to finally meet the entire family: Mama and Baba, Kokoo, Faith, baby Robin, all my brothers, Baba's second wife and her family, Mama Samuel and her family, as well as many neighbours who had heard they were coming.

As we drove down into the valley my parents were a mixture of nervous excitement in the back. Dad tapped his leg, fidgeting, asking question after question about how to be appropriate in front of the family.

As we pulled into the compound, we found them all awaiting us, and as we stepped from the car a cheer erupted. Morio, now nine years old, and Shaila's two boys, five and three, came running forward to help Mom and Dad out of the car. Mama and Baba came forward from the crowd's centre, embracing my parents in hugs. I almost wept; everyone seemed immediately at home.

Their visit coincided with my brother Kipulel's circumcision ritual, so there was double the cause for celebration. My father spent time with community elders in the bush as they killed and skinned a cow and two goats, then cooked them over a fire. For her part, Mom joined in peeling potatoes and stirring massive cooking pots with the women. Dad herded goats with my brothers and Mom cradled baby Robin in her arms.

The ribs were removed from the carcass and cooked over a fire. Mom and Dad were given the first pieces.

"Meat doesn't get much fresher than this!" Mom exclaimed.

While there, the two of them not only learned to use a oleleshwa bush for a napkin, but also successfully navigated our pit toilet, drank warm cow's blood and tried local Maasai brew. Dad marvelled at the star-filled night sky and at seeing in the flesh animals he'd only known from wildlife TV shows . . . though he also shed two layers of skin under the African sun.

The only thing missing was Samuel. I kept peeking from the corner of my eye for Samuel. I caught Mama Samuel's eye once and I could tell I didn't need to keep looking around. For five and a half years I'd waited for this moment, through all our trials and tribulations together. I wondered if it just wasn't meant to be. While Mom was with the women and Dad tried to pick up goat herding from my younger brothers, I took a moment to again discuss the situation with Mama Samuel, Daniel and Jacob. They told me they'd been given a tip of where Samuel might be, and they were preparing another search for the next day. Though the possibilities were promising, I told myself not to get my hopes up.

At the end of the day, we said goodbye to Nkoyet-naiborr and climbed back into the Land Cruiser. We promised we'd come back at the end of the week to say goodbye, spending the last day in the country all together. Mom, Dad and I went to Lamu, a fishing island off Kenya's eastern coast that was a popular destination for vacationing ngo workers. We went snorkelling, swimming and windsurfing in the Indian Ocean and relaxed together in the small getaway's peaceful, lazy environment.

Just as we'd sat down to a candlelit dinner of fresh crab by candlelight, gazing out at stars reflecting on the ocean's waves, my phone rang. I wasn't expecting any calls, so I almost didn't answer. But when I heard the voice on the other end, I almost dropped the phone.

"Naserian?"

Samuel! It was Samuel! With my heart racing, I rushed to the hotel's upstairs balcony so we could talk in private.

"Where are you?" I asked. "Are you okay?"

There was a long silence before he spoke.

"Naserian, I am never coming back," Samuel began, clearly in tears. He was alive. He sounded safe and in good health, but clearly distraught.

"Samuel," I said, breathing deeply to calm myself, "whatever's happened, whatever's driven you to leave home, we can solve it together. Your family needs you."

I pleaded desperately for him to return, or at least to tell me what had happened. After my repeated pleas, he agreed to meet me back in Nairobi in a couple days to talk things through. I knew Samuel was a man of his word, so I slept that night with relief I hadn't felt in three months.

Three days later we returned from Lamu for our last night in Nairobi before my parents' flight out the following night. I arranged for a driver to take Mom and Dad to an antique store they had wanted to visit while I went downtown to meet Samuel. There he was, looking thin and weary, but in one piece, waiting for me at our meeting point in the city at Afya Centre off Tom Mboya Avenue. After a quick embrace, we headed into a small restaurant to talk over tea. He was quiet and avoided meeting my eyes. But gradually, I was able to coax him to tell the story of his disappearance.

After the run-in with the landlord and his cronies, Samuel had reopened the bar for the time being before deciding where to move away from this landlord. One elder who frequented the bar and dropped by and given him some specific advice on buying alcohol in cost-effective bulk quantities (opposed to the single-serving packets commonly found in Kenya) and measuring more carefully the drinks sold to the customers. He told Samuel he knew where this alcohol could be purchased and offered to take Samuel to the big city of Nairobi to show him.

Anxious about trying to keep the business afloat, Samuel saw this as an opportunity to increase revenues. And since the man was an elder, Samuel innately trusted him. He collected all his money—about 25,000 shillings (about $320)—and travelled with the elder in hopes of purchasing this new inventory, dreaming of all the additional food and clothes he could give his family with the inevitable increase in profits.

When they arrived in town, the elder gave Samuel a piece of candy. Moments after Samuel popped it into his mouth, the elder instructed Samuel to hand over the money so he could go buy the alcohol. Just then, Samuel began to feel faint. Suddenly dizzy and nauseous, he was unable to speak. The surrounding streets seemed to spin, and he was only vaguely aware as the elder reached into his pocket to swipe the money. As the man hurried away, Samuel tried to call out, but was powerless. His vision glazed over and his body gave out. He slumped to the ground, watching helplessly as the elder disappeared into the crowd.

When Samuel regained consciousness minutes later, he immediately searched the immediate area for the elder, but it was a lost cause. This big foreign city intimated Samuel, and neither his eyes nor mind could focus properly. The elder had drugged him somehow and made off with the money. Instead, the situation continued to turn over on itself, thoughts somersaulting over one another like circus acrobats. What should he do? Samuel sat on the curb for hours, hoping for the elder's return. But he never came.

He had ten shillings left, just enough for fare to return to Soko. Samuel was filled with fear and stress, unable to think straight. From Soko he began walking the few hours back to the bar, he felt as though he was about to go crazy. He closed the bar and for two days simply sat there, thinking. He didn't eat or drink. All he could think was how he'd made a huge mistake.

Seated on my couch, he relived his thoughts at the time. "I can't tell anyone about this. I have to run away. I can never see my family again. I have shamed Naserian by losing her money, and she is the last person I would ever want to hurt. I can never face her again. I respect her too much to do that. I lost her money . . . maybe she thinks I've stolen it! Today, I have made the biggest mistake of my life."

Samuel began walking toward the open savannah, hoping to disappear forever into the bush. Whenever he came across a road, he feared I might potentially drive by, so he hid until no cars were in sight, then scurried across to continue on through the bush. Anytime he saw a white person— even a man—he immediately turned directions and went the other way. Every person he saw was a threat to his escape.

Day and night, he walked, for nearly 250 kilometres. He had no food or water, only what he could collect along the way before continuing forward. As darkness fell, he often found safe haven at churches, climbing in a window and sleeping on the concrete floor. At the first light of day, he'd disappear again into the bush, heading further and further from the shame he'd left behind. He didn't know where he was going, only *away*.

Sometimes a friendly stranger offered him a cup of tea, or a potato sack on which to sleep. Other times he went days at a time without finding any fruit trees or sympathetic person to help him. In the small town of Suswa, Samuel met a man who felt sympathetic and offered him 500 shillings a month to chop meat at a butcher's shop. This was less than twenty cents a day, and it would barely cover rent, food or clothing. But in his desperation Samuel accepted the offer. He was determined to work until he'd replaced the 25,000 shillings, then return to back to me what he'd lost. Only then, Samuel felt, could he redeem himself and return to the life he'd left behind.

"But most of all, to you, Naserian," he told me. "I would never want to do anything bad to you, to hurt you in any way."

As weeks passed, Samuel knew that his family would be looking for him, and the pressure of constant worry and shame at being discovered only increased. He felt he couldn't take the stress anymore. He thought if he could work up the nerve to call me, to hear me say whatever it was he believed I needed to, it could then all be over.

After two more weeks he had worked up the nerve to call, only to hear a recording: I'd recently replaced a damaged cell phone and had a new number. Samuel felt defeated, resigned to a life of shame, and he tried to adjust to his new surroundings.

In Suswa, Samuel had befriended a mama named Veronika, who made weekly visits to Nairobi on Tuesdays to sell her beadwork at the "Maasai Market," an area provided to Maasai from across their country to sell their handicrafts. Several mamas from Nkoyet-naiborr also went there, and one day Veronika overheard their conversation about a boy named Samuel who'd mysteriously disappeared. Veronika heard about how upset the boy's mother was: no longer eating, not sleeping, barely able to do the day's chores, afraid for the worst. Veronika didn't say anything to the women, but called Samuel to her home upon her return to Suswa.

"Samuel," she said, "I know you have run away from home."

Samuel tried to deny it, but the truth was clear in his face.

"Today at the market, I heard people talking about you. They said you have been missing for almost three months, and everyone is confused. They don't know why you've run away."

Samuel continued to avoid further discussion, but a few days later, Veronika called Samuel to her home. Stepping inside, he stopped short halfway through the door. Seated on Veronika's couch were his brothers, Jacob and Daniel. Hesitantly, Samuel walked in and greeted each of them with a handshake. Seeing his brothers was too much of a surprise. Samuel said it felt as if the room was losing oxygen.

"I'll be back," Samuel told his brothers and left the house.

He didn't get very far, as at that very instant a commotion was breaking out in the road outside of the home. A group of prostitutes were attacking one another with glass bottles, cursing and screaming while a crowd of curious onlookers mobbed. Momentarily stunned, Samuel paused. Not wanting to look behind him at his awaiting brothers, nor ahead of him at the fight, Samuel looked down at the ground.

As if waiting for him, a discarded phone card lay in the dirt, enough for a short call. Samuel instinctively bent and picked up the card, just as Jacob and Daniel, having heard the fight breaking out, came running to see what was happening. After a moment of not knowing what to do, Samuel agreed to leave the crowd and join them at a hoteli for tea. They tried to act nonchalantly, so Samuel wouldn't be alarmed and run away.

"We came to see a friend of mine," Jacob lied. "He is going to help me find a place to rent land here to grow maize. We are just as surprised to see you as you are to see us."

They sat together, talking about nothing in particular and watching news from a TV bolted into the corner wall. Seeing Samuel more relaxed, Jacob asked him to go outside with him for a moment to talk.

"Samuel, we are not here to scout land," he confessed. "We were sent by someone to look for you."

Samuel was taken aback. "Who?"

"Naserian."

Samuel was shocked and confused. He could hardly believe what Jacob was telling him. He'd assumed I'd never want to see him again. But there he was, running from the very person who wanted him most.

"The family is worried and wants you to come back home," Jacob said. "Return home with Daniel and me tomorrow morning."

Samuel knew he had to speak with me himself before making a decision. He remembered the phone card, seemingly a gift of fate. Suddenly it seemed possible. He asked Daniel for my new number and to borrow his phone. With his stomach in knots, Samuel dialled my number.

Listening to his sad story there in Nairobi, my heart broke. Until then, Samuel had told no one what had happened. I assured him it was all a huge misunderstanding, one that was now long over. He'd done his best; it was just bad luck. I didn't care about the money. It wasn't Samuel's fault—it was the elder's, who had deceived him so cruelly.

"Samuel," I said. "Businesses succeed and fail all the time. We can start over and try again. What's most important is you return home." Finally Samuel agreed, but he didn't want to return to Nkoyet-naiborr without me.

"All of my heart is for you," he said. "What can I give to you, to thank you for being in my life?"

I smiled and shook my head. "Nothing. Just believe that we will always be together, for better or for worse, whether near or far. Whatever problem we come across, we'll get through it together."

Samuel and I may be from different cultures, but together we've found a bond that transcends boundaries. (Photographgraph courtesy of Tony Hauser)

That evening we all went out for dinner. Finally, Samuel and my parents could meet one another. Samuel greeted them as if meeting royalty, and they reciprocated his appreciation.

My parents being who they are, after their steady diet of Kenyan food over the previous days they requested we visit a more Western-style restaurant, a pizzeria. The place was cozy, but Samuel was horribly out of his element. Nervous and hoping to impress my parents, he told a long-winded story of how he and I had met. I dutifully translated while my parents listened, nodding patiently.

When our food arrived, Samuel looked hesitantly at the foreign food in front of him. Reluctantly took his first ever bite of pizza, cheese dripping from his mouth. He looked like he was going to spit it out in disgust. But he managed to gulp it down with a half smile on his face to be police. He whispered to me, asking if he really had to finish it. Laughing, I told him he was off the hook. My parents joked they felt the same way about drinking the cow's blood!

The next day we drove back down together to Samuel's home for my parents to say their goodbyes to everyone. Samuel was naturally anxious about his return, and he clenched his shoulders with tension as we lurched down the bumpy road, down the valley and toward Nkoyet-naiborr. I held his hand and did my best to assure him it would be okay and that everything would work out. Once again, Samuel placed his complete trust in me.

The moment Mama Samuel laid her tearful eyes on her son, all past worries dissipated. She held him in her arms, and everyone heaved a sigh of relief at seeing Samuel safe and sound. While his family's problems were far from over, and many challenges still lay ahead, for now he was just happy to be back home.

It was time to celebrate. His family slaughtered a chicken for my parents and borrowed plastic chairs from neighbours so they wouldn't have to sit on cow hides. Neighbours flocked to welcome Samuel home and bid my parents farewell before their trip back to America the next day. We ate, sang and laughed together as the afternoon receded to evening, another sun setting on the boma and humble Nkoyet-naiborr.

Seeing my two families united as one was the fulfillment of a wish I'd had ever since I'd first come to Kenya. Now my journey had come full circle.

After a heartfelt round of goodbyes, I left with my parents for the drive back to Nairobi. We were just reaching Soko when my father suddenly cried out.

"Stop! Stop the car."

Our driver pulled over and Dad hopped out of his seat before we had even come to a complete stop. We watched as he hurried to the roadside, then simply stood there, gazing at the blazing sun setting across the vast plain. After a moment, I got out of the car and joined him there. The wind was the only song across the vast empty land.

He took a deep breath, then turned to me.

"You know, Robin," he said as he cleared his throat to hide his cracking voice ,"I was always hard on you as a kid, so you would be an independent thinker and fight for what you had to say, so you'd stand up for yourself.

"I always tried to be an example of asking 'big' questions, trying to be a 'big' person. I always thought I was big. But I'm not. The world is big, and I am small. But I look at you . . ."

Just like the morning before I'd first left for Kenya, I was surprised to see my father cry.

". . . and I see a giant."

I didn't hide my watering eyes.

With a choked voice, he said, "I just want to remember this." He said, sweeping a hand across the view of the valley below. "This is a beautiful home you've created for yourself. We're so proud of you, Robin . . . Naserian."

We hugged one another tightly, staring off at the sun together.

A few hours later, we were at the airport in Nairobi, saying our goodbyes. Watching my parents head off toward the departure gate, I was reminded of that scene when they saw me off on my first trip to Kenya. But this time I was the one sending them off on an overseas journey. This time, I wasn't leaving to search for home—I was already there.

I went to Africa to seek freedom and independence, to simply get to a place where I couldn't rely on any person, language, technology, cultural norm . . . anything. The journey was about forcing myself to decide what my morals, ethics, priorities and values really were, not anyone else's.

But along the way, I found a new name, a new identity, a new culture.

I came to see that self-discovery isn't about what sets us apart, and achieving independence isn't about creating distance. It was about learning to see how one fits into a greater whole, and it was about strengthening those bonds that bring us together.

Not so long ago I'd written that note to myself, saying how I felt tied to a monotonous life, to decisions I hadn't made and that I was facing a destiny I hadn't chosen for myself. In Kenya, I found that destiny, and a new home. A home, I'd learned, is not where you are, but who you're with. And the home I'd found was not only in Kenya or America, but with the people with whom I shared this life.

What's Next?

Looking ahead, I'm not entirely sure what's next—for Kenya, for Nkoyet-naiborr or for myself.

My initial decision to travel to Kenya seems like a lifetime ago now. In many ways, I feel like a completely different than when my journey began. Looking back, I can admit it: yes, I was far from an ideal kid. Like every young person, I had yet to learn many of life's lessons—just as I continue to keep learning today. When I was young, I was simply seeking an outlet for my passions. I could only find it by leaving home and travelling halfway around the world.

At the time, my parents were genuinely worried about my future. "We didn't know what direction you were going," Mom told me recently. "It was kind of scary, what way you might choose."

Mom and Dad may have gained a few wrinkles and more grey hair from worrying about me. My life of development work overseas certainly wasn't exactly what they'd imagined for me. But today we can joke about how things turned out. Mom says they are proud of what I do and what it took to get where I am today.

"How many people do we know that are happy in what they do and believe in what they do? How lucky you are to find something you love. Who knows where you'll be in ten years? There could be a whole new goal. Who knows? You are still an evolving person."

It's true. We are all evolving in our own unique ways, taking on new tasks and assuming different roles in this world. By following the rebellious urge I had felt, I've done things I never have done before, and been in situations I've never been in, therefore I've played new roles. I've been the sincere learner; the competent traveller; the naive tourist; the blind mover—both bold and scared; the capable mama; the mystified lover; the imprisoned body; had a child-like heart; the patient spirit; the casual liver; the on-the-edge thriller; the selfish and selfless; the graceful woman; the flustered analyst; the worried grown-up; comfortably independent; the apathetic pretender; the fed-up socializer; the entertained visitor; the nervous child; a fated by-product; a devout minimalist; an obedient daughter; and a humble thinker.

I've been tired and worn; invigorated, moved and fascinated; comfortable and depressed; empowered yet stepped-on; stupid and confused, but intelligent and clever; shy yet daring and bold; hungry for life but at times too satisfied to eat any more of life; confused but at ease with that. I knew the world is so wide, yet the system made it feel so narrow. Not anymore.

Things don't always wrap up neatly—that's what life is all about. Still serving as Free The Children's Kenya Program Director, I remain in Kenya for most of the year, overseeing our many development projects.

As a result, I've seen first-hand the tough realities people face and, despite many advances, Kenya still faces enormous challenges. Roughly half the population lives below the poverty line. Over a million Kenyans are officially documented as living with HIV-AIDS, though the real numbers are probably much higher. Twice as many women than men have the disease, and more than 85,000 Kenyans died of AIDS and related causes just in 2006. Malaria and tuberculosis, among other tropical diseases, are huge problems. Orphanhood rates stand at about eleven percent. And even though the political situation has stabilized for now, the violence surrounding the recent elections shows that it took very little for the citizenry to lash out.

Clearly there are many issues we in the West need to address in order to ensure the survival of Kenya and its neighbours.

If you are reading this book, you are among the world's privileged elite. According to UNESCO, there are an estimated 771 million illiterate adults globally, or eighteen percent of the world's adult population, according to the latest estimates. The lowest literacy rates are found in Africa, South and West Asia and the Arab States—some of the poorest places in the world.

If you purchased this book, you are far better off than the more than one billion people who live off less than a dollar a day. Your standard of living is undoubtedly much higher than the 800 million people who go to bed hungry every night, and the estimated 50,000 people who lose their lives daily from poverty-related causes.

Reading this, you are most likely able-bodied. Yet some 2.5 billion people worldwide live without proper access to sanitation. The International Monetary Fund and World Bank have said that Kenya is suffering a health care crisis "twenty years in the making." Average life expectancy in Kenya hovers at around fifty-three, compared to about seventy-eight in the United States and eighty-one in Canada. Infant mortality rates are on the rise, and one-third of Kenya's children are developmentally stunted due to lack of proper nutrition and health resources.

I state these facts not to present a dismal view of the world, or make you feel guilty in your good fortune. My goal, both in this book and in my development work, is to inspire change. We are in a position to do something about these problems. I often think back to the question posed to me by the man in the market in Nairobi, years ago now: why did you come to Kenya, if not to help people? The question can be asked of all of us, on a broader scale: what is the mission of our lives, and what are we to do with the opportunities we are given?

Everybody has a unique role to play in making our world a better place, and there are many places where you can make a difference. My story shows that one can visit as more than just a tourist, observing from outside. Volunteer, do research, reach out and meet people in their home communities—there are countless ways you can get involved.

The American friends I made while in Kenya during my one-year cultural exchange all found their own discoveries, and they had put the insights they'd gained to use in a myriad of ways.

Sandra is now married and living in Lombard, near Chicago. She works as a nurse in palliative care at an oncology hospice wing. It was her experiences working with nurses in Meru that led her to similar work in the States.

I asked her how she saw Kenya's future unfolding, coming from a medical perspective. She said for progress to be made in improving lives, particularly in controlling HIV, it would come from educating and empowering women. In particular, when girls are attend school and hold jobs, they are more likely to raise sons and daughters who agree that women should have the right to negotiate safer sex practices. Only awareness and understanding could prevent the further spread of the deadly disease.

After graduating from university, Brenda volunteered with Americorps VISTA (Volunteers in Service to America) and worked with refugee women and children in Boston. She's now studying nurse-midwifery at Yale.

I posed the same question to her: what's next? She said she believes that the tumultuous elections and the peace-building initiatives that followed, Kenya has shown that it can take development into its own hands. The continued lack of dependence on foreign donors, she felt, will be accelerated by the world-wide economic depression.

But she reminded me of the traditional African concept of ubuntu: I am because we are. All humanity is interconnected, and only as a whole do we grow stronger. We must continue to listen: to the individuals who we meet along the way, to the stories of those who go before us, to those who wish to come after us.

I didn't know what I was getting myself into when I left for Africa. But I continually see how we can fundamentally change the world and people's lives. By opening myself up to the Maasai people's generosity, I was embraced by their love. To them I am forever indebted.

The community is still very much a part of my life, and I'm with them at least once a month. Samuel continues to look after his household, watching out for his mama, his brothers and sisters until they are old enough to start families of their own. He also continues to look after Mama Toti and her four children, as she has since left her husband.

These days Samuel is able to eat on a daily basis, to visit a doctor on most occasions when sick and he has enough clothes to wear. He constantly strives for others to be able to afford others the same luxuries he is now able to enjoy. As a respected member of the community, he is often asked to join committees, easily mobilizing his community around any wedding, funeral, circumcision or issue. Recently, Samuel held another mama in his arms while she passed away from AIDS. The dying woman asked him to ensure her two children, two and four years old, would be cared for. Samuel honoured that promise. He is now the chairman of a committee within the community to ensure the safety of those two children.

"In all my life, my biggest dream is to help others," he tells me. "Throughout my life, people have helped me when otherwise I would have died. Ever since I was a child, I've always had the heart to work with and assist others."

I had the chance to ask Mama Samuel about her hopes for the future. True to the Maasai spirit, her beliefs remain modest and hopeful.

"To make a safe, secure home," she says. "To welcome visitors, whether from Nkoyet-naiborr or from far away. To not be disturbed by rain, and to build a tin roof for the home. To help the Maasai receive education and have food when hungry."

Faith is in the middle of her high school education, rising higher and higher to the top of her class. Baby Robin will start preschool in a couple of years. Ambitions here are simple. But these basic beliefs help to remind me what's really important in life: love, safety, health, compassion and working for the future of our community—together.

Our family continues to grow: Mama has given birth to a baby girl,

Mesa. The life of baby Mesa will be vastly different from that of the other women in the community. Unlike generations before, she will have opportunity for an education and the support of a community in transition. She will, I hope, live free of some of the constraints women and girls face in Maasai culture, yet also find support in its core beliefs of family, respect and generosity.

I've seen how cultural values are changing in Maasailand, and I am optimistic that the lives of the Maasai people will continue to improve. But there are still huge leaps we need to take in terms of addressing environmental challenges, cultural conflicts, political violence and disease. In the Thinking Further section I've included some of my favourite books, movies and resources to help you start finding those issues that will inspire you.

You never really know what twists and turns your life's path will take. But I've learned that I was able to sit in the back of a pick-up truck as it clunked down the dry, red-dust road en route to market, surrounded by elders, chickens, milk cans, goats and children because I *chose* to do something different. I found my own path to travel in Maasailand and in working to help improve lives in this country I've come to love so dearly.

I hope my story shows that finding the direction your life might take isn't necessarily about falling in love with any particular place. It's about seeking those opportunities to find what truly defines, enlightens and inspires you. I invite you to seek your own path, wherever it might take you.

Notes and Background Information

In Chapter 2, Culture Shock in Nairobi, the statistics about the number of people worldwide who leave rural areas and move to cities—about 1.5 million every week, 70 million every year—are taken from a report by the *BBC News* entitled "The challenges facing an urban world." Find it online at http://news.bbc.co.uk/2/hi/science/nature/5054052.stm (accessed April 21, 2009).

The alarming trend that, within twenty years, the number of the Nairobi's squatters is expected to double, can be charted through the United Nations' *World Urbanization Prospects: The 2007 Revision Population Database*. Some more interesting in-depth facts and numbers can be found through the International Fund for Agricultural Development (IFAD) and their ruralpoverty.org site.

The information about HIV-AIDS rates, guessed to be as high as 50 percent, with 50,000 of the Kibera slum's children left as AIDS orphans, is taken from the UN Office for the Coordination of Humanitarian Affairs, which published a survey of global trends in urban child poverty called *Youth in Crisis: Coming of Age in the 21st Century*, with an in-depth look at Nairobi's street children.

Recalling the plight of homeless people in North America, I was saddened to learn in school that children make up about a third of the United States' homeless.

According to the National Coalition for the Homeless, in 2003 children under the age of eighteen accounted for 39 percent of the U.S. homeless population; 42 percent of these children were under the age of five.

In Chapter 3, My New Family, most of the Maasai background I initially gathered was from oral accounts and conversations with Samuel, elders and others. But in the writing of this book we turned to several sources on the subject. You can read more about Maasai culture in such books as *The Last of the Maasai* by Mohamed Amon, Duncan Willets and John Eames; Tepilit Ole Saitoti's *The Worlds of a Maasai Warrior: An Autobiography*; and Cheryl Bentsen's *Maasai Days*.

Estimates of the current Maasai population, anywhere from only about 150,000 to almost a million throughout sub-Saharan Africa, are difficult to verify, as historically the Maasai have been misrepresented in Kenya's censuses. This is due to many reasons, from the challenge of counting individuals in households that often shift in size, to the resistance of some Maasai to be counted by government outsiders. Yet they still remain mostly marginalized from mainstream Kenyan culture, both economically and politically.

Before leaving home, I'd known next to nothing about Kenya. I didn't even know what language Kenyans spoke. But as I came to know the country better—both in classes during my time in Nairobi and reading history books, but also from speaking with Maasai elders—I knew I needed a better understanding of its history and its people. So I began acquainting myself with the country, its history and the issues the Maasai faced within the larger culture.

I learned that for a long time Kenya thrived free of outside influences. Then during the age of European exploration, Islamic and Portuguese visitors had traded with and influenced the country's early inhabitants for centuries. Though the slave trade existed throughout sub-Saharan Africa for generations, most people outside of Africa hadn't glimpsed the largely unexplored territories of East Africa until British colonists established trading posts in the late 1800s. These colonists described Africa as "The Dark Continent," and its people as "primitive," "savage" and "backward"—setting the stereotype for how the rest of the world would view it and its people for decades to come.

My reading told me that the first objective of these early visitors was exploration. The second was missionary work on behalf of the Christian church. As Europeans began settling in East Africa en masse in the early 1900s, one of their first moves was to survey all of the land to identify any exploitable resources there. This colonial scramble resulted in divisions of Africa's land and people into mostly arbitrary boundaries.

The borders drawn around the land that would be known as Kenya encompassed more than forty very different ethnic groups, who were then divided and placed in so-called "reserves": all Maasai together in their reserve, as well as all Kamba, Kikuyu, Kalenjin, Luo, Luya and so on in theirs. The elders I spoke with told me that the reserve system caused widespread landlessness and degraded the environment as cows, previously free to roam, grazed on the same land over and over. Pastoral communities, which had never before faced boundaries dictating how to keep their herds, faced losing their livelihoods and lost any real political power.

The Maasai, with their background as warriors, were one of the first groups to resist the British colonists. But a spear is no match for a rifle, and the British punished the Maasai with sanctions and unfair taxes. Specifically, it was made illegal for anyone to buy Maasai cows, their main commodity. With their meat unsold, communities faced inevitable losses. Samuel told me of elders saying one could tell where Maasai boundaries lay, due to the lines of dead cattle on the edges of their reserve, waiting for customers who never came.

This continued until 1952, when Kenyans began a seven-year uprising called the Mau Mau Rebellion. Though the rebellion was unsuccessful from a military standpoint, it inspired a drive for Kenya's independence that would finally be realized in 1963. The first Kenyan government was formed, and Jomo Kenyatta of the Kenyan African National Union (KANU) became president in May 1963. With this move, those more than forty different ethnic groups with no loyalty to anything larger than their own home communities were lumped together into this new idea of a Kenyan "nation."

The Kenyan government built roads, schools, government buildings and institutions. They developed infrastructure and health care, and they inspired Kenyans to fight for their rights. Though still united first with their individual ethnic group, over the years Kenyans gradually opened to the idea of a unified nation. A group of elderly men I met in Soko told me they remembered the 1960s as a very exciting, uplifting, hopeful time. Growth and posterity seemed on the horizon.

However, the KANU ruled for nineteen years as a single, domineering party, and Kenyatta remained president until his death in 1978 at age eighty-four. The successor he named, Daniel Arap Moi, carried an image as a young, strapping, enthusiastic leader. Moi was embraced by the Kenyan people with open arms, and the beginning of his reign brought further success and development.

But over time, Moi's name became increasingly involved in political scandals. Accusations flew of "Moi's cronies" being responsible for mysterious deaths in the night, human rights violations and worse. The once-promising government increasingly resembled a dictatorship.

People sought to resist this trend, and small movements rose over the following decades, but open elections would only finally happen in 1997. Seemingly overnight dozens of rival political parties sprang up. But this abundance of voices only served to divide potential opposition, and Moi still won by a landslide. Many suspected the election had been rigged, but nothing came of the following investigations.

By 2002, the economy was in decline and poverty was on the rise. The dichotomy between Kenya's rich and poor classes was widening and people were deeply unsatisfied with the lack of promised opportunities. In the meantime, after twenty-three years of uninterrupted rule, Moi stepped down for an election to be held on December 26, 2002, and he named the man who would be his successor: Uhuru Kenyatta, son of Jomo Kenyatta. "Uhuru" means "freedom," so "Mr. Freedom Kenyatta" was being primed to take over the KANU party and the presidency.

The opposition parties adopted a new cooperative strategy, dropping their individual agendas to form a coalition that posed a first serious threat to the dictatorial administration. In the weeks leading up to the election, *The Nation* made breathless announcements almost daily of new parties joining the coalition. The name of the coalition continually until the formation of the NARC, the National Alliance Rainbow Coalition. Led by Mwai Kibaki, a former member of Moi's cabinet who had split from the KANU, the possibility of a new, democratically elected regime was the hope of Kenya and of Africa.

When I'd first arrived in Nairobi, the hope in the streets was pure and alive. It was the only thing anyone wanted to talk about: taxi drivers, strangers on matatus, businessmen drinking tea—everywhere, conversations ran wild, with most Kenyans optimistic for their political futures. Across Africa, observers saw Kenya as a symbol of hope for the continent, a model they could follow to rise against the corrupt dictatorships that had held control for so long.

It seemed that Kenya would always go through peaks of hopeful beginnings . . . then valleys of despair. It was as if Kenya's history was an epic story with twists and turns unwinding—except this story was real.

In Chapter 7, Tradition and Change, I found information about the changing landscape of East African culture in the mid-twentieth century in the novel *The River Between* by acclaimed Kenyan author Ngugi wa Thiong'o. There he addresses the traditional practice of circumcision, in both males and females. Western missionaries, whose arrival at the time greatly influenced Kenyan society, called circumcision "wrong" and "barbaric," telling local communities it was a bad thing to do.

The perspective Thiong'o offered had struck me; he wrote, "I don't know how they can negate a custom of which they will never have the hope of halfway understanding." I was unsure where I personally stood on the matter, between my own upbringing and my desire to respect local customs.

While it has been a topic of debate for decades, only relatively recently has female circumcision, or clitoridectomy, become a hot topic of discussion in the international community. It brings into conflict questions of cultural tradition versus human rights, and one that makes many people squeamish. Most would prefer to not even approach the subject.

Female circumcision is practised widely throughout Africa, not only by the Maasai but in a range of cultures, as well as in numerous areas of the Middle East and, in some documented cases, South America and India. While some religious practitioners advocate it, circumcision is generally considered more of a cultural convention, rather than one of faith.

To outsiders, the practice is appalling and its immorality is unquestionable. Carried out on girls at any age between infancy and adulthood, it involves removing and often damaging genital tissue, mainly their sexual organs. There are no medical benefits from the procedure, and it can actually lead to many health concerns, including infection, haemorrhaging and later complications in childbirth.

On a deeper level, circumcision maintains repressive ideas about femininity and gender. It inhibits women's sexual pleasure and often imposes pressure to conform to a largely male-dominated society. There are associations between circumcision and "cleanliness," and an uncircumcised woman might be seen as an undesirable wife.

The situation grows even more complicated when trying to maintain cultural respect alongside preserving traditions. Circumcision is a convention that has existed in communities such as the Maasai for many generations, and it is considered the pinnacle of a girl's transformation into a woman. For other countries to pass judgment on this custom means imposing outside beliefs on close-knit communities. On the other hand, don't we, as believers in human rights, have an obligation to protect girls from unnecessary pain and irreparable physical harm?

As stories of women who had undergone genital mutilation have captured the public's attention, there has been a widespread outcry against the practice. In 1997, and again in 2008, the World Health Organization issued a joint statement with the United Nations, calling for the abandonment of this "archaic" practice. This was Deputy Secretary-General Asha-Rose Migiro's bold remark in an address to the un, claiming, "with sustained effort, female genital mutilation can vanished within a generation."

And yet Amnesty International estimates that more than 130 million women today worldwide still undergo some form of circumcision, and more than two million procedures are still performed every year. According to irin humanitarian news and analysis, a project of the un Office for the Coordination of Humanitarian Affairs, available online at www.irinnews.org/IndepthMain.aspx?IndepthId=15&ReportId=62462

(accessed April 21, 2009).

Global migration patterns have found instances of the practice showing up in expected places; in 2006, Khalid Adem became the first man in the United States to be prosecuted for mutilating his daughter. Without a doubt, it remains one of the fiercest societal debates in the developing world.

In addition to the information about HIV-AIDS presented in Chapter 8, Research, HIV-AIDS information can be found in the United Nations *2008 Report on the Global AIDS Epidemic*, in 2007 an estimated 22 million people were living in HIV, with approximately 1.9 million infected that year alone. More than eleven million children have been orphaned by AIDS deaths. As many as two million Kenyans have HIV.

In Chapter 9, A Boma of My Own, the passing of my January birthday brings reflection on the comparative mortality rates in Kenya and America. As an American with a comfortable, middle-class upbringing, my future was wide open compared to that of most Kenyans, who face a life expectancy of fifty-one years. Learn more about health issues facing Kenya and its neighbours through the WHO's Statistical Information System, available online at www.who.int (accessed April 21, 2009).

Statistics from the UN's Food and Agriculture Organization that almost a third of all Kenyans are malnourished are taken from the FAO's country profile on Kenya. You can see more about Kenya's situation at www.fao.org/es/ess/yearbook/vol_1_2/pdf/Kenya.pdf (accessed April 21, 2009).

The quote from the United Nations where Kenya is described as "one of the most unequal societies in the world," with the country's richest ten percent controlling more than a third of the economy, comes from United Nations Development Programme, *2007/2008 Human Development Report.*

Information about the health status of Kenyans and others who lives in sub-Saharan Africa comes from the World Health Organizations Country Health System Factsheet for 2006, available at www.afro.who.int/home/countries/fact_sheets/kenya.pdf (accessed April 21, 2009). The numbers regarding malaria frequency in this chapter are adapted from reports by the Howard Hughes Medical Institute, found online at http://www.hhmi.org/biointeractive/disease/malaria/index.html (accessed April 21, 2009).

In Chapter 12, Return to Kenya, the estimate on world poverty is based on the World Bank's extensive data, and is often cited. But how we define "poverty" is still a heated, ongoing debate. Given the world's many different economies, is the "two dollars a day" really a reliable gauge of what it means to be poor? Looking at children's issues, UNICEF publishes a fascinating annual report titled *The State of the World's Children*, exploring the current realities faced by children and their families in some of the world's poorest places. In terms of the world's water crisis, WaterPartners International is a U.S.-based non-profit organization committed to providing safe drinking water and sanitation to people in developing countries. Their website, www.water.org, contains many valuable facts and reports. But as I told those students I hosted in Kenya, I encourage you to do your own reading and make your own conclusions.

Samuel's diagnosis with tuberculosis is not unusual. According to the World Health Organization, more than 140,000 new cases of tuberculosis were diagnosed in 2008 alone.

Neither is the diagnosis of glaucoma unusual. Samuel's sister, Mama Toti is not alone in her experience of sudden blindness. According to the World Health Organization, glaucoma is the world's second leading cause of blindness. About one to two percent of all Africans suffer some form of glaucoma, and many cases go untreated due to inadequate health care facilities.

Samuel resorted to bribing police to secure the release of his brother. While there have been efforts to restructure Kenya's police into a national network, in rural communities small local branches of police still operate mostly independently, and they are extremely corrupt. In 2007, BBC News reported Kenya's police were the most corrupt organization in a government notorious for widespread extortion and bribery.

Thinking Further

The path to learning about the many issues facing the developing world can take many routes. Here's a few recommended starting points, but don't take anything I describe as gospel. Doing your own exploration will take you to new discoveries and help you unleash your own personal passions.

If you're interested in discovering how the world's political situation evolved the way it did, a great read for a background on colonialism and global conflicts is *Guns, Germs, and Steel: The Fates of Human Societies* by Jared Diamond. Another book I can highly recommend is *The End of Poverty: Economic Possibilities for Our Time* by Jeffrey D. Sachs, former director of the United Nations Millennium Project. If you really want to see the world in a new light, have your mind blown by Stephen Hawking's *A Brief History of Time*. A really great series is the *No-nonsense Guide to . . .* series—sort of like a "Dummies" series for social issues, explaining such topics as globalization, human rights and world poverty in straightforward terms for the newcomer.

Sometimes a well-told story can say more than stacks of studies or statistics. Khaled Hosseini's *The Kite Runner* and *A Thousand Splendid Suns* are huge bestsellers, not only because they've exposed Western audiences to new, unfamiliar cultures, but because they also tell timeless stories of ordinary people overcoming enormous challenges. Books like Richard Bach's *Jonathan Livingston*

Seagull and *Illusions: The Adventures of a Reluctant Messiah* are powerful stories about how finding peace in one's self can bring peace into the world as a whole. I have also found simple philosophy about finding life's path in much of Paulo Coelho's work, including *The Alchemist*.

East Africa has a long tradition of oral and written literature, but only in the last few decades has the rest of the world opened up to some of the region's amazing authors. Probably the best known is Ngũgĩ wa Thiong'o, whose novel *The River Between* remains one of my personal favourites. His stories teach us the history of Kenya's transition from its rural, pastoral origins to the increasingly modernized culture of today. Other great African authors include Chinua Achebe and Peter Abrahams.

Finding trustworthy sources for news can be a challenge. In Kenya, the leading news source is *The Daily Nation* and its online companion. For international news, I listen to the radio constantly: BBC World Service and National Public Radio are the most common destinations on my dial. Online podcasts are also great when you're on the go. Magazines like *The Economist* and *Scientific American* provide the latest stories about our constantly changing world, while web sites like globalissues.org provide a good entry point for a broader discussion the issues that affect us all. Challenging the status quo with critical thinking is the way to get to the reality of the world's situation.

Even in mainstream culture one can find gateways to new cultures. Despite the glossy allure of Hollywood cinema, film can often be just as inspiring medium as books. *Blood Diamond* and *Hotel Rwanda* were recent high-profile stories about contemporary issues facing Africa. Canadian director Deepa Mehta's *Water* was a film I enjoyed about India's cultural issues under colonial rule. *Beyond Borders* was a recent depiction of a Western woman's decision to devote her life to humanitarian work. Even an Oscar-winning sensation can have an effect; the success of recent hit *Slumdog Millionaire* can be attributed just as much to its depiction of urban India's terrible poverty as its stirring love story.

Films can also point out truths of which we might not be aware. Documentaries like Al Gore's environmental call-to-arms *An Inconvenient Truth*, or Ted Braun's investigation into the horrific genocide in Sudan *Darfur Now*, take us to places we normally wouldn't get to see, and they can be the wake-up call that starts us taking action on social justice issues.

And importantly—don't always watch these movies by yourself! Watch with friends and family, and discuss not just the plots or characters, but the deeper issues being discussed. Don't take everything at face value. Talk to an expert, or do your own research, so you can discern fact from fiction. Probe the real truth behind the headlines, and pass on this knowledge to others.

As you open your eyes to the world's realities, there are many issues that might ignite a spark inside you. And the more we learn, the clearer it becomes that the problems our world faces are deeply interconnected. For example, by purchasing fair trade products like coffee or chocolate, we help enrich the economies of those communities seeking livelihoods independent of multinational corporations. This also promotes eco-friendly practices in harvesting and production, which helps in the fight against climate change. In a stable environment, vulnerable communities have a better chance of prospering, and can then afford to send children to school rather than work in dangerous conditions.

Beyond development work, the world needs compassionate, smart people of all walks of life: entrepreneurs, writers, artists, musicians, fashion designers, scientists, educators, parents—whether your passion is anything from frontline activism to skateboarding, gardening to spearheading an international charity, you can change the world in your own way. Don't swallow cultural norms; find your own path. Pass on the knowledge you gain. The world needs you!

Questions for Discussion

1. What did Robin's story teach you about Kenya? Were there any surprises? What elements of its culture and people would you like to learn more about?

2. What would be the main differences between the life of an ordinary American young woman and that of one in Kenya? What are the positive and negative elements of each?

3. How do you see the relationship between Robin and Mama? How does it progress throughout the book? How does it reflect on Robin's growth as a person, and as a woman?

4. How does Samuel as a person represent Maasai culture as a whole? How do you think Samuel would see a North American city, like the one Robin where grew up? Could he function, even prosper, in such a place? What would be the main obstacles he would face?

5. Rather than object to scenes like the circumcision that she finds shocking, Robin chooses to use it a learning experience. Do you think this is the right approach? Should she have tried to convince her family that it is an unethical practice? What would you have done in her position?

6. Robin's travels take her to a wide range of places that face unique challenges. What causes lie at the heart of

these challenges? If you had to design a development solution for an impoverished Kenyan village, what would it take for it to succeed?

7. When she returns to North America after her time away, Robin finds it difficult to fit in. What do you think has changed? What has stayed the same?

8. In Maasai culture, women are assigned specific roles in the household and in the community; even Robin, an outsider, is expected to follow these rules. How is this different in Western cultures? Are there similarities?

9. What brings Robin and Samuel together? How do you see their relationship evolving after the end of the book? Could they find happiness together?

10. How has Robin's view of the world changed over the course of her story? What do you imagine her future holds?

Acknowledgements

If you look for Nkoyet-naiborr on a map of Kenya, you will be out of luck. This is because the names of my adoptive village, and several other names, places and individuals throughout the book, have been changed. I have made the decision to do so out of respect for the community I have come to love. When the process of writing this book began, I discussed my plans with several elders in the community, as well as my Maasai family. Many of them expressed their trepidation about the project and were wary of drawing unwanted attention to the community from the outside world; other past accounts of Maasai culture have framed it in a negative light, and they have become skeptical about introducing any further controversy to their home. After much deliberation and discussion on this issue, I have decided to honour their wishes.

This book is the culmination of many peoples' experiences, efforts and love. I would like to personally acknowledge and thank all the communities, families and individuals who were involved in the creation of the book.

I would like to humbly extend my gratitude to all rural Kenyans with whom I have worked over the years, especially within Nkoyet-naiborr, who have welcomed me into their homes, lives and hearts. They are my teachers and continued inspiration. I couldn't have completed this work without their openness, love and blessings.

This book would not have come to fruition if not for the personal mentorship and assistance of Marc Kielburger and Roxanne Joyal. They believed in me and the message throughout the process, and I will be forever grateful for the commitment, dedication and passion they've brought to this project. Rob Benvie has been an overwhelmingly supportive editor and friend throughout the process of the book—travelling to Kenya and working back-and-forth across oceans. His expertise, patience and work ethic has transformed stories and experiences into an actual book. Ann-Marie Metten's editing prowess has touched each page; her long hours of editing have added greatly to the book.

A big *asante sana* (thank you) to Chris and Tania Carnegie, David Baum, Shelley Lewis Hood, David Thomson, Jo Mosby, Pat Justice and Professor Jonathan and Shelley White for their guidance, support and encouragement. Thank you to Tony Hauser for his travels to Kenya and sharing his gift of photography. My humble appreciation goes out to the special contributions of Jane Goodall and Les Hewitt. Thank you to the Me to We Books team: Russ McLeod—who has gone above and beyond in his support—and Stephanie Shea. Thank you to Andrew Garcia and Frances Data for their talented design and to Alec Bozzo for his photography.

The personal assistance of Eva Denny, Linnea Toftness, Sandra Olson and Karen Schultz made it possible to explore further into Kenya. I would also like to extend a warm tribute to Professor Mohamud Jama for his encouragement and supervision during my initial time in Kenya.

For keeping my feet firmly planted on stable ground, I want to thank my friends for their never-ending support. My neighbours in Schaumburg, as well as the Rovin, Kunkel, Florczak and Gimbel families have always allowed room for my adventurous side to have a voice, although it wasn't always easy for them. Thank you for allowing me space to explore.

My team members within the Free The Children and Me to We families continue to inspire, education and challenge me to live the best life I can imagine possible, especially everyone on the Free The Children Kenya team: Peter Ruhiu, Michelle Hambly, Langat Richard, Mugo Francis, Beverly Kandie, Loice Kerich, Edna Mutai and everyone on the Kenya team. You all teach me so much every day. Thank you for being my role models.

Finally, I would like to thank my mom, dad, sister Erin and brother Adam. You allowed me to follow my dreams, even when it was one of the most difficult things to let your child and sister do. I owe everything I am to the love you showed me, from birth through to this day; I love you all.

About Free The Children

Free The Children is the world's largest network of children helping children through education, with more than one million youth involved in its innovative education and development programs in 45 countries. Founded in 1995 by international child rights activist Craig Kielburger, Free The Children has a remarkable record of achievement, initiating community-based development projects around the world and inspiring young people to develop as socially conscious global citizens. Today, through the voices and actions of youth, Free The Children has built more than 500 schools in developing countries around the world, providing primary education to more than 50,000 students every day. Visit **www.freethechildren.com** to learn more.

About Me to We

Me to We is a new kind of social enterprise for people who want to help change the world with their daily choices. Through our media, products and leadership experiences, we support Free The Children's work with youth creating global change. Every trip, T-shirt, song, book, speech, thought, smile and choice adds up to a lifestyle that's part of the worldwide movement of *we*.

Me to We offers choices that allow people to create ripples of positive change. What's more, through significant financial and in-kind donations, Me to We supports Free The Children's development work in marginalized communities worldwide. Visit **www.metowe.com** to find out more.

Also from Me to We Books

The World Needs Your Kid: How to Raise Children Who Care and Contribute
Craig Kielburger and Marc Kielburger and Shelley Page

This unique guide to parenting is centred on a simple but profound philosophy that will encourage children to become global citizens. Drawing on life lessons from such remarkable individuals as Jane Goodall, Michael Douglas and Archbishop Desmond Tutu, award-winning journalist Shelley Page and Marc and Craig Kielburger demonstrate how small actions make huge differences in the life of a child and can ultimately change the world.

Free the Children
Craig Kielburger

This is the story that launched a movement. *Free the Children* recounts twelve-year-old Craig Kielburger's remarkable odyssey across South Asia, meeting some of the world's most disadvantaged children, exploring slums and sweatshops, fighting to rescue children from the chains of inhumane conditions.

Winner of the prestigious Christopher Award, *Free the Children* has been translated into eight languages and inspired young people around the world.

Take Action! A Guide to Active Citizenship
Marc and Craig Kielburger

Want to begin changing the world? *Take Action!* is a vivid, hands-on guide to active citizenship packed with the tools young people need to make a difference. Accomplished human rights activists Marc and Craig Kielburger share valuable tips and advice from their experiences as founders of Free The Children and the Me to We movement. Ideal for Grades 8–10, *Take Action!* shows that young people don't need to wait to be the leaders of tomorrow—this journey begins *now*.

Take More Action: How to Change the World
Craig and Marc Kielburger with Deepa Shankaran

Ready to take the next step? *Take More Action* is our advanced guide to global citizenship, empowering young people to be world-changers—around the world or in their own backyard.

Brilliantly illustrated and packed with powerful quotes, stories and resources, *Take More Action* includes invaluable material on character education, ethical leadership, effective activism and global citizenship. Ideal for Grades 10 and up, *Take More Action* paves the way for a lifetime of social action.

The Making of an Activist
Craig and Marc Kielburger with Lekha Singh

Warning: this book will change you. Full of vivid images and inspiring words, travelogues, poems and sparkling

artwork, *The Making of an Activist* is more than just a scrapbook of Free The Children's remarkable evolution. It's a testament to living an engaged, active and compassionate life, painting an intimate portrait of powerful young activists. Explore the book. Catch the spark.

It Takes a Child
Craig Kielburger and Marisa Antonello; Illustrated by Turnstyle Imaging

It was an ordinary morning like any other. Twelve-year-old Craig Kielburger woke to his alarm clock and hurried downstairs to wolf down a bowl of cereal over the newspaper's comics before school. But what he discovered on the paper's front page would change his life—and eventually affect over a million young people worldwide.

It Takes a Child is a fun, vibrant look back at Craig's adventures throughout South Asia, learning about global poverty and child labour. This incredible story truly demonstrates you're never too young to change the world.

Follow in Robin's footsteps and take your own journey to Africa

In a unique, life-changing experience, Robin's choices took her to Kenya where she found courage to redefine her purpose in life.

Travel overseas with Me to We Trips for a volunteer adventure of your own, and radically change your perspective while transforming the lives of others.

Go on an adventure to Free The Children development sites around the world. Get your hands dirty as you build a new school, or watch a child's eyes light up as they learn their first lessons inside a classroom. Better yet, learn what true compassion really means.

In Kenya, you can follow in Robin's footsteps as you volunteer in the Maasai Mara, meet mamas and their children, haul water on your back and learn about issues related to extreme poverty.

Volunteer programs are available for families, school groups, corporate retreats and youth in:

- Kenya
- China
- India
- Ecuador
- Arizona-Mexico

For more information, visit **www.metowe.com/trips** or e-mail **trips@metowe.com**.